A Passionate Life

A Passionate Life

STEPHANIE COLE
WITH LIZ BARR

Hodder & Stoughton
LONDON SYDNEY AUCKLAND

The following sources are gratefully acknowledged:

Hermann Hesse, *Gertrude* (Penguin, 1990)
Laurens van der Post, *About Blady* (Chatto, 1991) and *Jung and His Story of Our Time* (Penguin, 1978)
Ned Sherrin, *Sherrin's Year* (Virgin, 1996)
John Dover Wilson, *The Shakespearian Scholar*

British Library Cataloguing in Publication Data
A record for this book is available from the British Library

ISBN 0 340 63019 1

Typeset by Avon Dataset Ltd, Bidford-on-Avon, Warks

Printed and bound in Great Britain by
Mackays of Chatham plc, Chatham, Kent

Hodder and Stoughton
A division of Hodder Headline PLC
338 Euston Road
London NW1 3BH

To my mother, to my daughter and to Peter

A Passionate Life

by Stephanie Cole

Act One

A sleep and a forgetting

From birth to marriage

Interval

During this interval, members of the audience are cordially invited to come backstage and meet Miss Cole behind the scenes

Act Two

But will you wake,
For pity's sake?

Later, the same life

Curtain Speech

Prologue

Stephanie Cole is a remarkable woman so it is no surprise to find that she has lived a remarkable life and now offers it to us in a remarkable autobiography.

Ms Cole is an actress, much admired and much loved. Part of her book is a record of her progress to the peaks of her profession. Setting aside her talent and her dedication, how she achieved it remains something of a puzzle since she was so busy on other important, demanding and vividly described journeys at the same time. Although with beguiling frankness she takes us lightly through her professional career, she is even more revelatory about her personal and spiritual progresses.

On the latter track Buddhists and devout Christians, nuns and monks (especially the venerable farting monk in the Pondicherry Ashram) are all loved or criticised with an open mind and viewed with a benevolent eye. We can only admire and envy the understanding at which she finally arrives.

Joining her on her *personal* odyssey we encounter a depth of pain, passionately felt and ultimately understood. Her confusion and the suffering of those near and dear to her are unsparingly recorded. Schizophrenia, tinnitus, claustrophobia, agoraphobia, low self-esteem and shyness and the quest of a child uncertain of her exact paternity are described in a tone contained and compassionate.

We are treated not only to her triumphs in *Waiting For God*, *Keeping Mum*, *A Passionate Woman* and her definitive performance in 'Soldiering On', perhaps the subtlest of Alan Bennett's *Talking Heads* plays: but also to an account of an apprenticeship which any young actor who wants to know what he or she missed from not playing and learning a craft in repertory in the 50s and early 60s would do well to study – and sense their loss. Those who do remember will smile and feel a keen nostalgia as she reveals the antediluvian tricks of stage make-up and the trials of the backstage provincial life of the period.

This passionate life has also been quite saucy – but that too makes for excellent reading.

Ned Sherrin

Act One

A sleep and a forgetting

From birth to marriage

Our birth is but a sleep and a forgetting:
The Soul that rises with us, our life's Star,
Hath had elsewhere its setting,
And cometh from afar;
Not in entire forgetfulness,
And not in utter nakedness,
But trailing clouds of glory do we come
From God, who is our home:
Heaven lies about us in our infancy!

William Wordsworth, from '*Intimations of Immortality*'

1. The matriarchy

I come from a long line of survivors. The Hirsts, my maternal forebears, were an army family from way back. One of the Hirsts, family legend has it, came alive out of the Black Hole of Calcutta, another was mentioned in dispatches after serving through the whole of the Boer War, another was presented to Queen Victoria, and there is a monument in Netley to honour the courage of yet another. But the strong women who married into succeeding generations of Hirsts have been the real survivors.

My great-great-grandmother came from another army family, the Gibsons, and grew up in South Africa. She married my great-great-grandfather Hirst, and almost immediately had to cut up her wedding dress into bandages and assist in nursing the wounded, as well as serving ammunition in the trenches at Fort Hare under General Somerset during the Kaffir Wars. Her mother and father were murdered by Kaffirs while eating their Christmas dinner, and she helped her younger brother escape by dressing him in girl's clothes.

She had one daughter and five sons, who all joined the army, three becoming captains. Her daughter married a Colour-Sergeant Favell and had two sons who both joined the army. When my great-great-grandmother was on her deathbed, in 1902, she received a message of gracious sympathy from His Majesty King Edward VII to his loyal subject, Mrs Hirst, and 'an expression of hope that she

3

would recover from the serious illness from which she was suffering' – apparently a great gratification to the old lady, who lived only a few days after receiving it.

One of her sons, George, married my great-grandmother, Kit. Unfortunately George doesn't seem to have had the same stamina as the other Hirsts, and died quite young of typhoid or diphtheria or one of those things people rarely get nowadays, having left the army literally only a few weeks before, leaving Kit with six children still growing up and no pension. It must have been a time of considerable hardship.

Kit had been a nurse before she married, so she went back to nursing in York. She was a very talented pianist and played the organ in the church in the little village of Gate Helmsley where they lived, and any artistic ability that I have probably comes from her. I think I would have liked Kit enormously. The photographs of her, as with all Victorian photographs, show a rather gaunt, stern face, but I suspect she wasn't like that at all.

She had two sons and four daughters: my grandmother, my three great-aunts and two great-uncles. Of the latter, Harry was gassed in the First World War and suffered from ill health for the rest of his life, and the other, William, was the black sheep – every family has one – and had to leave the country. I don't know what he was supposed to have done, but off he went to Canada, and there's still a branch of the family living there. He was quite a bit older, and his four sisters were still living at home when he left. Irene and Ella, the eldest, both left school at fourteen and went out to work. My grandmother and the youngest daughter, my great-aunt Peg, also had to find work as soon as they were of an age.

Rene and Ella weren't beauties, but they had lovely personalities, and so were attractive. They both married early and I believe happily. Of the four sisters, my beloved great-aunt Peg was the only one who never married. The great love of her life, Jack, either disappeared or was killed in the war, and I think she never got over it. It left her with a lot of love to go round, and my mother and I were later to become the happy recipients.

My grandmother was the second youngest, and had been christened Anna Gladys, but everyone called her Peter – nobody knows why. She was the most beautiful of the girls, and very eye-catching as a child, with large, deep-set violet eyes with double lashes, and fair, red-gold hair. The story goes that when she was a little girl, playing in the barrack yard at army headquarters in York, where her father was stationed, one day Prince Arthur of Connaught came to inspect the troops. He saw this sensationally pretty child, and gave her a box of chocolates. I don't know whether it was this, or through being spoiled by her brothers' adoration, or the result of being jilted at the altar by her first and perhaps only love, but something set the seal on the rest of her life, because she grew up into a selfish woman who found it impossible to show affection, but nevertheless one who always delighted in beautiful things and good food.

On the rebound from being jilted, my grandmother married someone whom she didn't love but who had a great deal of money, my grandfather, William Sheldon. His parents had been Birmingham people, who had a tobacconist shop, but they couldn't read or write, so I don't quite know how they carried on their business. His father, however, seems to have had a great talent for making money, and William, being better educated and literate, succeeded in making a great deal of money. There were luxurious holidays for my grandmother in Paris and St Moritz, and they lived in a large house in the then rural and highly desirable village of Solihull. They had everything money could buy. My mother and her brother were both sent to expensive public schools. Then, unfortunately, Grandfather Will took to the bottle, driven to it by my grandmother so everyone says, and got the DT's and died when my mother, June, was nineteen, and her younger brother, Harry, was fifteen.

My grandmother was an enigma. On meeting her, she

appeared charming and sociable, but she had a side to her which I have never understood. She was never kind or loving or generous to my mother. On the surface, whenever I went to see her, she would seem pleased enough. There would always be some treat, like an ice cream, or she would let me sit and play with all the fascinating objects she had collected, because she had a great eye for beautiful antiques, and there was always something new and wonderful to look at. But there was something about her that was chilling. I don't think she knew how to show, or perhaps even feel, love. All the rest of the sisters – Ella, Rene and Peg – were tremendously warm, loving and giving; only Peter, my grandmother, wasn't.

She always thought of things in terms of monetary value. I was very conscious of that when I was young, and I hated it. She gave her daughter, my mother, no affection, but she spoiled and apparently adored her son, my uncle Harry, who unsurprisingly soon became another black sheep. She would always pay off his debts, of which there were multitudes. That was her way of doing it. You bought someone something, gave them money, and that meant you loved them. Where she got that idea from, I've no idea. She died only about fifteen years ago, in her mid-eighties, but to the end, I never fathomed her.

Some time before I was born, she married again, a wealthy stockbroker. He reminded me of a fat Field Marshal Lord Montgomery and I never liked him very much. He was a weaselly sort of man. I'm probably being very unfair, because he was always kind to me, endlessly patient when I was little, teaching me to read and write and do sums, and I know he gave Peg good and helpful advice about her financial affairs, but somehow I never trusted him or felt comfortable with him.

Because she died only recently, aged ninety-six, my great-aunt Peg is the one I've heard most of the family history from. In 1914, when the First World War started, she left school and went and rolled bandages. Then she worked in the Queen's Hotel, Leeds, in the war ministry office, moving troops around the country. She saw the first Zeppelin over Leeds. Peg always thought herself very ugly when she was a child. She wasn't. I can see from the photographs that she was a very attractive young woman, with her dark brown hair in a long plait down her back, and bright blue eyes.

Unfortunately, as we've got older, my mother and I, unlike Peg, both inherited the 'stout' gene in the Hirst/Sheldon family. The sisters and brothers were divided. There were two stouties and three thinnies. Peg, Irene and Ella were all thinnies. Will, the black sheep, and Peter, my grandmother, were stouties.

All our family are Celts. My mother, like my grandmother, is red-gold, where Peg, like me, was very dark, and we all have violet or blue eyes. Our eyes are very deep-set, which makes life rather difficult for make-up artists first thing in the morning. These days, when I sit down at the make-up table and they say, 'Is there anything particular you want?' I always say, 'It's a matter of complete embuggerance to me what else you do, but please would you find my eyes.'

By the time the Second World War started, my mother was a vivacious, very pretty, freckle-faced, young art student, with a great gift for water-colour painting and embroidery. She had a lovely smile, and loved dancing. She has a face and a personality that people warm to immediately, and has always had an easy gift for friendship.

Most of the young men in those days were in uniform, all looking very dashing. It was a time of dance bands, romantic music, and tomorrow may never come. My mother's marriage to Leslie Cole, like so many others of the time, was rushed into in a frantic haze of champagne and we'll-meet-agains and Hollywood happy-ever-afters. She was nineteen. She had known too little affection in her young life, either from a father, drunk and suffering from the DT's, or from a volatile mother whose love for anyone other than

7

herself, if she showed it at all, was showered in cash form on her son. My mother wanted real love and warmth, a family of her own, a home, stability and happiness. Unfortunately, wanting these things too much is not the ideal recipe for the wedding cake and before I was born, she and my father had gone their separate ways.

I was to grow up in a matriarchy, brought up almost entirely by three very strong women – my mother, my grandmother and my great-aunt Peg – who always gave me the precious gift of her unconditional love.

2. Enter Stephanie stage left, upside down

I realise now that I have left it too late to die young. This comes as something of a shock. As a child, I never believed that I would reach thirty, never mind fifty-six. On the morning of my twenty-first birthday, I remember being enormously surprised to find that I'd made it even thus far. This morbid fancy probably came from an insatiable appetite for poetry, with a leaning, particularly in the days of my youth, towards the nostalgic and the tragic-romantic.

I was born on Sunday 5 October 1941 in, I have always believed, a bedroom above a small grocery shop in Cornyx Lane, Solihull, in Warwickshire. The shop belonged to Great-Aunt Peg, and my mother had gone to live there after she and Leslie Cole had split up, several months before I was born. Apart from bearing his name, all I know about him, or have ever wanted to know, is that he served in the RAF during the war and that he and my mother had not been at all happy together in their short marriage. The rest is my mother's story.

I have a belief that our souls hover in a great energy from which we come and to which we return when we die, deciding what lessons need to be learnt next time round, and which set of circumstances and parents would be the best classroom to learn them in. I suppose even from the security of the womb I may have picked up messages that all was not going too well with the world I had chosen, and maybe this not-so-small baby embodying my soul grew nervous about going to this particular college. Certainly I made my way into it with extreme reluctance, and facing the wrong way. So unwilling to be born was I that after a very long labour attended by Nurse Win Watson, a doctor had to be summoned to drag me out, feet first, with his foot braced against the end of the bed. It was an unconventional entrance into life, which did my mother no good at all and she needed to be looked after for a long time afterwards by Nurse Win, who continued to dot in and out of our lives from then on, offering remedies, advice and hot water bottles, right up until the day she died.

Before I go any further, I must make you a formal confession that my memory of events does not always exactly coincide with the memories of others, in particular those of my mother. I hated history at school, and I'm not particularly interested in exact dates; my memories are extremely vivid, but they come in terms of sensations, changes of light, pictures and nostalgic smells, and of the deeper significance that past events have for me; I have a tendency to mythologise the past.

My mother, on the other hand, likes to get things straight. For instance, she tells me that I wasn't born in the flat over the little grocery shop at all – I was born in my grand-mother's house, in Broad Oaks Road, Solihull, and we only moved to my great-aunt's flat later, after my mother had had a row with her mother. I dare say that is something she would know more about than I do, but I always thought that I was born in my beloved great-aunt Peg's cosy flat, and not in my grandmother's cold, unloving household, and now I don't think I want to change my warm, happy memories for mere facts.

My earliest memories of childhood are all flooded with the sensual joy of being alive. I have vivid pictures, which are not photographs, of lying on the hearth-rug in the back room of Peg's grocery shop, playing with a set of lead figures of Snow White and the Seven Dwarfs, and I can still recall the delightful taste and biteability of lead, an extremely dangerous joy that fortunately was quickly put a stop to when discovered. I remember perching in the huge, creaking basket on the front of Ron the delivery boy's bike; the delicious taste of wartime sausages, more bread than meat I'm told, but nevertheless a great treat; the smell of wax crayons, particularly the bright purple-pink one which was my favourite and in which everything from sky to grass would be coloured.

I can remember, although I can't have been more than a year old, lying in the dark, in my cot, and someone coming in and waking me up, and it was not my mother. An aunt who I didn't know had come to see me and woken me up, and I was terrified in the dark, and screamed. I was always very afraid of the dark from then on.

I remember the dog we had, a Samoyed, with the original name of Sam, and of burying my face in his long, white, warm fur, and the drenching experienced when he shook himself after I had been bathing him, with my mother's help, when I was less than three. There were French windows into the garden at the back of my great-aunt's shop, and they hung a baby bouncer there for me. I can remember the feel of the canvas chair under my bottom, the sensation of bouncing up and down, looking out on to the garden.

I remember the raspberry canes, and picking the raspberries; feeding the hens my great-aunt kept, and looking for eggs under the hedges. The little garden led on to fields, because in those days Solihull was still a village, and I would go for long walks with great-aunt Rene's daughter, my aunt Joan, who was wonderful at telling stories. She used to read me *Winnie the Pooh* and then tell me the stories all over again as we walked by a little river.

One of my pleasures in those days was to play on the floor behind the counter in the shop, where the smells were intriguing and enticing, and on rare and joyous occasions people would come in with presents for the 'dear little girl'. Once I was given a really beautiful doll from France by a young soldier who was missing his own family. She still sits in my bedroom to this day, although her beauty was somewhat marred by a very drastic haircut I gave her when I was six.

One day my great-aunt Peg received a small consignment of bananas, an almost unheard-of luxury during the war years. They were shown off to me with great delight and were regarded as a huge treat, to be kept under the counter in reserve for regular and favoured customers. On the Day of the Bananas I was in my usual place, underneath the counter, when a customer came in. Had she heard aright, that Miss Hirst had some bananas in? This lady was neither one of Peg's favourites, nor a regular customer, so my great-aunt denied all knowledge, at which, to her chagrin, I popped up from below, helpfully waving a large bunch of the coveted fruit. Exit a delighted customer, and exit Stephanie, propelled fast into the back room.

My mother said to me very recently, 'Now you're not going to say that we were bombed out of the flat in Solihull and moved down to North Devon because of that, are you?'

And I said, 'Well, actually, I was, because I thought that was what happened.'

She said, 'Well, it wasn't.'

I don't know if I knew at the time that there was a war on, or even what war meant, but a recurring nightmare I had for many years during my childhood was in fact a reliving of an actual experience. I used to dream that I was at the top of a staircase, needing, wanting, having to get down, but I couldn't because the staircase had come away from the wall and from the landing I was standing on.

There really was a bomb. Very early one morning, I think in the summer of 1942, a German bomber, presumably returning home from a raid further north, dumped a bomb very near the end of our back garden. I was less than a year old and I had been sleeping with my mother in her bed; she had just got me up to go downstairs to the shelter when the bomb went off. The blast blew out all the windows, and great shards of glass were driven into the bed we had just vacated. She took me to the head of the stairs and looked down, and there was a huge gaping hole where the staircase should have been.

But, my mother says, in spite of the bomb, we didn't immediately leave Solihull. We all decamped to my grandmother's house while the damage to my great-aunt's shop and flat was being repaired.

She must be right, because now I do remember a year or two later, at the age of three or four, going to a little nursery school, Windilows, in Solihull, where we wore rather natty red blazers, and drank wartime orange juice out of mugs with pictures of little fluffy chickens on, while the teacher played the viola. Would that all education could be so pleasant. Milk has always made me spectacularly sick, but that wartime orange juice was lovely. I also loved the great spoonfuls of Virol and Radio Malt children were given in those days, and I've had a sweet tooth ever since.

So it must have been when I was nearly five, just as the war was ending, that we moved out of Solihull. What with the bombs and the bananas and the ration books, shopkeeping wasn't getting any easier, and my great-aunt decided to sell up and buy a cottage in Croyde, on the North Devon coast, near to where my grandmother and stepgrandfather, having sold their house in Broad Oaks Road, had already ensconced themselves in a beautiful little thatched cottage.

Before the war, a lot of Birmingham people used to go to Devon for their holidays, and near Croyde there are Saunton Sands, several miles of dunes running along the Atlantic coast of North Devon, where there was and still is an amazing 1920s art deco hotel, frightfully grand and very much the place to go in those days. Very wealthy people from Birmingham used to go there as an alternative to Torquay, and naturally my *nouveaux riches* grandparents were among them. So when they decided to move out of

Solihull towards the end of the war, that was where they looked for a place to live.

Croyde was – and is – a lovely seaside village, undisturbed by tourists in those immediately post-war days, and for quite a few years afterwards. I virtually spent my childhood on the beach. I learned to swim as soon as we arrived, and an abiding image of childhood is of being barefoot on the sands. To this day, whenever I see a beach, I want to whip off my shoes. I was taught to be respectful of the sea at a very early age, for obvious reasons, but I also learned to adore it. I particularly love that very dramatic pounding water of the North Atlantic shore. And sand. I don't like pebble beaches.

My great-aunt Peg was small and birdlike, but in those days she was very strong and had the heart of an ox. She was always a great walker. She used to think nothing of tramping along for five or six miles a day, searching the lanes for blackberries and the fields for mushrooms. She gave me my own great love of the countryside.

One of my chief joys when I was little was being carried piggyback on her shoulders across what were called the burrows at Saunton Sands, miles and miles of miniature desert – but you had to be careful because some of the area had been mined against an invasion, and the army was still using the dunes as a training ground for flame-throwers, tanks and amphibious craft. We used to play the Grand National – with me as the jockey. Towards the end of her life I could have lifted Peg with one hand, she was so tiny.

Peg's cottage had once been a pub and legend had it that there was a smugglers' run from somewhere in the house to a cave in Baggy Point, a great place for wreckers in the old days. I never found the secret passage, perhaps because I was too scared of the ghosts of the old rum-runners to search properly. In my grandmother's cottage, too, there was a haunted staircase, its entrance covered by a curtain. I was so terrified by stories of 'a lowering presence' and 'a sudden cold clamminess' that I never dared even peep behind that curtain.

My great-aunt's generation were full of superstitions and stories of other worlds. One of her sisters, Great-Aunt Ella, a marvellous, spine-chilling storyteller, always said that she had seen her husband at the foot of her bed on the very night he died in the trenches in the First World War. Ella told fortunes with tea leaves and cards with amazing accuracy, and taught me how to do it. I don't do it now, but she taught me that the cards are just something to concentrate on to keep your brain busy, leaving you free to receive mental pictures from the person whose fortune you are telling. The same thing happens with the shapes made by the tea leaves. I still don't know why it works, but it is astonishing how often the pictures that come into your mind seem right.

All this folklore was allied to a strong, family, churchgoing tradition, and it was in the middle of this heady mixture of superstition and religion that I first heard tell of God. I was five years old, kneeling on a scratchy, hard cushion, with my head under the narrow hymn-book shelf. There was an odd, musty smell, not much light; the adults above me were mumbling together in low voices. I wasn't at all sure that this was for me. Then suddenly everyone started to sing a song about sailors being lost at sea. I cheered up immeasurably. I knew about the sea. I loved playing in the waves and the rock pools. I also knew about the dark side of the sea – the strong undertow and the strength of the breakers. So I loved this song for the sailors.

But when in Sunday school they told me about a very old man who lived in the sky, who was very, very good, and who was watching us all the time, and who set us very high standards of behaviour and always punished us if we didn't live up to them, I knew instinctively, at the age of five, in some deep part of me, that they had got it wrong, and that God was more like the sea, dark and light, giving and receiving, there to love and play in as well as to be in awe of.

I was also introduced to Jesus at Sunday school, and I loved the stories about him. Here was someone I could talk to, tell my troubles and sadnesses to, someone who would exact no retribution for known or unknown wrongs, someone who loved children. Jesus and Danny Kaye were my first heroes.

I have many good memories of that time. Just after the war, when sweets were all on ration and not part of one's life, my great-uncle Will, the Hirst family black sheep who had gone to Canada, came back to visit us in Croyde with a large box of candies. I didn't know what 'candies' were, and I was a little disappointed to find that they were not chocolates but little fondant sweet biscuits with coloured sugar on the outside. But once you'd got over them not being made of chocolate, they were delicious, as well as a feast for the eye – pale greens and pinks and yellows, all in little paper cases.

Walking with my mother on the old back road from Braunton to Croyde and finding the first primroses and violets was one of the great joys in my life, along with searching for cowrie shells in the rock pools, and American ice-cream sodas, chewing-gum and sausages grilled on the beach barbecues, all provided by the American airmen from the nearby base, who showered us local children with delights. The airmen's homes and families must have seemed a long way away.

That's how it was, in my childhood. It sounds sort of idyllic – and it was, and it wasn't. There are two dark memories. I had my tonsils out when I was about eight or nine. I had no time to prepare or ask questions about it. My mother thought it best not to tell me until the day before that I was going in for an operation. I went into a little hospital run by nuns, and it was a nightmare. I now have some friends who are nuns, but they are very different. I pity anybody who was educated by nuns in those days. There I was, a little girl with a very painful throat, not able to swallow, and a stern-faced sister with a bit of a hormone problem swept into my room the morning after the operation, and said severely to me, 'Have you had a bowel movement?' I had absolutely no idea what a bowel movement was.

A much more unhappy event preceded the tonsils saga. I didn't remember until I was in my forties, undergoing analysis, the actual moment of parting from my mother when she first took me to boarding-school. I was just five years old. In the analysis I remembered, in a flash, what I was wearing, what my mother was wearing, and where we were standing. I had on a little smocked dress, and she was dressed in blue. We were standing in a hall with Victorian tiles on the floor, at a boarding-school called Tyspane. There was a big staircase leading up to a gallery, a huge window, a big front door. We were standing in a group, the headmistress, who I was told to call 'Auntie Ba', was holding my hand, and my mother – was just leaving.

I was overwhelmed with grief. I was to be a weekly boarder, so of course my mother told me that she'd be back in a few days, but at that age you have no concept of time. At five I couldn't understand why I was not allowed to go home. To have to wait a week to see my mother and my great-aunt and Tibs the cat felt like a life sentence. For a child, every separation has all the sadness of a death and a few days, a day, even a minute, are all unimaginably long. If anyone has any doubt of that, you have only to remember what it was like, as a child, waiting for Christmas. Even on Christmas Eve it felt like an eternity of waiting, until that moment when you fell asleep and woke up the next morning and there were your presents at the end of the bed. That hugeness of time. So to be left in a strange place 'for a few days' was a desolation.

I didn't cry. Without doubt, a child of five, silently screaming for her mother, has remained a part of me. I know now how to take care of that child. That sounds pure Californiaspeak – but it is true.

My mother's generation were brought up on the book by Truby Whatshername – you only fed the baby at certain times, you didn't pick it up when it cried, you imposed discipline from birth onwards, and you didn't explain things. It wasn't their fault; they were told that these were the right things to do. There must have been so many mothers in those days standing by the cots of their screaming babies, wringing their hands with longing to pick them up, but not daring to, because they had been told it was the worst thing they could do for their baby.

I think my mother thought that Peg was spoiling me, and that I was running wild. She didn't have much money to live on, so she needed to work. She did various things, including working in a dress shop in Barnstaple. She was still very, very young. I used to blame her for leaving me at that school, but I don't now. I remind myself that she was only in her twenties. What did I know in my twenties? I later discovered that Mum spent days sobbing over the parting.

She did what she thought was right at the time, for reasons she believed were right. In those days a lot of people sent their children away. The village school was not an option, for reasons of pure snobbishness, really. Nobody of that class – middle class – sent their children to the local village school. At Tyspane I would get the most wonderful education. It would not have been possible to take me there and back every day; petrol was on ration, and there were very few buses. So if you add all those things up, it made perfect sense.

After the first shock of parting from my mother, I was very happy at Tyspane. Auntie Ba – I have no idea what her real name was – turned out to be a lovely, motherly lady. Miss Huxtable and Miss Hodges were born teachers. Miss Huxtable was tall and willowy with one of those hairdos where you tied a stocking round your head and bunched the hair all the way round like a halo. She had an elderly mother in Ilfracombe. Miss Hodges was short and stout with dark hair and an incipient moustache. They were both gifted teachers who adored children. There was also a sweet, plump, local girl, a children's nurse called Violet, who looked after the boarders.

They made reading and writing fun, and even arithmetic seemed magical. We read out loud in class, and I hankered to be asked to read all the time. The sound and feel of words in my mouth, the pictures and emotions the writer and I could conjure up were an addiction I have never been cured of.

I even fell in love for the first time, when I was five, with two boys at Tyspane. One was Robert Capstick who had dark brown eyes. I swapped him my Dinky set for his set of medals. (When my mother discovered what had happened, the swap was reversed.) I also fell for a beautiful, fair-haired boy called Richard. There was a hit parade song at the time called 'Open the door, Richard – and let me in', and I used to go round the school singing this all the time, because I was totally in love with Richard. And with Robert.

The house was surrounded by a huge garden which ran into a meadow. There was a high seesaw among some beautifully scented pine trees, and if you sat at the very end, which took some courage, you went up almost to the sky. There was a Wendy house, an old, wooden, switchback ride and the heaven of making houses in the meadow at hay-making time. The only uniform was white aertex shirts and red shorts for the beach. They were easy to get in and out of, whereas liberty bodices, worn at other times, presented something of a challenge to my fingers.

We went regularly to Saunton Sands. It was said that every kind of wild flower to be found in Britain grew on the spongy grass behind the barriers of wind-carved sand. The two Miss Hs, like Great-Aunt Peg and my mother, were a fount of information about flowers and birds. I was so proud when I could name the ragwort, full of furry caterpillars, the great sea stock or the tiny creeping scarlet pimpernel, and recognise the differences between the thrush's and the robin's song.

Tyspane became a home from home, but it wasn't home. I had never felt lonely on my own. I had been happy to play for hours by myself on the beach, in the dunes, in the garden, and I would carry on long conversations with trees, plants, birds and animals. When I went to school, this habit of conversing with ants and mending the broken stalks of plants was something I found it wise to conceal. Now I couldn't ever be alone. Living at boarding-school, I had to spend all my time among a lot of other children, who naturally asked questions.

One thing this meant was that for the first time I had to try and explain what had happened about my father. He'd gone away. Why? It wasn't too difficult, because at that time nearly all the children had been brought up for their first five years by mothers and aunts, while their grandfathers, fathers and uncles were away at the war. Many of them had fathers who had been killed or captured or were missing in action. Two of the children were refugees. We were all in the same boat, so I wasn't a particular object of curiosity. But I began to wonder myself, for the first time, if there wasn't something a little bit different about my family.

Probably there were a few children that I played with in the holidays too, but I don't remember them. The times I remember most clearly are of a happy, almost solitary life, very busy, jam-packed with events like going off to the dunes to play Germans versus English, by myself. I was an agent, dropped by parachute, behind enemy lines.

3. The facts of life

At the very beginning, I wanted to be in a Disney cartoon. Aged three, what I really wanted to be when I grew up was Donald Duck. I would sit for hours in the bath, getting wrinkled skin, trying to imitate his voice. Luckily this was just a phase, or my later career might have been somewhat limited. But the cinema had cast its spell, and when I was taken to the theatre, I became well and truly hooked on the idea of becoming an actress, although, in fact, my very first visit to the theatre was not an unqualified success. I was taken, aged three or four, to a pantomime at the Birmingham Alexandra Theatre. I was enthralled, right up until the moment when G. H. Elliot, the Chocolate Coloured Coon, deeply un-PC now, appeared; and the sight of this black man who was not a black man, who waved huge white hands about, terrified me. He was weird. He was alarming. I was rushed screaming from the theatre.

I loved words from a very early age. The first poems I learned were in A. A. Milne's *When We Were Very Young*, and Robert Louis Stevenson's *A Child's Garden of Verses*. I also loved Kipling. I still think he's a good poet. When I was eight, my mother gave me a big, fat, green book, which I still have, called *The Golden Staircase*. I had two favourite poems in that, and over them I would weep copiously. One was Burns'

> My heart's in the Highlands, my heart is not here;
> My heart's in the Highlands a-chasing the deer;

21

Chasing the wild deer, and following the roe,
My heart's in the Highlands, wherever I go.

I thought that was so moving. And the other, that I now
regard as a simply frightful poem, was by W. E. Henley:

What have I done for you,
England, my England?
What is there I would not do,
England, my own?

Part of their attraction was that when I was young, I always
had a tremendous feeling of nostalgia for something that I
couldn't remember, and a feeling like homesickness but I
didn't know where for. When, at the age of eleven, I first
came across Wordsworth's 'Intimations of Immortality' –
'Our birth is but a sleep and a forgetting . . .' suddenly
everything seemed to fall into place, and I recognised a
description of my own feelings, and that perhaps I was
homesick for the mysterious place from which I came.

Homesickness was also fuelled by life, of course. Crying
copiously over 'My heart's in the Highlands . . .' was a great
way of expressing the grief I felt about being at boarding-
school and away from the people I loved most. John
Masefield's 'The West Wind', and the anonymous poem at
the end of my copy of *The Wind in the Willows* called 'Ave
Atque Vale' always reduced me to tears. But only when I
was alone. At school, in front of the others, I would be
stoical. I cried my eyes out reading *Black Beauty* for myself,
but when Miss Hodges read it out to us in class, and came
to the part where Ginger died, I found myself laughing. I
wanted to sob, but was afraid that that might not be acceptable. My diaphragm had to do something, so I laughed.

I read voraciously anything I could get my hands on.
When I moved into a new flat a couple of years ago, and
was putting the books back on the shelves, I picked up the
first edition of the complete works of Shakespeare that I

had ever owned, a present from my mother, in three volumes, and it had on the fly leaf, 'To Teff, on her ninth birthday'. (Teff was my name for myself before I could manage Stephanie, and it has stuck as my family pet name.) I probably understood very little of the meaning of the plays then, but I was besotted with them. I would sit and read and read and read them. It was better than any drug – I just got high on the glory of the words.

The combination of this love of words and reading, with many visits to the theatre and the cinema, put the seal on my ambition to be an actress from a very early age. I was lucky, because my mother has always loved the theatre, so we would go regularly, whenever it could be afforded, and to the cinema. It was to do with another world, with fantasy, with not being in this world, not having to do this life, and it was being part of something which was magic and wonderful, removed from the pain and ordinariness of life. I couldn't have put words to it then, but I'm certain now that that was why I was fascinated by acting, from a very early age, and very attracted to the idea of being someone else.

I would imitate voices all the time, try out what it felt like in your mouth to talk in a certain way, usually in front of the mirror, or just to myself as I mooched about. I was always riveted by accents. At home we all spoke ordinary Queen's English, or whatever you like to call it, King's English in those days, but we were in a Devon village, and in those days the Devon accent was very broad, because it was quite isolated and hadn't been diluted by the voices of outsiders.

I remember a farmer's daughter, Kath White. Her father, Farmer John, was an enormous man, and they were real Devonshire. Kath, a mountainous figure, had a companion housekeeper, called Doll, who was a tiny little clothes-peg of a woman. I often used to go to see them and Kath would say, 'Ow are you, ma little med? Cum in, ma little med, cum in.' So I would try this out, practising her voice, wondering what it must be like to be Kath, up to your elbows in flour, making cakes and bread, with great bowls of milk turning to cream.

Until I was seven, the pattern of our lives at Croyde remained more or less unchanged. I grew accustomed to staying at Tyspane all week during term, and was happy there. At weekends and in the holidays my very happy, secure little world consisted of Peg, my mother and Tibs the cat; and my grandparents, although not exactly my favourite people, were part of the warp and woof of familiar, everyday life. And then one day, into the comfortable routine of our lives came the tall, elegant figure of Colin Lees.

The first time I met him was when he came to call on my mother at Peg's little two-bedroom cottage in Croyde. Instinctively children pick up what the real story is. I was called downstairs to come and say 'Hallo', and I'd just been given a jack-in-the-box. I was thrilled with this little wooden box. I thought it was just the best thing ever, so I took it downstairs with me, put it round the door and opened the lid, Oomph! And he took no notice. He completely ignored me. I know now that this was very uncharacteristic of him. He was a kind man who loved children, and normally he would have played for hours with any child. But on this day, he was concentrating on my mother. As far as I was concerned, that was it. I could see he was taking up all my mother's attention.

Colin's sister was married to a doctor in Ilfracombe. When the National Health Service started, my grandmother had wanted to sign on, and Colin had come round to the house with his sister and brother-in-law for a drink. That was how he met my mother. It was quite a small social world.

Because my mother was divorced, she and Colin had some difficulty in finding a vicar who was willing to marry them, which even then I thought was sublimely stupid, but in the end they did, and they had a full white wedding. My mother was still only twenty-eight. I was a bridesmaid, along with two new cousins – members of Colin's extended family. I wore an extremely pretty blue dress and a headband made of flowers. The plan was that at the end of the reception at an Ilfracombe hotel, they were going to drive me home to my great-aunt's in Croyde, and then they were going off on their honeymoon. So there we all were. All the photographs had been taken, the bride and groom toasted, the bouquet thrown.

Suddenly my mother and stepfather got into a car and disappeared. They had left me behind. My great-aunt and I careered down the hotel drive waving our arms and shouting after them. All was not lost. They came back and picked us up.

All those little things set the seal on how I was with my stepfather. I never let him in. He tried so hard, but I wasn't to be won. With me, Colin didn't stand a chance, in spite of bringing into our lives a wonderful black Labrador dog called Jo, whom I loved very deeply, and in spite of his being infinitely patient with me, teaching me to fish and canoe, and making bows and arrows, and carts for Jo to pull. Inside me there was a huge amount of resentment. For the first seven years of my life the family – my world – had been my mother and Peg and me. Suddenly there was this stranger coming in, and he was taking up all my mother's time.

In any case, I *had* a father somewhere; a real father, who was a prince, or at least a knight on a white charger, who would come along one day and make everything wonderful for me. Since going to Tyspane, I'd acquired this fantasy father. I'd made up my own idea of him. What I knew of Leslie Cole didn't sound terribly romantic to me. At first I used to tell my friends that he had been a fighter pilot who had been killed in the war. Then I used to imagine that my *real* father was probably Jack Buchanan – or, though I hardly dared hope, Danny Kaye – and that was the reason he couldn't come to see us, even though he wanted to. But it was a secret. I never told anybody. I just waited and hoped for the day when he would come and claim me.

Jack Buchanan had entered my fantasy life courtesy of my mother's pre-war wind-up gramophone. I can still remember its smell when I opened the little doors, the HMV dog on a label on the lid, the little metal cup full of steel needles. I would wind it up laboriously and put on Bing Crosby, Al Jolson, Cicely Courtneidge and, one of my favourites, the cool, sophisticated Jack Buchanan.

We all liked music and singing in the family. One of my sweetest memories is of my mother singing 'Ma curly-headed baby' to me as a lullaby. Peg taught me 'Blaydon Races' and 'Did you ever hear tell of Long Barney?' and we both would cry when we sang 'Sweet Polly Oliver' together. I was taught to play the piano; endless scales and 'Sur la Glace à Sweet Briar' failed to inspire, but at least it taught me to read music, which has stood me in good stead.

About a year after Colin and my mother were married, came even worse news. We were to move to a house in Gloucestershire, and leave my beloved Peg, and the sea, and I was to go to a new school, Clifton High School for Girls.

We moved to a place called Golden Valley, near Bitton, a tiny little village on the upper Bristol to Bath road, where it runs through the countryside from Bitton to Beach. There had been a little coal mine there in late Victorian times, like the one in the Forest of Dean. The mine consisted of a single ten-foot tower, by now all overgrown with ivy. Our house had originally belonged to the pit manager, so it was rather nice very-early-Victorian, but with a Georgian look to it. At the back there was a huge barn, with a smaller barn attached to the side which had a sliding window where the miners used to come to be paid. There can't have ever been more than a dozen miners, because it was such a little mine.

In many ways, home life continued to be just as idyllic as it had been in Croyde. We had our own water, which came from a spring on the hill just behind, and at the bottom of the garden was a river. In those days, children could roam the fields, as long as we always remembered to close the gates. We learned to be careful if there were bulls, and we knew that if it was a field of wheat then we must walk round the edge. We were never destructive, but it was wonderfully free. The river made up for there being no sea. I learned to fish, and would spend hours building little dams and swimming. My stepfather had a couple of blow-up dinghies, and we used to go for boat trips.

There were two quite separate societies in the village. There were the 'village' people: the farm workers, the people who served in the dairy and the shop, or who worked in a tiny paper-mill at the end of the river. Then there were 'the nobs', the gentry: the doctor, the vicar, the lawyers and the owners of the farms and the paper mill – the folks that did indeed live on top of the hill.

There was a very big house on the hill where the Kings and the King-Smiths lived. In fact, Dick King-Smith, who wrote *The Sheep-pig*, which became the film *Babe*, was one of the family that owned the paper-mill. He's a bit older than me, so he was grown up when I was a child, but I do remember seeing him. Coincidentally, another great children's writer, William Mayne, also lived there. He was the local doctor's eldest son.

The two halves of society only saw each other socially at church or at the village cricket match. The rest of the time they lived in different worlds. It was where I first met snobbery head on and, instinctively and intensely, I could not bear it. I became very rebellious and rude.

I had a foot in both camps. I had village children friends, and up-the-hill children friends. The up-the-hill friends had ponies. My parents were as poor as the proverbial church mice so we couldn't afford a pony, but because, being 'middle class', they were regarded as members of the up-the-hill society, I was allowed to ride their friends' children's ponies. On one occasion, no pony being available, my friends Jacynth and Trudi and I tried to ride a large goat that belonged to a local farmer. We came off very much the worst.

With the village friends I would play wild games, and we'd make dens in the hedgerows, but I still preferred to do some things, like badger watching, on my own. I was then – as I am now – both very gregarious and incredibly solitary. I remember reading Margaret Rutherford's autobiography, in which she said that between jobs she had to go away, because the strain on her of being with people was so huge that she could recuperate only by being alone. I understand that. When I'm working, I love being with people, but if I can't have some time to be on my own, it's as bad as not having water or bread.

Living in a small rural community, there was not a lot going on in the way of a social life, especially for young people – just the occasional village hop, and cricket in the summer. So most people, even the young, went to church, more as a social gathering place than anything.

My best friend Jacynth and I decided to join the bell-ringers. We were about twelve by then, and we thought it might be more exciting than Sunday school, where you did just the same sort of things as you had to do at school all week. There were all those thrilling legends of people hanging themselves from the bell-ropes. We soon discovered there were real dangers – that if someone accidentally let go of their rope, it was quite frightening. You all had to leap back into the deep windows of the tower while the rope whipped itself into a violent frenzy round the ringing chamber.

There was a very po-faced captain of the bells, who taught us how to ring, and we all met one evening a week to practise, and then again on Sunday mornings to ring for the service. Sometimes we would go on trips to other churches to ring their bells; it all greatly added to my enjoyment of reading the Dorothy Sayers detective story about bells, *The Nine Tailors*.

The downside was that every Sunday we were expected to stay for the service after we'd rung the bells, and there was even a special bell-ringers' pew reserved at the back of the church. By then I'd had two years at Clifton School for Girls, where we had church twice on Sundays, daily school assembly with dull prayers and duller hymns, and where, every morning as soon as we got up, we had to read tracts from the Bible Society with the relevant passage in the Bible. The combination of all this had completely done for any embryonic Christian faith I might have picked up from Great-Aunt Peg, and turned me into an ardent humanist. Jacynth and I used to play cards in the bell-ringers' pew, until we were caught and it was banned, so it all became very boring.

I don't think we were ever really cut out to be bell-ringers. There weren't a lot of laughs, and we were not highly regarded by the other ringers, who quite rightly took it all very seriously. The end came one sunny summer Sunday morning when we had biked down early, and were playing around waiting for the others to arrive. We found a pile of bell-ropes and thought it would be a neat idea to use them to haul our bikes up the tower. We didn't think we could be seen, but we hadn't taken into account the people in the nearby alms-houses, whose windows looked out on to the church. They woke up to the sight of an old Raleigh bike, with no visible means of support, rising slowly and majestically up the side of the church tower. The matter was reported to the captain of the bells, and Jacynth and I were banished from ringing from then on.

As childhood slowly became adolescence in rural Gloucestershire, I began to experience, with some of the wilder village boys, the dangerous and thrilling pleasures of kissing games. I really enjoyed it. But I never spoke about it at home. My mother had told me the facts of life, and I had got the message, rightly or wrongly, that it was definitely a thing no one ever talked about.

4. *Shades of the prison-house – bottle-green and grey*

In spite of an almost idyllic home in the Gloucestershire countryside, the years from when we moved away from Croyde until I left home at sixteen were very difficult. The main reason was that I was encased, from the age of nine, in the bottle-green and grey uniform of Clifton High School for Girls. For the first two years I boarded at the junior department of Clifton, while my parents were making the new house habitable, and I experienced the truth of the saying that an English public school is the perfect preparation for prison life: appalling food, living by numbers, and a complete disregard for the growing individual. I grew fat and rude and very, very rebellious.

My first school, Tyspane, had been loving and allowing and understanding and was, as much as any school could be, a home from home. I suppose there must have been school rules, but I don't remember any punishments; I remember it being a place of sunshine and happiness, where the only sadness was that I wasn't with my Mum.

So it was a terrible shock when, at the age of nine, I went to board at Clifton High School for Girls. In the first place it was only girls, which I thought was silly; second, there were all these bloody rules and regulations and third, we had to wear a hideous uniform. At Tyspane we'd just had our white aertex shirts and red shorts to wear on the beach, and even that was really only so that we could be spotted easily among the sand-dunes. Now there was a long list of all the things I would need to have.

There was something rather exciting about buying a proper new school uniform. I'd read my Angela Brazil books and Enid Blyton's *Mallory Towers* stories. I didn't know what was in store for me. We had to go to Daniel Neal's to get blazers and socks, under-knickers and over-knickers and divided skirts for games, all in unbecoming shades of bottle-green and grey, with summer dresses that were mind-boggling in their thoughtlessness for girls reaching puberty. With white Peter Pan collars and white cuffs on the sleeves, and little belts, made in ugly green gingham, they were simply hideous even by the standards of the early fifties. We had to wear hats which, on our last day, we carried ceremoniously to Clifton Suspension Bridge and threw off with a great cheer. People downstream must have been amazed to see all these grey, felt, pudding basins come floating past. It was a fitting end to a rotten time.

But at the beginning I was enchanted by the list of things, and they all had to be marked, so my mother spent hours sewing in Cash's nametapes. She is a very good needle woman, but it still took her ages. On the list it said that you could take only one book and one toy. I took a beautiful copy of Robert Louis Stevenson's *Treasure Island*, which I still have, my teddy bear and my paint-box. When I arrived at the school I discovered that everyone else had taken all sorts of things, books and sweets and toys and all their familiar things from home. Because we weren't allowed an exeat for the first three weeks, I couldn't get anything else. I was a voracious reader, and I had to go for three whole weeks with just one book.

I'm not very good at physical challenges, I must confess. I am a physical coward. There was a fire drill soon after I arrived at the school, and they had recently installed an escape system called 'Davey ropes'. The boarding-school house was about five storeys high, and we had to descend out of the top-storey windows. When you are nine years old, that's big, that's high, that's terrifying. The webbing belt was put round you, under your arms, attached to a rope, which was on a winch. You had to sit on the sill of the open window and swing your feet out, so that you were sitting, looking down. Then you had to ease yourself off the window-sill, let go, turn round and, as you slowly descended, you had to push yourself away from the building with your hands and feet – like abseiling down a mountain.

You are being asked to launch yourself into space, and it is petrifying if you don't have much faith in the teachers behind you. I had no faith in them whatsoever. I thought they were utter idiots and that I should not be putting my life into their hands. I was right. Outside some of the windows were horizontal window bars, to prevent us, pre-sumably, from committing suicide because the food was so bad. As I went down, my foot got caught in one of these bars . . . and they didn't notice. They continued to let the rope go, and I was left hanging upside down by one leg, screaming. The mere idea of mountaineering has been anathema to me ever since.

In those days they did such bizarre things to children, and the lack of psychological insight was quite breathtaking. We decided to have a midnight feast – just some rather hard rock buns and various things we'd brought back from the last exeat. We were caught, of course, and gated – that meant not allowed to go home for the next exeat, which for me was the worst punishment possible. It never stopped me from being naughty; it just made me angry, because I thought it was so unfair. It still makes me wild when people, particu-larly children, are kept from something they love or need or that makes them feel secure.

Food really was bad in school in those post-war years. I remember we were given rissoles for one meal, which were simply disgusting. I quite like rissoles now – good, well-made rissoles with organic beef and lots of herbs – but those I could not eat. Those same rissoles were presented to me for every meal until they eventually went off, but they couldn't make me eat them. In the end they gave in, because it would have been dangerous not to. What a bizarre set of values to think that this could teach a child anything.

I always questioned the rules and regulations at school. For example, there was the rule that when you walked down the corridor, you were not allowed to touch the walls.

'Why not?'

'Because that's the rule.'

If somebody had said, 'I'll tell you why not. Because it makes the walls greasy and dirty if everyone runs their hands along them, and we have to keep washing them down,' that would have made perfect sense to me and I would not have touched the walls. But instead they treated us as lesser beings, who didn't deserve the courtesy of an explanation. You always started from a place of guilt, as a child. You were always guilty until proved innocent, no matter what.

I loathed Clifton with a loathing that I can still recall quite fiercely. I was bright, but not conventionally so, and I was written off by most of the teachers at an early stage as lazy and a wastrel. I still loved, in English, being asked to read aloud. I had done quite a lot of that at Tyspane, and did a certain amount at Clifton, because we had a wonderful English teacher called Miss Locke, who was sweet, and one of the few teachers who could see that there was something else going on behind this unhappy rebelliousness, so she would take enormous trouble with me. Under her aegis, I even acted in a play, *Friar Bacon and Friar Bungay*. There was also a French mistress whom I admired, and I adored the French language, so I happily did French plays, but I never went in for the end-of-term school plays, because they were amateur. I knew, unwaveringly from the age of four, that I was going to be a professional. How smug!

Reading – especially poetry – increasingly became my solace and escape from the pain of daily life. The poets were my friends. They were my teachers about life, especially when I discovered T. S. Eliot, W. H. Auden and Dylan

Thomas. And even before that there were Wordsworth and Keats. I just worshipped Keats. Many years later Robert Gittings, who wrote the definitive book about him, became a friend.

So much poetry is about the inner life, which I've always somehow known is much the most important for me. I still collect poetry books and read poetry much as other people read novels. I do read novels too, of course, but poetry has always been the thing that sang to me most. In a very small shell they present to you something that is important in your own life. And there are a number of poems which I always keep by me these days, in my organiser, which remind me of the principles that I try to live by.

I also came across a piece of prose when I was at school, with which I immediately identified and have treasured ever since. It was in a book of Shakespeare criticism, *The Shakespearian Scholar*, by Dover Wilson, which is an academic work, but in it there is this wonderful piece:

Upon this planet there dwell two strange races of people. The first is a tribe small of stature and delicate of limb, the members of which make their way into civilised society one by one, arriving among us entirely unable to look after themselves, and quite ignorant of our language. After a little while they learn our speech and something of our habits, but they take little interest in the things we prize most. Their ideals are not our ideals. They see a universe quite different from that which is familiar to us. Our eyes are lamps in which the oil of reason burns. Their eyes are charmed casements through which the moon of imagination pours . . . until we teach them to forget.

We have to teach them to forget, or the work of the world would never get done. And yet there are a few, a very few, who do not forget, and these form the second race of strange beings, they are the super-children, they are the Johnnies Head In Air at whose stumbles the world laughs, because it cannot see the stars on which their gaze is fixed. They take no part in that all absorbing task of our civilisation, the acquisition, transformation and distribution of matter. But they are the true creators. They bring cosmos and beauty into a world which is without form and void, and so they have the name Makers or Poets.

I think all children have that potential, but most of them learn to forget. But the few are lucky, who are able to keep on creating, in however small or large a way. It can be a Picasso, or it can be you or me. I've always identified with that, and known that that's what I want to be part of, not caught up in the work of the world, except as a maker or poet.

Perhaps that was also one of the reasons I became increasingly wayward. I was unhappy at Clifton from the start, but my real rebellion didn't begin until I became a day-girl at the senior school, when I was eleven. When I think back now, I often wonder why on earth, when I first went there as a boarder and hated it so much and was so deeply unhappy, I did not simply save up my pocket money, get on a bus and go home. It would have meant two buses, but I could have done it – and I never did. There was a part of me that was too scared.

My own daughter became streetwise at a very early age, because she was at a London day-school. But I went to boarding-school from the age of five, and I didn't know how to do buses. Occasionally I'd travelled on one with my mother to go into Bath for shopping or the cinema, but I never really noticed how we did it. I didn't know how you caught a train. I was scared of those things, of all sorts of things. I was scared of being independent, and yet I hated authority.

The hatred and the rebelliousness really began to take me over at eleven, with the onset of puberty. You can't hold in your emotions then; it all goes haywire. My rage extended to home. My mother and I had many, many battles royal, shouting and screaming. I threw a heavy ski-boot through my (closed) bedroom window once. She had locked me in my bedroom, and I screamed. It was very dramatic. My behaviour was appalling. I hated my parents, and all their friends. I was constantly rude and wouldn't do anything I was told.

At school I was forever in detention. I spent so many hours waiting outside the study of the headmistress, Netta Glenday, that I became deeply familiar with a copy of Van Eyck's 'Adoration of the Lamb' which hung on the wall by her door, and I swear that to this day I could reproduce that famous triptych myself, brush stroke by brush stroke, with no trouble at all. When I saw the original in Ghent or Bruges years later, it sent a shudder down my spine.

Netta Glenday was a remote woman, innately shy, with a stammer, who collected paper-weights. She had a rather plump, unattractive, extremely rude girl constantly presenting herself at her desk, and she had no idea how to deal with me. She would say, 'Don't do it again.' But she never asked, 'Why do you think you keep doing it?'

Psychology didn't come into it in those days. You either toed the line or you didn't. Team spirit, and letting the side down – there was a tremendous amount of that. Whenever she said I'd let my mother down it would add guilt to my general feeling of rage, and made me even angrier. I didn't give a damn about letting the blasted school down.

On the one hand, my mother really wanted me to toe the line, but on the other hand, once a year, if we had the money, we would take the train up to London for the Ideal Home Exhibition, which she loved. We only did it a couple of times, because it meant my taking the day off school, which was absolutely forbidden unless you were ill, so for once we were in league against authority. Then we were spotted, on Bath Station, and we didn't dare do it again. But I had seen there was a bit of the maverick in my mother too, which encouraged me in a way. My mother had been to Malvern School for Girls, but she had never been as rebellious as I was.

The final straw that broke Netta Glenday's back was the episode with the Latin mistress, one Miss Weedon, who had a very sharp nose and frizzy hair. (Why did one almost never have attractive role models at school in those days? There was one, our French mistress, who was rather glamorous, which was probably the main reason why I came to like French so much. She was a good role model of an attractive, married woman with a career, but she was the only one.) We were working towards our O levels, and Miss Weedon was taking us for Latin. It must have been infuriating for her, because really I was very bright, but I wasn't in the least bit interested in Latin, so I didn't do any work. She said, 'You'll need Latin for university entrance.'

I said, 'I'm not going to university.'

'Oh, yes, you are.'

'Oh, no, I'm not.'

'Well, what are you going to do?'

'I'm going to be an actress.'

And she laughed. That was it. I picked up my Latin dictionary and hurled it at her, right from the back of the classroom, where I always sat. Unfortunately it missed, but even so that was probably the reason I was expelled.

At this point, my mother would like it put on official record that I wasn't actually expelled. I was always going to leave after taking O levels, and I did take them. My mother also doesn't want you to think that she was the only parent who couldn't control her daughter – there were four of us in my extremely unruly, rebellious gang, all from irreproachably respectable families, including a surgeon's daughter. The four mothers all wrote to Clifton to ask that, if our O level grades were not good enough, we might come back for another term and retake them.

You must admit that my version does make a better story. In any case, both versions end with the chilling words of the letter my mother received back from Clifton: 'When

Stephanie has taken her O levels, she will not be welcome back at the school.' Hurray!

I passed all my O levels except one. I hated history so much that I hadn't wanted to take it at all, but they made me, so I just wrote my name at the top of the paper, and then sat there for two and a half hours, twiddling my thumbs.

A part of me now completely understands, and feels that I was justified in being so difficult, because there was nobody who understood me. I can look back with great compassion on my unhappy, younger self. It wasn't only me. There were many other miserable girls, and there was nobody there with the breadth of vision, the foresight, the imagination, the love of learning and education, to recognise, not just in me, but in so many others, the splendid potential. Many girls were simply completely cowed by the system.

I was lucky, because I had some fire inside me that made me fight the injustices. The way I did it, by rudeness and rebellion, was the only way I could, because you're very limited as a child in your means of demonstration against what outrages you. It was absolutely the wrong sort of school for me. I don't know where I should have gone, but not there. My mother had originally thought of sending me to Cheltenham Ladies' College, but she was afraid she might let the side down by getting the giggles when being interviewed by the headmistress who she learned gloried in the name of Miss Poppem. So I was spared the sage green. From what I've heard, I doubt very much that it would have been any better.

I think if anything could drive me really mad it would be to find myself again in a place or a situation of deep injustice about which I could do nothing. I have huge empathy with people who are wrongly imprisoned, or denied their rights in whatever way, or operated on in a way that ruins their lives . . . I can't bear it. It fuels my anger and drives me to support, among other things, the National Schizophrenia

Fellowship and Age Concern, because the injustices that are still being done both to the elderly and the mentally disabled are just horrendous. I have to do something, or I get so frustrated that I feel I might go mad.

And I'm sure that much of that frustration and anger grew out of things that prevailed in my boarding-school in the early fifties.

5. Peter and Paul

I've never got over the thrill of being able to say, 'My brothers . . .' It still makes my heart turn over.

Whatever troubles I was having at school, and however rebellious I had become at home as puberty set in, a truly wonderful thing happened when I was eleven that made our family life hugely, immeasurably happier.

My brothers came into our lives. Jo, the black Labrador who had arrived with Colin, was a great companion and joy, but I had always longed to be part of a proper family, with brothers and sisters. My mother had a series of miscarriages, and it seemed it could never be. Along with several other families in Bitton they had a Dr Barnardo's boy to stay for the summer holidays once, but that wasn't the same thing at all. He was a rival, not a brother, and I was furiously jealous.

Then one day my mother's younger brother, Harry, arrived on our doorstep, and left his twin sons – Peter and Paul, who were then about eighteen months old – for my mother to look after, because he and his wife were going through a bad patch in their marriage. The boys stayed with us for about three weeks, and then Harry came back and took them away again.

Later we heard that Harry and his wife had split up, and he told my mother that the boys were staying with his wife's relatives. What the wretched man had actually done was to put them into a Church of England children's home. At the same time, we are pretty sure, he was using them as a lever for getting money out of my grandmother. He may have thought that if she knew that we were looking after them, she wouldn't go on supporting him. It is hard, even for the sake of my brothers, to think of anything nice to say about my uncle Harry. He wasn't even gloriously, anti-heroically wicked; he was just dangerously weak, cowardly and feckless. He is one of the reasons that I used to be so unforgiving about my own fears and fearfulness.

The boys were nearly two years old by the time we managed to trace them, at a children's home near Chester, on the Welsh borders, and we were able to go and bring them home. I'll never forget it. There they were, these two sad, blonde-haired, blue-eyed angels, Peter Maitland and Paul Russell, sitting in a bare, comfortless room with several other little children, all listless, with a scattering of toys strewn around them. No one was playing with the children or encouraging them. Somewhere down the line the twins had been terribly ill-treated – we don't know by whom. Pete had had his arm broken in two places, and Paul had had his nose smashed.

We took them home. I'd always wanted brothers or sisters – and now, there they were. I loved them to bits. They were my living dolls. I used to play for hours with them, with Dinky cars and Lego, and as they got older we built dams together down in the river, and went on boating trips; I could show them all the things I loved doing. We became a proper family.

My mother was never so much of a churchgoer as my devout, Anglo-Catholic great-aunt Peg, and still never talks about religion, but she was always a great one for family celebrations and rituals. Easter, Christmas, birthdays; they were always marked in a tremendous way. In Devon at Easter we had always gone along for the traditional egg rolling, and she would paint boiled eggs very beautifully for our breakfast, and hide little, coloured, chocolate eggs all over the garden for me and my friends to hunt for.

At Christmas the entire house was decorated, and my stepfather would dress up as Father Christmas. My mother made him the outfit. She went to huge trouble to set the scene, and I think she enjoyed it enormously. Buying Christmas and birthday presents for the boys became an extra source of fun and joy for all of us.

I think if I hadn't been living back at home by then, if I'd still been a boarder, the story might have been different, but I was at home, going to school as a day-girl, and I can honestly say that I was never in any way the least bit jealous or resentful of my brothers. From a very young age, like so many children, I loathed injustice, and I could see that these two completely helpless little boys were victims of great injustice. They were so needy that my heart quite naturally and spontaneously filled with the sort of overflowing, unconditional love that Great-Aunt Peg had always shown me.

When they first arrived they were, naturally, very frightened, disturbed young creatures, who had been shunted from pillar to post, and it was very hard for my parents to reassure them they were now permanently safe and loved. They had lots of illnesses, and would frequently bang their heads against the wall because they were emotionally disturbed. Very little was known about this in those days, and as we were living deep in the country, there wasn't any professional back-up. All my mother and Colin could do was love the boys and do everything they could to *show* them they were loved, which they gladly did. They wanted to adopt the boys immediately, but Harry put all sorts of obstacles in their way. Eventually, however, the adoption went through and their name was changed from Peter and Paul Sheldon to Peter and Paul Lees. I had long ago opted to remain Stephanie Cole, keeping my connections with my mysterious, fantasy father.

My stepfather was wonderful with the twins, and truly loved them. He made a little cart for Jo the dog to pull the boys along in when they were tiny, and Jo loved that.

Whenever the cart came out, his tail would wag and he would be there immediately, waiting for his harness to be put on. Jo, too, was completely devoted to the boys. He would lie in the middle of the road outside the back gates of the house, and when a car came along he would rise slowly to his feet and walk majestically along in the middle of the road, making the car crawl behind him for the few yards past the front of our house, until all danger of the boys being hurt had passed.

Gradually life calmed down. They were much loved and somewhere their souls knew it, so they grew more confident, and soon became two smashing, attractive, mischievous boys. Paul was always into mechanical things. From the age of ten he could take a car apart and put it together again. He was phenomenal. He was left-handed and possibly very slightly dyslexic so, although he got by, he found school work difficult. But because he was so good mechanically he had an area in which he absolutely shone, and he and Colin would spend a lot of time together. The barn was always full of DIY materials. Colin was very handy, and was supposed to do all the do-it-yourself work for the house, so he spent an awful lot of time standing and looking at it. He would get it done eventually, but it always took ages. Thus the barn was full of machinery, workbenches and bits and bobs, and that was another bit of paradise for the boys, especially Paul.

Pete was much more academic, dreamy and creative. He loved words and painting, so in some ways he and I were naturally closer in the things that interested us. Later he became fascinated by history and archaeology. When the family moved to Keynsham, they were building the famous Keynsham bypass – well, it's famous in Keynsham – where they had to dig out a chunk of the hillside. Pete started to collect ammonites, and when he was still only a teenager he actually discovered the first full skeleton of an ichthyosaurus ever found in the West country, which was a terrific thrill. It's now in Bristol Museum.

* * *

As they grew up they both went through difficult teenage years, which, having been such a rebellious adolescent myself, I completely understood and sympathised with. But of course, by that time, I had long left home, and was hardly ever there, so it was my parents who had to bear the brunt of it.

It was always very obvious what Paul was going to do: he left school at fifteen and became an apprentice in a garage. Pete's adolescence was slightly more difficult than Paul's; it didn't seem that he would ever come to the end of it. From being a loving and charming little boy, he became increasingly remote and unhappy, moody, difficult, angry, impossible to reach, and he didn't seem able, or even to want to explain.

Pete eventually decided, when he left school, that he would like to work backstage in the theatre. It fitted in with his main passions, which were painting and gardening, and playing the blues on a bottleneck guitar. So he went, following in my footsteps, to the Bristol Old Vic Theatre School, took the technical course there, and found work among the sound and lights of the theatre. But his troubles had only just begun. It was to be another five years of painful struggle before we discovered what the matter with Pete really was.

6. Leaving home

One day, when I was fourteen, my stepfather, Colin, was travelling to Cardiff by train. He found himself sitting opposite a small, bright-eyed Jewish man, and they started to talk. Colin asked him what he did, and the man, who had a thick Berlin accent, said, 'I teach movement and basics at the Bristol Old Vic Theatre School. And also I teach at Cardiff.' It was Rudi Shelley, one of the finest drama and movement teachers of our time. Among others he taught Anthony Hopkins at Cardiff, and many of our top actors today owe all their basic knowledge and understanding of their craft to Rudi. Colin said, 'Oh, my young stepdaughter wants to be an actress. Have you got any advice I could pass on to her?'

And Rudi said, 'Yes. Tell her to learn to sew.'

When Colin came home and told me this I thought, 'Oh, bloody hell! Do me a favour!'

I wanted to declaim dramatic poetry, lose myself in another world, not sit about making costumes. My mother was such a wonderful seamstress, cook and gardener, so naturally I hated doing all those things. There had always been that bit of mother–daughter competition, and I felt that whenever I tried to do any of the things that she was good at, I was never good enough.

There I was, fifteen years old, thrown out of Clifton Girls, but still too young to go to drama school, even supposing one would take me. My public school education, incidentally, had been paid for in a rare spirit of generosity by my grandmother – just another point against her as far as I was concerned. My mother now insisted that I do a year at the College of Commerce in Bristol. Any girl who grew up in the fifties will probably recognise the pattern – a mother who holds it as incontrovertible truth that, having given your daughters as good an education as your sons so that they could live fine, free independent lives in the brave new world, you then insisted that they train to become secretaries so that they would always have 'something to fall back on'. I know so many girls whose mothers made them do this. I don't know of any men.

I never did come to be at one with Pitman's shorthand, but the typing has been invaluable, and I continued with French and gained a smattering of German, although it never appealed so much to my romantic soul or felt so good in my mouth. But I'm glad I did it, and I had a good year.

Occasionally I was to be grateful for having something 'to fall back on', but not too often, thank goodness.

We didn't have to wear a uniform, and it was up to us whether we turned up for the classes or not, so consequently I always did, even enduring the tedium of double-entry bookkeeping, although I can't say I ever penetrated its arcane mysteries. I went to lots of parties. We even did a play at the college, *The Importance of Being Earnest*, and I played Miss Prism for the first time.

In the meantime, I was doing what I could to prepare for an audition at the place I had set my heart on going to. I could have tried for any of the drama schools, but I was terrified at the thought of going to London; the old fear thing again. I was so lucky, because one of the greatest drama schools in the country, the Bristol Old Vic Theatre School, was in my own home city. It was the only drama school I wanted to go to, and the only school I wanted to audition for.

I went once a week to a man called Hedley Goodall, a

radio actor who held private tuition classes for people of all ages. I also went once a week to a lady called Edith Manvell, who had been married to Roger Manvell, the film critic, although they were long divorced. I read poems and bits of Shakespeare with her. They both did their best for me, but I was conscious, even at fifteen, that their rather rule-bound way of teaching produced a kind of acting that was not what I saw radiating from Peggy Ashcroft, so I knew that for my audition I would have to go my own way.

The wonderful thing was that my mother was completely and utterly supportive. She never admonished me for being expelled from Clifton, and there was never any question that I shouldn't go for the thing that I had set my heart on. We continued to go to the theatre together whenever we could, and to the cinema, opera and ballet. Once a week we would go either to the Bristol Old Vic Theatre or the Bath Theatre Royal, or to the Bristol Hippodrome. Once or twice we went to Stratford, and a couple of times we had huge treats, and went to London. I saw Laurence Olivier, John Gielgud, Sybil Thorndike and Edith Evans all at the height of their powers.

My stepfather and I both loved variety, so we would also go to the variety theatre as often as we could. I've seen all the greats of the older generation: Norman Evans, and lovely Beryl Reid, who was so glorious, Cicely Courtneidge, Joyce Grenfell, Ruth Draper, Morecambe and Wise, live, not just on television . . . They were all astonishing and wonderful to my eyes. To this day I just love to see a past master alone on a stage, working an audience. I always secretly wanted to be a stand-up comic myself, but I knew that I would be far too scared. Acting a part is like putting on a mask, which of course the first actors in the Western world did. Standing alone in front of an audience, talking directly to them, strips you of all disguise and takes enormous courage.

For years I used to have a recurring dream of having to keep an audience entertained for half an hour because something had gone wrong backstage. I would open my mouth and start to speak, and in my dream I would always be a huge success. The house would be rocking with laughter as I woke up. The odd thing is that it has more or less come to pass. I have several times in recent years had to talk off the cuff to an audience when there's been a crisis, and found that I can quite happily keep talking to them until whatever has gone wrong backstage has gone right again; or do the warm-up of a live audience before recording a television situation comedy. I love doing it. It is great food for the ego! I never believed, when I was young, that I would ever have the chutzpah to do anything like that.

My mother and I had always haunted the second-hand bookshops whenever I had a birthday or it was Christmas and people had given me money; now I started to search for the biographies and autobiographies of all the old actors. I read everything there was to read about the theatre, no matter how out of date. I read plays, old and new, and my knowledge became quite wide. I took the magazine *Theatre World* from the age of twelve and I would read it from cover to cover.

I do so love the way things come around. About two years ago, when I was in the West End in *A Passionate Woman*, I received a letter enclosing a photocopy of a page from *Theatre World*, with a name written in a very young hand several times in the margin – my own name, Stephanie Cole – where I had been practising my signature. I can't have been more than thirteen or fourteen. My correspondent said in his letter, 'I would love you to have this, if it is indeed your writing.' Indeed it was, and he has sent me his copy of *Theatre World*.

I went along for my audition when I was fifteen and a half. The Principal of the Bristol Old Vic Theatre School in those days was Duncan (Bill) Ross, who had trained with Michel Saint-Denis at the London Old Vic School, and whose teaching was in a direct line from Stanislavsky's. You had to take along two pieces, one Shakespeare and something contemporary. I chose a speech by Doto in Christopher

Fry's brilliant, comic play, *A Phoenix too Frequent*. I can't remember which bit of Shakespeare I prepared.

I have vivid recollections of a very long and practical interview, first discussions, then 'get-up-and-do-it', and a man with flaming red hair who talked a language I understood and who somehow saw, in this dumpy, incredibly shy girl, a passion and a raw talent just about peering through. The redhead was Bill Ross, of course. He asked me to read the opening of *The Merchant of Venice* with him, Solario and Solarno, 'the two salads' as they are called. Then he said, 'Now, tell me, what you think they are like.'

I answered off the top of my head, 'One is rather flowery and one is more down to earth', and I think that caught his attention; here was a would-be actor who could read character from the written word.

My mother sat in the car outside for an hour and a half, and was just on the point of marching in to demand what they had done with me, when I appeared, walking on air, feeling like a butterfly who has just emerged from the chrysalis, still squashed and dripping, but with the colours upon its wings ready to be unfurled for the world.

'What happened?' asked my mother, stubbing out her umpteenth cigarette.

'I did it – I'm in!' I yelled.

And we both sobbed all the way down Pembroke Road!

Somehow or other, bless him, bless him, bless him – to this day I bless him – Bill Ross had recognised something in me that something might be done with. And saved my life. I know that sounds melodramatic, but if I hadn't been accepted, I think my world would have fallen apart.

The odd thing was, I never doubted it. Not through arrogance – I was far too shy and unsure of myself for that – but because this was the point my whole life had been steering me towards. It was as though, through all my school days, I had been trudging across thousands of miles of dry desert knowing that somewhere ahead was the Golden City, and now I had reached it.

* * *

The list of things I had to get was even more exciting than when I first went away to boarding-school – black footless tights and leotards, a ballet support – ballet! – ballet shoes and various books. I bought them all and tried them all on and read them all and found the waiting unbearable. And then there was finding digs near the school – a vast room in Edith Manvell's lovely old house in The Paragon, with an electric ring for cooking, huge windows with exotic hangings, a bed, and table to work at.

I had to go to Gloucester for an interview to get a grant. Three elderly people sat at a table in front of a window in a dimly lit, wood-panelled room in the Council House. I couldn't see their faces. Would I do a piece? I had already been accepted by one of the most prestigious schools in Britain. What more did they want? I had nothing prepared. They found a book of poetry, and gave me Wordsworth's 'Daffodils' which I knew well and duly read for them. The three good burghers of Gloucester must have been satisfied, because I got the grant – fees paid and three pounds a week to live on. I was all set to spread my wings.

A significant thing happened one day during the year between leaving school and starting at the Vic School. For the first time, I asked my mother to tell me about my father. We were on our bicycles, riding down to the village when she told me. She said that she had been in a state of great unhappiness when she realised that her marriage to Leslie Cole had been a mistake. She had fallen passionately in love with someone else, and I was the child of that romance.

She asked me if I would like to meet him, but I felt that if my father didn't want to know about me – I certainly didn't want to know about him. Actually, the chief feeling I remember is one of relief. I was free of the fantasies that I'd woven about my father. I didn't have to wait for Danny Kaye or Jack Buchanan to come and find me any more. I think unconsciously I had always known that the story I'd been told as a child was not the whole story.

In those days, I don't think it was just us; most families were much less demonstrative, less openly affectionate than say, I am today, with my daughter. I don't remember anyone saying to me as a child, 'Oh, I do love you.'

It wasn't that they didn't feel love. Mum and Great-Aunt Peg loved me warmly and devotedly, but they weren't particularly tactile people, nor was my stepfather. Yet somehow, being sensual and loving physical contact must be written somewhere into my DNA. Among the most important things in my life are the sensual things, and they were always incredibly important to me as a child. It still happens to me now. When I go past trees, for example, the palms of my hands actually tingle, and I have to touch. I have to put my hand in water. These were things I could never share as a child, because, as far as I knew, I was the only person who felt like that.

When I joined the Vic School, and stepped into the world of the theatre, there were all these people who felt as I did. I started to understand myself for the first time. These were people who were not afraid of hugging, of expressing how they felt about each other, and to do it often. To outsiders we are sometimes seen as people who wear our hearts on our sleeves, who are not sincere, but this is not true. I have met more genuine love, more support and more caring for their fellows from people in my business than anywhere else in the world. Because of my work with various charities, and the way I live my life, I know quite a lot about other businesses, other professions, other communities, even Christian communities. And I believe that I see more tolerance, more real allowing of other people, in the theatre than anywhere else. For me, at sixteen, it became my family – everything I thought I ever wanted or needed.

7. Playing the now

The first days at the Vic School were terrifying. I'd always been shy, and if I hadn't wanted to act so much, I could not have done it. One of the things I was most trepidatious about was appearing in my leotard and black tights for the first time. There were only about twenty new students, plus a small technical course, and fourteen or so second years, including Patrick Stewart now of *Star Trek* fame, and Robin Phillips, who ran Stratford, Ontario so successfully for many years.

We were all welcomed by Bill Ross, and he talked about the school and its methods. Then we had to sit round in a large circle, not yet in the dreaded tights, thank heavens, and a piece of knotted rope was handed round. As it was passed to you, you either undid it or knotted it up, while saying whatever words came into your head, starting with the last word of the person before. I loved it. 'This is so easy!' I thought. I remember mine had to do with fox, brush, red, not immensely inventive perhaps, but passable when almost catatonic with nerves!

I still remember the awful moment, that I had been dreading, of putting on The Tights. I was desperately self-concious, and I thought I was so fat. Years later I was sitting with some friends from those days, who, wonderfully, are still in my life, comparing notes. One of them, Ann Morrell, an ex-Bluebell girl, confessed that she had been just as embarrassed and terrified – and she has the longest, slimmest legs you can imagine. I *had* put on weight at Clifton, and had become unattractively plump, but as soon as I was happy and doing what I loved, I discovered that I had an enormous capacity for self-discipline. I would go in at a quarter to eight every morning and exercise for an hour before everyone else arrived. I spent hours lying on my back on the floor, holding a Swedish medicine ball between my feet and doing 'Swedish rolls'. The weight soon melted away, but in my own eyes I remained far too fat. I was always convinced – and it has taken me years to get away from the idea – that I was horrendously overweight. Now, when I look at photographs of myself then, I can see only a perfectly slim, attractive young girl with long brown hair.

From the day I arrived, I worked and I worked, and it was like the most wonderful love affair. I was gloriously happy. I became a model pupil. It was just so easy. I was where I should be, with the people I should be with, doing what I wanted to do. I discovered that because I loved it, I would work every hour God sent, and do everything, over and above the call of duty. My real schooling began again. It had started at Tyspane with those two wonderful elderly ladies who had imbued in me a love of reading, and oddly enough, a love of numbers and puzzles. I even loved algebra. To this day, when I have to sit down and do my accounts, although I loathe the idea, once I start I love the actuality, and that I owe entirely to them.

The Bristol Old Vic Theatre School was my university. I had always read voraciously, but suddenly I was given a proper book list, including *Medieval People*, then a famous Penguin book about people in the Middle Ages. I'd always hated history at school, but this was different. This was history seen through the eyes of real people. I became fascinated.

I won the Sarah Siddons Award. It was only instituted for about two years, and it was for the person who had worked hardest on themselves, and God knows, I did work hard on myself. It was a book token for ten pounds, which was riches in those days, and I went straight down the road and bought *My Life in Art* by Stanislavsky, which I still have. I read it immediately.

I can remember – when I was still only about sixteen and a half – I was cast as Madame Arcati in a production of *Blithe Spirit*, so I wanted to know all about psychics. I went to the library, got out a huge number of books, and read them all, cover to cover, including, for some reason, a book about Buddhism by the great Dr Suzuki. So I read and read and read, and everything was meat and drink to me. I started to read Sartre and the existentialists . . . It was all such pleasure.

And that was just the work. The social side was even more heaven. The parties, the friends, the learning new things together, the flirtations, the falling in love. I started to go out with an actor called Terry, a fair, wild Welsh/Yorkshireman, who at that time rather fancied himself as another Dylan Thomas. He wore corduroys and ate raw carrots out of a brown paper bag. We would walk past the front of the zoo together every morning on our way to school, and became friends. And one day we became lovers.

While I was going out with Terry, even though I was madly in love with him, I continued to flirt wickedly with everyone else. When he passed on to another girl, the pain of rejection and need was so great I almost fainted. But I was not capable of showing it. I didn't think I even knew why I needed him so much, because that would have been too frightening. My failing has always been an inability to show my vulnerability. I still find that hard to do.

I got over it. I was too enamoured with my new life, and the new, sultry Juliette Greco look that I had begun to cultivate, to be sad for long. And in every other compartment, life was utterly wonderful, mainly because the great ethos of the school was: the play's the thing. For the first time in my life I discovered the glory of true 'team spirit' – of everyone working together for a wonderful end. Every one of us had an important part to play, and there were no stars, no prima donnas.

One of the most moving theatrical experiences I have ever had was when the amazing Ninagawa Theatre Company of Japan, came over for a season at the National Theatre with their production of *Medea*. There was a chorus of about twenty members who were all dressed in white and all wearing masks, all absolutely identical – the height, the look – and they moved as one. And yet, somehow or other, each member of that chorus came over as unique.

We are all unique, and we must, it seems to me, explore our uniqueness, but at the same time, we have to be able to say, 'I am a member of this family.' I guess that is what I feel my life has been about, trying to find my uniqueness, in a way that encompasses both loving and being loved, including the darkest side of oneself, and, at the same time, never losing the awareness of also being part of a greater whole.

Growing up until I was seven in an all female household, except for a step-grandfather whom I didn't like very much, and then with a stepfather whom I was committed to ignoring, no matter how kind and sweet he was, I had never learned to understand or communicate with men. I just didn't know what they were, these strange beings. Now at the Vic School, I began to learn.

Bill Ross was an incredibly important figure in my life. He was an inspired teacher. He could be quite acerbic, with the fiery temper of the redhead. He was always absolutely truthful and to the point, but it was tough love.

The other huge influence has been Rudi Shelley, who has become a legend in the theatre. Rudi is a small, slightly bandy ex-dancer, with very thick, wavy hair, and a lined, clever, expressive face, who had been a ballet dancer in Berlin. Being Jewish, he had had to get out of Germany before the war, and had gone to Palestine. From there he came to England. He is gloriously theatrical, always wore a huge ring on his left hand, and in those days he smoked endless Gauloises. All his ex-students will remember phrases like 'Squeeze your lemon' and 'Up with your bolero'. He always used to say to us, 'Acting is the art of re-acting. Learn to listen, not to act listening, but really listen.'

The day after I'd given a performance in a student show of which I was inordinately proud, I asked Rudi what he thought, and can still hear him saying to me, in the rich Berlin accent he has never lost, 'Ducky, you looked like a pregnant nightingale!' His house was called The Slipped Halo. The rooms were dark, crammed with African masks, Mexican figurines, a beautiful reproduction of Rodin's *Hands*, and there were piles of books and records and tapes galore in a hugely eclectic collection. The rest of the staff at the Vic School: Paula, the secretary, was a tall, slim, elegant woman who was cool and could be cutting, but also funny and incredibly efficient. She was very supportive and encouraging to me. She was a demon bridge player and had played with Omar Sharif on several occasions. The singing teacher, Nell Moody, could make a frog sing like Callas, and was a person of passion and wispy hair. She loved my contralto voice, and I started to see that there were bits of me that were beautiful. She encouraged a passion in me which has lasted all my life for music and singing. And there was Daphne Heard, with her vast, magenta-jumpered bosom, and a pill-box on a chain round her neck for the ash and stubs of the Woodbines she smoked continually, and which affected her magnificent voice not at all. Her best advice was this, 'Always take something valuable with you to every job, in case there is no money and you can't get home. You can hock it.'

Rudi and Bill said to me from the beginning, 'Try this book', 'Read that book', and opened up the world for me. They were like that with everybody, of course, but I was particularly keen, and they were not bored by that. They were all my theatre parents. They guided me and gave me much good advice over the years.

The great thing we were all taught about acting at the Vic School was to 'play the now'. I believe that's for life, too.

Living the now is so difficult. People think that it's easy, because it is children who quite naturally live in the present, but adults don't. We're always so busy thinking about what we should be doing, or are about to do, or what we've just done. But we were taught to play – and live – the now. It makes coffee taste better. You hear and understand better what people are saying to you. You start to feel the ground beneath your feet, the texture of everything you touch; smells become more smelly, blossom more blossomy.

8. Sarah Siddons' ghost, and other stars

After two years of real happiness at the Bristol Old Vic Theatre School, I got my first job as an acting ASM (assistant stage manager) in the company, the Bristol Old Vic itself. It was just a glorious extension of being a student. There was a tradition for students at the Vic School to play supernumeraries and help backstage during runs at the theatre, which is the best way of learning what the business is really like, and so it was at the Theatre Royal, King Street, where I'd first stepped on to a proper stage.

It is an astonishing theatre to start your career in. It spoils you for anywhere else, because it is the oldest continually working theatre in this country, and it is has the most beautiful auditorium anywhere. Bath comes a close second, along with one or two others – the Haymarket in London, for example – and if you've spent the first years of your working life in a theatre like that, nowhere else will ever quite live up to it.

In those days, before it was rearranged in the 1970s – or wrecked, depending on your point of view – there was an amazing flying system backstage, which Fronk, the Polish flyman, was in charge of, with the original hemp lines which were wonderfully efficient. He had built it using the old cannonballs from the thunder run as counter-weights. (The thunder run was a channel running above the ceiling of the auditorium from above the gallery down to the wings. Cannon balls running down this would sound like thunder

– hence 'the gods'.) Everybody who ever worked there would remember Fronk. His name was really Frank, but he always said, 'I'm Fronk,' so that was what he was called.

In the seventies, the powers-that-be decided that the Bristol Theatre Royal needed refurbishing, and indeed it did. Unfortunately, they didn't do what they did with Bath Theatre Royal, where none of the original equipment has been ripped out. At Bristol, Val May decided to keep only the shell of the auditorium and the stage and almost everything else was demolished. Wonderful things disappeared, like the old stalls for the ponies and Fronk's old flying system with its original hemp ropes. Fortunately, most of the equipment under the stage, like the old grave trap and the star trap, are still there.

The star trap can never be used and was declared illegal years ago, because it is so dangerous. In the old days, a star trap was used for the villain in the pantomime. It is a circular trapdoor in the shape of a star, hinged round the rim, and all the segments fit in as if you are linking your fingers together. It would open like a star, and the villain would be shot through it; then it would close very quickly under him, and he would land on top of it. That is how any trap works, but if a star trap didn't close properly, the danger was that you'd land back down and catch your leg or your ankle in the sharp points. You could do yourself terrible damage, and people did. The grave trap is so called because it is always upstage centre, where the Grave-Digger's scene in *Hamlet* is traditionally played. That is still there. Everything else was replaced with a modern backstage and modern front of house, and it is all perfectly practical, but oh! What it could have been if they hadn't mucked about with it. I think it was an act of total desecration.

What is extraordinary about every single theatre is that each one has its own unique smell. There are certain smells they all have, like the lingering smell of size, but there's always something else, and each theatre is different. In the early nineties, I returned to the Bristol Theatre Royal to be in a 'Save the Theatre' charity show. I walked through the old pass door for the first time since I'd left, and I hadn't smelled that smell for over thirty years. The nostalgia was so overwhelming that I nearly burst into tears.

The geography backstage was completely different, but when I walked on to the stage, it all came back. I had forgotten how small it was, and how small the auditorium. The Bristol Theatre Royal auditorium hugs you as almost no modern auditorium does. Most of them are triumphs of civic pride over theatrical sense – with a very few honourable exceptions, like the New Orange Tree Theatre in Richmond and the Tricycle Theatre in Kilburn.

Sarah Siddons is supposed to haunt the Bristol Theatre Royal and when I was there in the old days, Fronk swore that he had seen her many times. Very late one night in 1960, I was clearing out the big props from behind the stage and at that time, on the OP (opposite prompt) side of the stage, there were the old dressing-rooms, including what had originally been Sarah Siddons' dressing-room, which was now being used as a prop store. I went in there to put some props on the shelf, and as I was leaving there was a loud noise behind me. I turned round and saw there was a paper carrier bag swinging violently against one of the shelves. I supposed I must have knocked it. I went out and got the next load of props, returned to put them on the shelves and, out of curiosity, went over and looked more closely at the carrier bag. It was on a wall with lots of big nails to hang things on and, unless you actually lifted it out and swung it deliberately, there was no way you could actually move it by knocking it. No one ever believes me, but I have always sworn that it was the ghost of Sarah Siddons, visiting me in her dressing-room.

The first time I'd ever gone down to the theatre was when I was still a student, to be in a new play called *The Woodcarver*. A very young Leonard Rossiter was playing the lead, and an even younger Prunella Scales was directing it. At the age of sixteen, I played a ninety-year-old woman, who came on, shrieked at Len, who was carving a figure of Christ, 'Papist! Papist! Heathen Papist!' and tottered off again.

Also during my student days, I had gone down to the theatre as dresser to one of the actresses in Ned Sherrin's and Caryl Brahms' *No Bed for Bacon*. I have a perfectly clear memory of being in the company pub, the Old Duke, one lunchtime during rehearsal, when a tremendous argument blew up between Caryl Brahms and Malcolm Williamson. The climax came when the Master of the Queen's Music emptied a pint pot of beer over the head of Caryl Brahms, while Ned tried to restrain him. Recently, when Ned and I worked together on *A Passionate Woman*, I told him that that glorious flash of Bohemia had quite confirmed my belief that I was in the right profession!

I'm a dead loss as far as memory is concerned. I only ever remember odd tiny specifics. The Bristol Old Vic was a very exciting company to be in. I would have done anything anyone asked. I would stay up until four in the morning on 'working weekends' as they were called, when you were changing the set for the next week's play, and I would still come in again at ten the next morning, to walk for the lighting. I was totally in love with it all. All the greats had worked there, were working there, or came to visit there. We had a lovely girl in charge of props, called Siobhan O'Casey, who was Sean O'Casey's daughter, and the legendary man himself came a couple of times.

Also in the company at the time there were Freddie Jones, Annette Crosbie, John Standing, Benjamin Whitrow and Eileen Atkins. I did *Roots*, in which I played Jenny, Eileen Atkins' sister, which was a great thrill because it was the first time that I had been given a big part. Eileen Atkins was young but very experienced by then. I was young and not very experienced.

A once-very-big star came down to play the Fairy in the V. C. Clinton Baddeley Christmas pantomime at the Old

Vic. I was working as ASM, although I wasn't in it. One freezing wet night as I was leaving the theatre, this star was walking down the rackhay – the lane from the street to the stage-door – just in front of me, swathed in furs, teetering in her high heels down to her waiting limo. I rounded the corner at the end just as she got in. She leant out of the window and said, 'Oh! Stephanie, dear . . .'

She lived in Clifton, where I had digs, so I was thinking, 'Oh good! She's going to offer me a lift.'

I said, 'Yes, Miss——?'

She handed me some letters and said, 'Would you post these for me on your way home, dear?'

That's how it was in those days. Stars in cars got ASMs, who were on foot or schlepping up in the bus, to post their letters for them, while they swanned home in their furs and limos. Which is why I didn't, and don't, like that sort of star system, or any sort of star system, very much.

The season at the Bristol Old Vic was quite long in those days, about ten months and, gosh, I got £9 a week – it was riches. It was a very happy year, doing everything from pantomime to Shakespeare. Nat Brenner, the theatre's general manager, was another father figure, with curly red hair and a wonderful, sensitive, crinkled Jewish face, another great man of the theatre. He was Peter O'Toole's mentor, and until Nat died Peter would always go to him for advice.

At the end of my year, I could have stayed on for another season as an acting ASM, but I had been offered the chance of going to Lincoln Rep, to head one half of the company, because it was a fortnightly rep. They would play a week in Lincoln, and then a week in either Loughborough, Scunthorpe or Rotherham (suntrap of the north) so they had a double company. Penelope Keith led Company A, and I had the chance to go up and lead Company B. When I say 'lead', I mean we usually played the female leads. I went to Nat and said, 'What shall I do?'

He said, 'Steph, darling, find out what you can do. Go to Lincoln.'

So I did.

Before I left Bristol, we took a new play called *The Tinker* by Lawrence Dobie and Robert Sloman to London, to the Comedy Theatre. It starred Edward Judd, who later became a film star, and the young Annette Crosbie. I was the acting ASM. A lot of very famous people came to see the play in town, but unfortunately we only lasted a rather ignominious five weeks. At the end of the show one night, I was packing up in the prompt corner when through the pass door came John Gielgud, who was not quite Sir John then, but still – hugely famous. I was thrilled to the core and he asked me if I would kindly show him to Mr Judd's dressing-room. Yes, of course I could, of course, of course. I led him to the number one dressing-room at the Comedy. In those days there was tremendous formality and a strict hierarchy obtained backstage. If you were at the bottom of the ladder, like me, you addressed all the actors and actresses as Mr Someone or Miss So-and-So. It was important to get it right. I turned to John Gielgud, just as I was about to knock on Eddie Judd's door, and said, 'Who shall I say it is?'

I was so embarrassed, because of course I knew exactly who he was, but he was so sweet, he just said, 'John Gielgud.'

I said, 'Yes, of course, of course, of course, sorry, so sorry . . .'

We now dissolve to thirty-seven years later, 1996. I'm in *A Passionate Woman* at the Comedy Theatre, and I'm in the number one dressing-room. A few nights into the run, there is a knock on the door, and David Pugh, our producer, is standing there. I come out into the corridor to say 'Hallo,' and David says, 'I've got a couple of friends here,' and introduces me to Kenneth Griffiths.

I say, 'Oh, it is a *great* pleasure to meet you. You are one of the great mavericks of our time.'

We exchange a few more words, and I notice a very tall

figure standing behind him, facing away from me. The tall figure turns and David says, 'And this is Peter O'Toole . . .'

I realise one second afterwards that I am standing on exactly the same bit of floor as thirty-seven years before, as I say to O'Toole, 'And it's an *even greater* pleasure to meet you . . . Well. No. I don't mean it's a greater pleasure than meeting *you*, Kenneth, but what I meant was . . .'

I got myself into deeper and deeper water, and I was thinking all the time, 'What is it about this spot, in this theatre, that brings out the faux pas in me?'

9. Repertory days

When I first went into rep, the contracts stipulated that you should provide all your own clothing, except for period pieces – obviously you weren't going to possess your own crinoline. Men had to have a dinner jacket and a business suit and a tweed jacket. Women had to have an evening dress, a cocktail dress, an afternoon dress and, if you played a lot of funny old things as I did, well, you had to have a lot of funny old things to wear.

My mother made me a huge pair of old-fashioned expanding corsets with suspenders, which she padded on the inside. I travelled with a trunk packed with all the glamour and glitter, but also with these frightful corsets, two pairs of old ladies' black shoes, an entire outfit in black, and two pairs of lisle stockings. There was a trick I learned early on. You wound lavatory paper round and round your legs, and then you put your lisle stockings over the top – bingo – swollen ankles and varicose veins.

You used to grab anything you could from your mother, your grandmother and their friends: hats, brooches, any sort of tat jewellery, shawls and scarves, everything was fair game. And you'd cut things up. One week you'd wear an evening dress, the next week you'd put the hem up, narrow the skirt a bit, put on a different top, maybe with a cummerbund – hey-presto – it was a cocktail dress. So Rudi was right – knowing how to sew was essential. At night, as well as learning your lines, you were forever beavering away with needle and thread and a pair of scissors.

Nowadays make-up is minimal, but I always loved the smell of it. I've still got my box, with Leichner Number 5 and Number 9, and the thin little stick of lake. You ran the lake along your upper and lower lip, half way into the lip, so the outside was white. Then you'd get a sixpence, and run the sixpence down from your mouth, and the ridged edge would drag some of the lake down and up, and you'd get the lines of an older face. If you were getting on a bit, and playing younger than yourself – which I never did – there was a wonderful thing that worked with the old-style lighting. You put a dot of red in the corner of each eye, and a dot of red in each earlobe. You had the full slap as well – the rouge, the eyeliner and the mascara and everything, men and women – but the red dots worked some sort of magic. I can see how they might have brought out your eyes, but what they did on your earlobes, God alone knows.

My face became a canvas. I remember playing in Shaw's *Caesar and Cleopatra* at Lincoln. I was playing the old nurse Ftatateeta and being reasonably well-read and thrilled with my newly acquired little bits of knowledge of history, I decided to base my make-up on the paintings of the Egyptian god Ra. I made a false nose, and got quite carried away with a very elaborate make-up. I thought it was simply wonderful and terribly effective, quite breathtaking in its magic. I walked proudly into the dress rehearsal. The director took one look and said, 'Steph? Er . . . Why have you made yourself up to look like a parrot?'

At Lincoln, there was no heating, only cold running water, and occasionally one would come face to face with a cockroach. For one or two weeks of the year, the repertory theatre would be given over to the local amateur dramatic society. On one particular occasion they were putting on *The King and I*, which Valerie Hobson had famously played in London. We, the resident professional actors, were asked if we would mind coming in and helping with the make-up and wardrobe for them, particularly the children. Several of us volunteered to go in. The dressing-rooms were tiny at Lincoln, they still are, and I was trying to make-up this myriad of chattering, overexcited children. The woman playing Anna was in the midst of all this, in her crinoline, a frightfully grand Lincoln lady, and she was suddenly driven beyond all endurance and said, 'Oh! I can't bear this! How on earth did Valerie Hobson manage?'

In those days, because it was a double company, you'd play a week in Lincoln and then, for the next week, every night at five o'clock you'd get on to the coach which would take you either to Loughborough, Scunthorpe or Rotherham. Scunthorpe was the worry, because we were warned, 'Do not run water during the performance.' The cistern was directly over the auditorium. I remember being in a production of *The Cat and the Canary*. At one point a character is standing on stage holding a séance, saying in an eerie voice, 'Tell me the name . . . Tell me the name . . .' Someone offstage pulled the loo chain, and all you could hear for the next two minutes was the cistern filling up.

Rotherham was chiefly memorable for a butcher shop which we passed on the coach, which had 'tripe de luxe' advertised in the window.

Loughborough Theatre was in a huge building in the middle of a park, and the sound and lighting were operated by the local cowman, who would never appear until he'd got his cows in for the night. It was miles from anywhere, a private theatre inside a vast house. One day there had been a blizzard, so we were snowed up and had to stay the night. The bathrooms were amazing. One was entirely encased in tortoiseshell. Another one was all marble. Another was gold.

I had huge fun at Lincoln. We were a young company, with ages ranging from eighteen to thirty or thirty-five. There might have been one or two older people, but very few. I fell in love – several times. And out again – several times. I played everything from A to Z. It was strange, but even if I was playing some eccentric old character, and was in love with the young male lead, it never impinged somehow or got in the way of romance. Because we all played different roles all the time, and the young male lead this week might be playing some doddery old butler next week, none of us ever gave it a thought.

From Lincoln I went down to Canterbury, to the Marlowe Theatre. I first had digs with an elderly couple; he wore a hearing aid on which he could get the Home Service. The house was near a tanning factory and the lavatory was in the back yard. So I moved fairly swiftly to a rambling house on the Old Dover Road, which was owned by a broad-minded lady called Frances. 'Live and let live' was her motto. When asked how to get rid of the ants, she handed me a powder which she said would make them go away – because they hated the smell!

Stephen Berkoff came down to the Marlowe to be in an Agatha Christie play. When I was in the West End recently with *A Passionate Woman*, I had a letter from him, reminding me of that deathless production. The Agatha Christie was *The Spider's Web*. What did he play in that? I'm just looking through my old programmes, and his name isn't in the cast of that . . . maybe it wasn't *The Spider's Web*. Maybe it was the next one . . . *Richard III*. No, he certainly wasn't in that. That I do know. Maybe it was another one. It *can't* have been *Love in a Mist*. It wasn't *The Crucible*. You see, we did terrific plays. It certainly wasn't *The Boyfriend*. *Tunnel of Love?* No. It wasn't *The Cocktail Party*. I bet it wasn't *Guardsman's Cup of Tea*. Was it *Goodnight Mrs Puffin*? No. I wonder if it was . . . I could have sworn it was *Spider's Web*. Maybe it was *Wanted – One Body*. No. It wasn't any of those. And it *wasn't Richard III*, of that I'm absolutely certain. If it wasn't *Spider's Web* – it was definitely an Agatha Christie. Maybe it was *Murder at the Vicarage*. I do know it wasn't *Richard III* . . .

I think I did about fourteen pantomimes in rep altogether. I played everything, from Principal Boy to Dame to the front end of the elephant – the last was while I was at Canterbury. What used to happen in commercial pantomime in those days was that the main figures – the Dame, Demon, Principal Boy – would come along with their own songs and comedy routines, and the writer would just write linking material. On one occasion at Canterbury, the management followed the commercial practice, so we had a visiting Principal Boy. She was a big woman. Each time she slapped her thighs they were still vibrating five minutes later. She had a rather scrofulous corgi dog with her and she kept large bottles of medicine for it in her dressing room which, it turned out, contained vodka. She had come along with her own song, to which we were not privy until the final run-through. So we were all getting very overexcited, waiting for the time for her to do her big number with the Principal Girl, Jan Carey – a good friend who is now married to Ian Mackintosh, the great theatre architect. Poor Jan had been rehearsing this song with her, but had kept absolutely mum about it to the rest of us. I can well understand why, because it turned out to be 'Now and then I'm a gay seventeen again.' As soon as she started, somebody shouted, 'No chance!'

I was the front of the elephant. The Principal Boy got very cross with me because I did a lot of swinging of my trunk, and she felt I was deliberately upstaging her . . . quite possibly I was.

From Canterbury I went to Hornchurch. My digs were in a house belonging to an Indian gentleman who made a rather frightening pass at me when I was in my curlers, filling my hot-water bottle, which seemed to me most unsuitable. I worked with Jane Howell, who had been at the Vic School with me, and was a wonderful director. She later went to the Royal Court. We did a variety of plays, including *Dandy Dick*. Jane was rather worried about the size of the audiences for the play, so we all had to go out on Saturday morning dressed up in our costumes and sing music hall songs in

Hornchurch High Street. The town had never seen anything quite like it.

Another great influence in my life has been Reggie Salberg, who ran the Salisbury Playhouse, where I went next. In those days Reggie always used to do interviews for new cast members at the premises of his cousin's wife, Sally Spruce, who was a costumier. You used to have to push your way through all the hanging costumes into a tiny office at the back of the shop, and Reggie would be sitting there. Tales abounded about casting couches and randy old men wanting to see your legs, all of which were untrue – well, most of them. I knew of Reggie as a great man of the theatre, and that it would be a good thing to join his company at the Salisbury Playhouse.

I arrived for the interview and he immediately said, 'I hear you're good, and I think I can offer you something. Have you done pantomime?'

'Yes.'

'Can you sing?'

'Oh, yeah.'

'What are you legs like? Show us your legs.'

I immediately thought, 'Hallo, hallo. Here I am, in the middle of these costumes – nobody around . . .'

I know now that Reggie would be the last person in the world to do anything, but I didn't know that then. Primly I raised my skirt a few inches and said, 'I think they're all right.'

'Oh yes. They're all right.'

And I got the job.

Oliver Gordon was the resident director. He was another who came to mean a great deal to me. He was a great amateur cricketer and spent half his life playing or watching cricket. He was an amazing spin-bowler. He had the biggest hands I've ever seen, with great spatulate fingers. He set a record for the number of wickets taken in a single over, which I believe has never been broken. But our friendship had an inauspicious start. He went to Reggie after the first day's rehearsal and said, 'It's no good, old cock. She's going to have to go. She can't do it.'

Fortunately Reggie insisted I had another chance. Actually, I was just still very shy in a new place, and a slow starter. I could do it. I stayed with them, very happily and productively, for the next three years.

The years at Salisbury are a melange of memories: playing every sort of part from Agatha Christie's Miss Marple, to Martha in *Who's Afraid of Virginia Woolf?*; in every sort of play from Greek tragedy through Restoration comedy, Shakespeare and commedia dell'arte, to panto and revue. I acted, I sang, I danced. I even played the recorder on stage and, less successfully, the ukulele. This last was in a seaside music hall scene where Jonathan Cecil and I, each on the uke, played a duet. Unfortunately, on the first night Jono forgot to take his white gloves off, and I was accompanied by a dull throbbing sound, made worse by the fact that I was not the one holding the tune!

Those were the days of the old building in Salisbury, which had been a cinema and was not entirely watertight. I remember sitting at the side of the stage in a passage way as the Nurse in *Romeo and Juliet*, wearing wellingtons and holding an umbrella over Juliet's head.

We did some new plays as well, but not always the best-written examples of contemporary drama. There was one political drama which was breathtaking in its ineptitude, but it had been written by a local patron of the theatre. We only played it for a week, and on the last night Reggie came round to say, 'I appreciate that you didn't enjoy yourselves very much and it was a very bad play, but the fact that cheers were coming from behind the curtain rather than in front was rather worrying.'

Then there were the times out of the theatre: steak and chips on pay-day at the Flaming O cafe; sunsets at Stonehenge; a trip to London to hear Bob Dylan and Joan Baez, seven of us crammed into my little mini-van; sitting over cheap wine and Nescafe talking acting and philosophy, art and music until the sun rose and it was time for rehearsal; trips to the sea; organising an egg-and-spoon race; sitting quietly in the deep, grey majesty of Salisbury cathedral, listening to the choir practising for evensong; discovering single malt whisky and dry sherry; cooking endless spaghetti bolognaises; the friendships, the quarrels, the laughter, the love affairs . . .

Two very important personal things happened to me during my time at Salisbury. One was that I met Oliver Gordon's younger brother, Henry, whom I was later going to marry.

The second concerned my father, my natural father. When I was sixteen and my mother had first told me the truth about him, I had felt that I didn't want to have anything to do with him. He wasn't interested in me, so why should I be interested in him? He had never supported us or given us anything or showed any concern about us – nothing, nothing, nothing. I was deeply hurt by what he had done or rather, not done. Any feeling of being intrigued about who he really was took a back seat to my anger, a huge anger that had been kept hidden for years behind fantasies of an ideal father.

But a few years later, I was beginning to feel differently. There is a part of the growing-up process, when you start to see that there are areas of your identity that derive ineluctably from your family. I could see that there were parts of me that came from my mother, but there were parts of me that weren't like anyone I knew, and I didn't know whether they were just me, or whether they were from my father. So I found that I was curious to meet him after all, just to see where those other bits of me came from, if indeed they came from anywhere. My mother knew where he was because she had kept a distant contact with members of his family, and she put me in touch with him while I was at Salisbury and so, we met.

His business had something to do with boats, so it was

possible for him to come down my way, en route to the South Coast. We arranged that he would meet me at the theatre one Saturday. There was a little alleyway between the theatre and the road; it was a bright sunny day, it must have been early summer, and I was waiting at the stage door. I saw this figure coming up the alleyway. I could only make out the outline of him, back-lit by the strong sunlight, and in that instant, as he came through the light, I could see exactly where a lot of my facial features had come from.

When I was a child, like all children, I used to adore going through family albums, and there was one particular photograph of a wedding that always fascinated me. There was an elderly lady in the picture, dressed in black, who reminded me slightly of Margaret Rutherford, with a large jaw. I was constantly asking my mother who she was. She always said that she was just the mother of the bridegroom, but years later it turned out that the bridegroom was one of my natural father's many brothers, and that this woman was my grandmother. I think my insistent wanting to know who she was, must actually have been a subconscious recognition of somebody that I was related to.

So, seeing this man, with my face, my nose and my jaw, was very strange. We went and had lunch; he was quite shy, and I was unbelievably shy, but we managed to hold a conversation. Two things stay in my mind about him. One was that he adored poetry, and so, always, have I. He told me how he used to go walking in the hills and speak poetry out loud to himself, which I also used to do, and I thought, 'Oh, so that's where that comes from.' He was rather closed in, quite private and didn't show much emotion while we were together; but I was very moved.

The second thing didn't properly register until quite a few years later. He told me that he had been married, and that he had another daughter, but that his marriage had broken up, and he was about to get married again. His other daughter, of course, would be my half-sister.

He and I corresponded for a while after our meeting, and

then he stopped writing. He never answered my last letter, and I assumed, rightly I think, that I was an embarrassment to him in his new family. I never heard from him, saw him or spoke to him again.

10. The wilderness years

After three years at Salisbury, I decided I needed to move around more. Over the next couple of years I played in most of the cathedral cities in England, and more besides.

At the Castle Theatre, Farnham, I was in *The Lodger*, a play about Jack the Ripper. I played the Landlady, and a friend from drama-school days, Chris Dunham, was the Lodger who puts poison in the Landlady's hot milk. The Farnham theatre is very tiny, the audience very close. One night I was pouring the hot milk into a mug, and about to drink it, when a hand, belonging to a little old lady in the front row, grasped my foot. She leant forward and hissed, 'Don't drink it, dear, don't drink it!'

What do you do? In spite of her timely warning, I had to drink it and die, but there you go.

At Guildford's Yvonne Arnaud Theatre, we were rehearsing an adaptation of a Chekhov short story. I was aware of not being very good and was dreading doing it, even praying the night before we opened that I wouldn't have to. The next day I drove down through torrential rain and when I got to the outskirts of the city I learned that the theatre was flooded. We never got to do the play. Be careful what you pray for – you may get it!

At Richmond I did the try-out of a new Ray Cooney play, and subsequently was offered the part in the West End but, for various 'political' reasons, the offer was withdrawn just before rehearsals. I got over that, but it was a small cloud, no bigger than a man's hand, on my horizon.

I was beginning to ask myself why I wasn't getting on as well as some of my contemporaries, why I was still doing what I had been doing twelve years ago – working in good reps with very good people, being offered work all the time it was true – but never really progressing. I became just that little bit less in love with the business. But I kept going.

I did the odd bits of TV. I did an early *Z Cars*, when it was still live. I was still in my twenties, and was asked to play a sick tramp, aged seventy. I went along to make-up, only to discover that they had decided I didn't need any! A few television parts came my way, but so many casting directors said to me, 'When you get to the right age there'll be lots of character work for you, but until then . . . sorry.'

I can't remember the exact sequence of events leading up to what I call my 'wilderness years'. What I do remember is becoming more and more browned off, and waking up in the mornings not with a feeling of excitement about a new day, but with a feeling almost of dread, of, 'Oh no, I don't want to do this any more. I really hate this.' In fact, of falling completely out of love with the theatre. I do know that I was in *The Mousetrap* from 1968 until November 1969, and things really started to go rapidly downhill from then on.

In 1967 I had broken off my relationship with Henry Marshall, Oliver Gordon's brother, whom I had met at Salisbury and been in love with, on and off, increasingly off, since 1964. They were recasting *The Mousetrap*, for 1968, as they did every year. This time Joan Knight was to direct it, and the management had decided, for the very first time, that it would be allowable to change the moves. The fact that it had already been running for nearly sixteen years with the same moves is fairly mind-boggling, but it had.

My old friend Chris Dunham was also offered a part in it, and we both decided that it might be fun to work with Joan, and that we should do it. Joan's idea was to take it back to the early fifties, in costume, with references to ration-books put back in, so it would become a period piece.

Joan was a good director, so Chris and I both signed up. In those days you couldn't sign for less than a year.

What I did know, having done several Agatha Christies before in rep, was that she was not a good writer of dialogue. Her plots don't hold together, and only the very thickest person in the audience can't guess who-dun-it in the first four minutes. Frankly, if you can play Agatha with any sense of reality, you can play *King Lear* at the National.

I knew all this, and was prepared for it. What I wasn't prepared for was that when we started rehearsing Joan was told that she could change the moves, but nothing else. In other words: no fifties period costumes, no script changes, no ration-books. Peter Saunders, the producer, kept a very tight control over it. However, it was a year's work, and there was light relief now and then.

We had an understudy, now long dead, who was eighty then, with very ill-fitting false teeth, and she had under-studied from the very beginning. She was utterly devoted to *The Mousetrap*. Because she had been doing it for so long she rarely went along to understudy rehearsals, and never under our regime. Unfortunately, she had to go on one night, and of course she had no idea of the new moves.

It didn't phase her one small jot or tittle. She came on and she moved to wherever it was she'd always gone before. You would be looking to the right and saying, 'Here comes . . . whoever . . .' And nothing. She didn't appear. You'd hear a clomp, clomp, and there she was, behind you. Nothing would deflect her from her purpose. Like a Sherman tank she would come across the stage right at you, and unless you moved out of her way, you'd be bowled over. Every time she delivered a line, her teeth were in danger of flying out of her mouth. It was *Acorn Antiques* made flesh.

We had a wardrobe mistress called Maisy, also in her eighties, very thin hair dyed purple-red, with bad feet so she wore carpet-slippers all the time, even on the street. In her youth she had worked on the halls with her husband. When her husband ran off with a chorus girl, she continued to work as a singer. She'd worked at the London Coliseum when it was a variety house. I love variety artists' reminiscences. She used to say, 'D'you know, Steph? I'm the only person that ever 'ad a lobster thrown at 'em at the Coliseum at the end of my act?'

'Really, Maisy? Why was that?'

'Well,' she said. 'They used to throw silk stockings and jewels and all sorts, the toffs did, if they liked you. And someone musta' thought I'd like a lobster . . . so they threw a lobster at me.'

She couldn't see properly, bless her heart, so the mending of the costumes tended to be a bit of a cobble-together. She had glasses held together with bits of Elastoplast. We all used to say to her, 'Maisy, why don't you go and get your eyes tested properly? You can get free glasses now.'

But she would always say, 'Oh no! These are all right. I can't be bothered.'

Bless her heart, eighty-something, and every day she would climb a huge flight of stairs up to wardrobe, singing away in her carpet-slippers.

One day I went upstairs, because we always had a cup of tea with Maisy when we first arrived for work, and she was wearing a brand-new pair of spectacles. I said, 'Maisy! How terrific! You've got new glasses. Well done! How are they?'

'Oo,' she says, 'they're lovely.'

'Did you go to your doctor?'

'Oh, no. I didn't do that.'

'Well then, how . . . ?'

She said, 'I'll tell you, dear, I was going home on the bus last night. I got on and I sat down, and there on the seat beside me was this pair of glasses. I picked 'em up and I put 'em on, and d'you know? I could see lovely. And I thought, "Well, there's a bitta luck." So I've got me new glasses.'

Maisy was a good deed in a naughty world.

But the end result of doing a year in that production was that I grew more and more desperate. I hated it so much. I had done it only to be in London earning money for a year, to give myself time to sort out my life after splitting up with Henry, all very bad reasons for doing anything in my profession, so I despised myself.

After *The Mousetrap*, I became reconciled to Henry, and moved in with him in 1969. It had played a very big part in my disenchantment with my profession. I did several things after that, but always in a rather desultory way, and always with a growing feeling of gloom and reluctance. I hoped every time that the feeling of joy in my work would come back, but it never did. I saw more and more of my peers working on TV and doing well, and the only reason I could think of for it not happening to me was that I was not very good. I had a crisis of confidence: I truly believed that I had chosen the wrong career; I shouldn't be doing it; I was lousy at it.

It gradually got worse and worse during 1971 and 1972, until the day of decision arrived and I thought, 'OK. That's it. It's not working. Give it up. Cut your losses and walk away, kid.'

What was the point? I'd done everything I could do to make it work, and it wasn't working. End of story. As far as I remember, I did a play in Swindon in 1972, and then I stopped.

I think that there were many reasons. Whenever I'm doing a new series or a play, and I sit at the other side of the desk, helping with the casting, I now understand one of them. It's to do with the way in which you do your interview. It has to do with having self-confidence – but not too much. Being able to talk – but not too much. Being able to be intelligent about something – but not too much. It is a craft in itself and I think that in those days I was not very good at it.

Another reason was quite simply that my time had not yet come. Some people's star shines brightly when they are very young, but then often fizzles out too soon; others may achieve celebrity after slogging away in the business for literally decades sometimes. It happens when it happens.

I also believe that the terrible years that followed – and they were terrible at the time, living through them was a nightmare – had a purpose, and now I thank God for them. Nothing that happened afterwards could have happened if I hadn't gone through them.

I started to throw myself into evening classes. I learned the guitar. I'd already been taught the basics of folk guitar in Salisbury by Brigit Forsyth, a guitar player and cellist as well as a wonderful actress. Now I went to day classes to learn classical guitar.

I also went in for more esoteric subjects. I learned to speak and read Welsh. Henry and I used to go twice a year, spring and autumn, to a place called Llanthony, in the Black Mountains, where I had discovered and read George Borrow's *Wild Wales*, which includes some appalling Victorian translations of Welsh poets. I tried to find better translations, but there weren't any, so I thought the only thing to do was to learn Welsh myself to discover what it was all about. I learned it well enough to be able to read Dafyd ap Gwilim in the original – he's the Welsh Shakespeare – and to get a little bit of the flavour.

My hobby had always been bookbinding, and I decided to try to become a professional bookbinder. I worked for a while at a bookbinder in the city, where women were only allowed to collate and sew – the most boring bit of the job. I also worked in a fine bindery back in Salisbury for a few weeks, where Henry was working temporarily, but it was still just collating and sewing. The bit I was interested in was the artistic side, even doing marble end-papers would have been quite nice. I soon realised that professional bookbinding wasn't for me.

I still find that when I'm not working for a few weeks, although I need a while to rest and recharge my batteries, after quite a short time I begin to get twitchy. Nowadays, I have learned to divert surplus energy into things like painting, playing the guitar or gardening. I do them all extremely badly, but they help me to keep calm. In those days, I was desperately searching for a substitute to use up my intellectual and creative energy that had once been poured into the theatre, and now had no outlet. When you cannot, for psychological, emotional, spiritual or physical reasons, give rein to your daemon, that creative drive within you, it will lead you to despair. That was my experience.

While I was in the midst of a very black depression and had, as I believed, given up the business for good, Reggie Salberg did a wonderfully encouraging thing. Reggie's father owned and ran the Alexander Theatre in Birmingham. Reggie and Derek, his brother, ran theatres all their lives, and they really were great men of the theatre, and very knowledgeable. When he heard what had happened, Reggie rang up one evening. He's got an unmistakable, slightly nasal voice, that everybody who knows him imitates – very badly.

He said, 'Can I speak to Stephanie?'

'Oh, Reggie! How are you?'

'I'm OK. Now, what's all this about you've given up the business? Now, why?'

'Well, I don't think I'm really talented enough, and I just don't think it's a good idea . . .'

He simply said, 'You mustn't give up. You have a great deal of talent, and you are not to give up.'

I didn't take it in properly at the time, or at any rate act on it, but it must have gone in somewhere.

11. Love and marriage

Henry's real name is Marshall King Battcock. His parents had named him Henry when he was born but two elderly aunts, who were near to shuffling off the mortal coil, said that they would leave his parents a lot of money if they named him after their dead brother, Marshall King; so he was officially christened Marshall King Battcock. But he was always known as Henry. You can't very well go into the acting profession with a name like Marshall King Battcock, or you couldn't then, so professionally he called himself Henry Marshall.

Henry started out as a composer and an actor. He had apparently been a fairly terrible actor, or so he says himself, so he'd given both those up and started to write, and had been quite successful. He'd even been talked of as the new Terence Rattigan, but then the post-war generation of angry young playwrights came along, and that put paid to Henry's kind of writing. He continued to write dramas for radio and television for a while.

Then, just when all his old BBC contacts were beginning to die off or leave or retire, and work was becoming thin, he found a new direction. He had worked in the past with Hugh Cruttwell at the Theatre Royal, Windsor, when Hugh was stage manager. Now Hugh had taken over as Principal at RADA, and they had just lost their fencing teacher, who had died. Hugh telephoned Henry and said the words that changed Henry's life, 'Madame Perigau is dead.'

Henry's great hobby had always been fencing, and as well as the practice, he was fascinated by the historical background. He did a lot of research, and I used to go along with him to the V and A and the British Museum, to look at the very old fencing books, and try to translate from the Latin and the French.

It was something we shared. When I was at the Bristol Old Vic Theatre School, there was an extraordinary fencing instructor called Professor Field. All fencing instructors are called 'Professor' as a title of respect. When I was there, for some reason most of the students preferred to do judo with Professor George Brandt, a real professor and an incredibly clever and intellectual man. He held a chair at Bristol University, but his hobby was judo, and he would come and teach us. I was useless. I remember him allowing me to throw him, and my standing over him after I'd done it, apologising profusely. He said, rather wearily, 'You have a certain old-world charm.' But that was not the object of the exercise.

So I started to take double fencing classes instead. Prof. Field had only about five of us left in his class, so as well as foil, which was normally all you learned, he started to teach us quarterstaff, sabre and épée. Thus when I met Henry, I already knew quite a bit about his great interest. I was even, one day, to direct the fights for a production of *King Lear* at the Salisbury Playhouse, about a year after Henry and I were – eventually – married in 1973.

Henry is naturally a very gregarious man, and writing is a solitary, lonely, difficult business. Suddenly he was catapulted into being a teacher of fencing. His whole life changed for the better with those words, 'Madame Perigau is dead.'

Henry and I had lived together before we married, but by 1967 our relationship had seemed to be more off than on, and I had felt I wanted some independence from him, which was when I made that fateful decision to go to London to do *The Mousetrap*. Afterwards, in 1969, Henry and I had a reconciliation and I moved in with him in London.

For years I hadn't wanted to get married. I had wanted romance, and marriage wasn't on the agenda, but it had started to get to me a bit when, every time I went home, people would say to me, 'Oh, so-and-so's married now . . . And so-and-so.'

It wasn't until I was in my mid-twenties that I seriously started to think about having someone else permanently in my life. Twice before Henry I had toyed with the idea of marriage. Both were actors. One was a sweet, gentle, loving, Jewish man, a wonderful human being; I recognise his great qualities now, but I didn't then. He didn't seem exciting enough to me. There was another man whom I had wanted desperately to marry. I met him many years later and thought, 'Thank God I was saved from that!'

By the time I had moved back in with Henry in 1969, that was what I thought I wanted; to be married with children. It was at the time when I was growing increasingly disenchanted with acting, and I believed that you probably couldn't both have a career and be happily married. Actually, I didn't want children at first, but after we'd been together for some time, it seemed a natural progression of loving somebody, to want to have their child. It was something instinctive rather than thought out. I felt it in my body rather than thought it in my head.

I'm an optimist, a fantasist, and an idealist, which is not a frightfully realistic combination. That is to say, I'm very practical, and have my feet on the ground, except where matters of the heart are concerned. Ever since I was a child, I would weave dreams and fantasies around people. I suppose I spent so much of my time with my nose in books, watching and reading plays, that I absolutely believed, despite many indications to the contrary, that marriage was wonderful and that everybody always lived happily ever after.

Interestingly, I notice now that when I got married I

perpetuated a pattern set by my mother, and probably my grandmother before her. In Colin my mother had married someone who was a very gentle, dear man, a bit of a bumbler, rather weak; and she was the driving force, she was the engine, she organised everything, decided what should be done, was absolutely the strong one. What I didn't know then was that I was like that, too. I still felt incredibly shy, and unsure of myself.

I too chose somebody who was very sweet. There was not an ounce of malice in Henry, never has been. He's a dear, kind man, gently pessimistic, and absolutely without ability to take responsibility for anything. That was not immediately apparent. He gave the appearance of possessing a certain self-confidence and strength, and I gave the appearance of being able to fit in and follow someone else's lead. He cured me of being shy. Quite early on in our relationship, we were going to a party which was all lawyers and I said, 'I'm terrified. I won't know what to say.'

Henry said, 'Just ask them about them. Let them talk about themselves.'

And he gave me a list of questions. It worked, and that was the beginning of the end of shyness. As the years went by, I grew up.

During the war, Hen had been a conscientious objector. He had become a devout Quaker when he was about fourteen, at school. I have never met a Quaker who was a rotten human being; I think they are exceptional people and I love to go to a meeting of the Friends. But then, in his twenties, just after the war, Hen became a fellow-traveller, a communist. He had read Frazer's *The Golden Bough*, which caught the imagination of so many people of Hen's generation, with its thesis that mankind progresses from magical, through religious, to scientific thought. It had made Hen reject any form of belief system, particularly Christianity. When I met him he was no longer a communist nor a Quaker, but an atheist, a strong believer in Nothing. That resonated with me – I could go along with that.

I moved into a house in Belsize Park with Hen in 1969. It was a big, early-Victorian house that had belonged to one of his brothers, Roy, who had bought a long lease from the Church Commissioners. Henry had moved in there when he had first come to London, and gradually amassed rooms around himself, that had sort of organically become the ground-floor flat. Above us was his brother, Roy, with his second wife, Jackie. Below us in the basement were two flats, in one of which was an artist, and in the other an Australian-Irish schoolteacher. They loathed each other.

On the upper floors were various people, including an ex-actor who was working on his PhD – it took him something like fifteen years but he eventually got it – meanwhile earning his living by entertaining gentlemen callers. He was absolutely enchanting, but he did keep very odd hours and some very odd company. Above him was a Pakistani gentleman, very sweet, in the Merchant Navy, chiefly famous for two things: managing to navigate his ship straight up on to the beach in Bombay, and a propensity for exposing himself to the girls in the flat opposite. It was quite an unusual household. We all lived in extraordinary harmony, however, and nobody impinged on the others.

Henry had been married before, but had never had children or wanted them; for him, terror was contained in those two words, 'your child'. So he took rather a lot of persuading. Nevertheless, I became pregnant in 1972. I had a miscarriage. Then I got pregnant again.

That rather took up my life. I didn't have to worry about my career for a bit. I went to all the classes; did all the exercises. Then, as the birth approached, I gradually became more and more terrified. I had been a breech birth and my mother had had a frightful time. Although the idea of having a baby was glorious, the whole thing was going to be heaven on wheels, a bit of me was absolutely panic-stricken at the idea of the actual birth.

So for the last few weeks I went to stay in Gloucestershire with my parents. It was deeply unfair to Henry, and gives

Me with June, my mother

Me with Emma, my daughter

Me with friends at Tyspane

My grandmother, Peter, with my great aunts Peggy, Rene and Ella

Bridesmaid at my mother's wedding, 1948: Me; Harold and Beatrice Lees; Colin and June, my mother; my grandmother, Anna Gladys; my step-grandfather, Harry Bacon; and my cousin Carolyn

Peter and Paul, my brothers, with Colin

My first major role – Arnold Wesker's *Roots* at the Theatre Royal, Bristol, 1960:
Me, June Jago, Eileen Atkins, Euan Hooper, Terence Davies,
Josephine Tewson, and Leonard Rossiter

Agatha Christie's *Murder at the Vicarage* at the Marlowe Theatre, Canterbury, 1963,
with Peter Badger and Stephen Berkoff

Sally Ann, 1978

In *Rose* at The Duke of York's, London, 1979: Diana Davis, Richard Vanstone, Jean Heywood, David Daker, Glenda Jackson, Me , Gill Martell, Tom Georgeson

Curtain call for Alan Bennett's *Monologues* at The Haymarket Theatre Royal:
Me, Sheila Hancock, Ian McKellen, and Imelda Staunton

Yorkshire Television's *A Bit of a Do* with David Jason and Tim Wylton, 1988

Noises Off at the Savoy with Chris Godwin and Michael Cochrane, 1983

The cast and team of *Steel Magnolias* at the Lyric Theatre, 1990

Open All Hours, 1982, with David Jason and Ronnie Barker

With Paul Chapman in Granada Television's *Return of the Antelope*, 1986

you some idea of how grown-up I was. But there was another reason: I wanted her to be born in the West Country, my adopted home, and to be conscious of her Celtic blood. When she was born, I gave her a Welsh middle name, Bechan, old Welsh for 'little woman'. It was all to do with roots.

I wanted Henry to be there when the baby was born, in the little local cottage hospital. He'd been to all the classes, and read all the books, so he was all prepared, only the baby was late and later . . . and three weeks late! Finally I went to the family doctor and told him I was overdue. I knew the baby was ready to be born. So I went into hospital and we waited. Then they broke the waters. The baby seemed to think it might be born then, and I went into labour. Nothing happened. We waited again.

The medics began to get worried, so they took me by ambulance from the cottage hospital to Bristol Royal Infirmary. The bumping of the ambulance helped the labour to get going again. They got me into hospital, and it went on and on and on. I was still only dilated a minute amount.

Then the specialist came in, looked at me and said, 'This is going to be difficult. It's going to be a breech birth – you know what that means? It's going to take a very long time. We're going to have to use the forceps – it's too late to turn her now. It's going to be jolly difficult for you, but there we are.'

He pinched my arm. I'd put on a bit of weight, as one does. My normal weight was about ten and a half stone in those days, but I was significantly more. He said, 'God, how I hate these women who eat too many éclairs.' And left.

Within a quarter of an hour, everything completely stopped – the labour, the dilation, everything. I'm convinced that my terror was so great that Emma and I just decided that we didn't want to do it. Then a divine Afro midwife came in. Mine was to be her first baby. She was gentle and loving and encouraging. She kept calling me Mrs Buttock, which made me laugh.

Finally, after about thirty-six hours, they decided the baby was in distress and they would have to perform a Caesarean section. They put me out – which they almost always did in those days. You very rarely had an epidural for a Caesar. At long last, on 8 February 1973, Emma was born.

Henry had come hot-foot down from London when I first went into labour, and had stayed with me all the time – in a state of total panic, but there. He was the first to see her.

They had told me it was going to be a boy, so Henry and I had agreed he would be called Oliver Benedick Battcock. As soon as I came round I said, 'Is Oliver all right?' and Hen said, 'Yes. She's beautiful.'

Then there was that moment of looking for the first time – all women who have had children will know this – at that little flower. I have never seen anything more beautiful in my entire life. Because I'd had a Caesarean, she hadn't had a struggle. She lay there like a jewel, like a newly burst rose, just unbelievably beautiful. She had her grandmother's huge, double-lashed eyes. A friend came to visit me and couldn't find us, and said to one of the nurses, 'I'm looking for Mrs Battcock' and the nurse said, 'Baby Battcock – oh, yes. The most beautiful baby in the hospital.' She really was – and of course I fell in love with her on sight, and burst into tears.

No Caesarean is easy, and unfortunately, as so often happens, then and now, the wound became infected. I also had problems breast-feeding her. Left to our own devices, I think we would probably have been fine in the end, but nurses had a habit of rushing round and expecting you to be able to do it immediately, and even if you've been to classes it's jolly difficult. They start making you worried, so the chance of the milk flowing becomes more and more remote. Then the milk does come in, but they will hover over you and make you tense, so it doesn't work properly. It was not an easy time.

I adored Emma, but I was immeasurably tired.

Caesareans always have this effect, but it's never properly taken into account. It's a major trauma, medically speaking, and even though the product of the operation is a baby, a cause for great rejoicing, your body somehow doesn't want to be up and dancing.

In the end I had to stop trying to breast-feed her. I'd hated giving up on it, but they weren't going to let me out of the hospital until she had regained her birth-weight. I was feeling very weak and strange and unwell, and worried about whether I was feeding her properly and knowing I wasn't and feeling guilty about that, and the scar was all abscessed and hurting like hell, and I remember them coming to me and saying, 'You can't go home.' I had been supposed to go home the next day, ten days after the birth. I just sat there.

Hen had gone home, and later that day he and my Mum came in together to see me, and I was in bed, but totally out of it – if you see what I mean. I can remember them standing there, and my mother saying brightly, 'How are you?' and feeling absolutely nothing.

I said, 'I'm all right.'

She said, 'Now, we're going to get you home tomorrow,' and I said, 'No.'

She said, 'But you're supposed to be being discharged tomorrow.'

'No.'

'What do you mean? You can't come out?'

'No. I'm not being allowed out. She's got to reach her birth-weight.'

I couldn't cry. I couldn't get angry. I could hardly move. I could hardly speak above a mumble. My mother was very frightened. She went home and rang our family doctor, Dr Field, and said, 'I'm really worried. I think we've got to get her home.'

Dr Field was wonderful. He rang the hospital and said, 'I will take complete responsibility for the welfare of this woman and her child. But you will send her home now.'

And I thank God for him, because I think I might have gone very peculiar if he hadn't got me out.

Before my pregnancy I had started to suffer from bouts of claustrophobia and agoraphobia, which had gone away when I knew I was expecting Em. It came back again with a vengeance, along with the postnatal depression.

After two weeks with my parents, once I was well enough and Em was feeding OK, I went back to London. Henry had been a brick through the whole experience. But the depression got worse and worse, combined with a claustrophobic feeling of being trapped by this tiny little thing, and agoraphobia about leaving the house. There was no dodging it. I'd never had a problem with duty and commitment before, but faced with this ultimate commitment, I was terrified.

Having found that I had no confidence in myself as an actor any more, I now found that I had no confidence in myself as a mother. I hadn't been able to give birth properly, or to breast-feed my child. It was a bleak time, dark beyond belief. Along with the overwhelming depression, the agoraphobia and claustrophobia also got worse. I became irrational and unpredictable, volatile, quick to tears, quick to anger. I was never violent, and I was fine with Em, but even this little baby couldn't stop me from thinking very seriously about suicide.

Somehow I got myself to the doctor, who said, 'Well you could go into therapy, but it would probably take years, and cost an awful lot of money.'

I said, 'No, I need something now.'

So he put me on tranquillisers, which were useless. They mask the symptoms, but that almost makes you worse.

Em was about five months old. I was having great difficulty in doing the shopping. I had to steel myself to go out with her in the pram to Sainsbury's, and sometimes I would have to turn round and come home when I was only halfway there. The panic attacks were frightful. I remember waking up one morning and looking at my life, just that day in my life, what that day would hold, and being suddenly overtaken by an astonishing anger about everything that was happening to me. The anger saved me.

I took the tranquillisers and threw them down the loo. I put on some trainers and ran twice round the block very, very fast. I went back to the doctor and I said, 'I've chucked those pills away. They're useless. They make me feel worse. There must be something you can do. There must be.'

He said, 'Actually, they've started something at the Royal Free. It involves hypnosis and a sort of process of de-sensitisation, a retraining of your patterned responses.'

I went along to the Royal Free, and was taught this incredibly simple method. It takes a long time, about four to six months, or even longer, depending on the severity of the case. And it doesn't work for everybody.

When you go to bed, you mentally divide your body into about five different sections and you clench and relax, clench and relax each part until finally you've relaxed every bit of your body. Then you breathe in, hold your breath, breathe out. You do this very slowly, three times, and then you start to visualise, for example, going shopping. You start from the moment you make your shopping list, all the way through. As soon as you start to have the slightest sensation of a panic attack, you stop the visualisation immediately. Then you re-relax your whole body, do the deep breathing exercise, and start all over again. Very often you fall asleep during the middle of this process, and that's fine. You go on doing it every single night until finally you can do the shopping trip there and back in your head, without any feelings of panic.

Then you try it in real life. And the amazing thing is, it works. You don't at that stage look for causes. You simply retrain your bodily responses. I didn't discover the true causes until many years later, in analysis. At the time I just needed to find a way so that I could live some sort of life. It worked for me. There were still places I wasn't keen on being. I still wasn't mad about travelling by tube, or being in a lift, and the thought of flying was complete anathema. But that was all liveable with.

Some years later, when *Tenko* was in the offing and I was going up for it, I knew that they would be filming part of it out in Singapore. I telephoned my agent and said, 'Even if I get the job, I can't take it, if it involves flying.'

God must have been smiling on me, because the wonderful part that I was offered was not involved in the location filming in the first series. I was in every episode, but I didn't have to travel to Singapore. By the time we were doing the second series, I knew I was going to have to fly to Malaysia, and I used the same visualisation method, mentally retraining my bodily responses for flying, and again it worked, and I was absolutely fine.

Henry and I were married at Hampstead Register Office on Haverstock Hill at 9 a.m., the first wedding on a Saturday morning in July 1973, and I think we were among the last couples married there, because it has long since moved. Present to witness the momentous event were my mother and Colin, a couple of chums and, of course, Emma. She was too young to attend the party we threw that evening, however.

While we were standing outside the register office, and a friend was taking our photograph, a group of young people passed, and one of them shouted out in fun, 'You'll regret it, mate!' to which my husband replied, 'Doesn't one regret everything sooner or later?' I laughed at such a melancholy attitude. But he was right.

My own attitude was that everything in the garden would be lovely. There was no question; it would work. I was taking the first steps to cure my agoraphobia, but I believed I was a complete failure as an actress and still felt deeply lacking in everything that was needed to be a successful human being. I thought that if there was somebody else in your life, they would make you into a complete person and everything would come right again. And for us, at first, it did work. For many years Hen and I had a very good marriage.

During that year after Em was born I did no acting, but Hen was earning enough for us to be OK. With a friend, Bill Hobbs, he had founded the Society of Fight Directors. Bill was the actual director of fights, and Henry was the researcher and teacher. Between them Hen and Bill changed the face of stage fights in British theatre, television and film; in fact, all over the world. They instituted a fight proficiency test for drama schools, so students learned the various forms of armed and unarmed combat and could be tested in it, and get their proficiency certificate, which would help them get certain kinds of jobs.

In 1974, when Em was a little over a year old, Henry went down to conduct a fight proficiency test at the Vic School in Bristol, where Nat Brenner was now the Principal, since Bill Ross had gone to teach in America, and he asked Henry how I was. Hen told him I'd given up the business. Nat said, 'Oh how ridiculous! Do you think she'd like to teach?' Hen said he would have to ask me, so Nat telephoned me and said, 'Would you like to come down here for a couple of days a week to teach?' And I thought, 'Maybe I would.'

Emma was a very good baby, especially considering what a neurotic, loopy mother she had, so I knew I would have no trouble taking her with me. I was to work as Rudi Shelley's assistant, which was joy. I began to think, 'Maybe this is what I'm supposed to be. Maybe I'll discover that I'm one of the world's great teachers.'

I didn't discover that, but it was a wonderful time. I would drive down to Keynsham with Emma on a Thursday morning, leave her with my Mum and Colin, go into Bristol to teach Thursday afternoon and all day Friday, then go home to Henry in London either Friday night or Saturday morning. It was great. I was paid. It made me look at my profession from a completely different angle; I had to get my head around the technicalities of it. It also taught me how every person requires a different language in order to communicate to them what it is you need to tell them. And it caused me to fall back in love with my business, acting, which was the greatest gift of all.

I owe all that to Nat and Rudi. I'm not at all sure that Rudi really needed an assistant. Maybe he did. It was wonderful to work with him. I adored him, and continue to adore him. It was bliss to learn directly from a great teacher, and then pass on some of the things to others. I taught voice and speech classes, working in areas that weren't quite covered by the other teachers.

I taught all sorts of people – and even if I taught them very little, I taught myself a great deal, and they taught me far more than I taught them, if that doesn't sound too pi. I was there for nine months, and then, undoubtedly because of the chance they'd all given me, staff and students alike, I started to grow in confidence. I realised that I could look after my daughter, well enough anyway; I realised that I was quite reasonable as a wife, I could cook, I could sew and do the housework. I had been trying to do it all far too well, and had got terribly tired; the old thing that all women know and must resist: trying to be a perfect wife, perfect mother, perfect everything and berating yourself for every failure, until you end up a perfect nothing.

When I was young, before I got married, I was perfectly capable of cooking a decent meal, but I wasn't that interested and didn't really do it very often. After we got married, I started to absolutely love it, and we had lots of people to dinner, which I enjoyed hugely, particularly during the wilderness years when I wasn't working. I needed somewhere to put my creative energies, and cooking gave me real pleasure.

We continued living at Belsize Park through the 70s. My depression became a thing of the past. Living upstairs there was now one of my great, great friends, Eileen Davis, known to all as Eyeline. Eyeline and I had met at the Vic School while I was teaching there. Eventually a room became free at the top of the house when an old lady tenant died, and

Eyeline took it. Then she met her now lifetime partner, David Hobbs, and he moved in as well, and we all became great friends. We would nearly always celebrate Christmas and New Year together.

One particular Christmas Eileen, David and Siobhan, Eyeline's daughter, were coming down, and various other friends were coming over and it was going to be a large Christmas lunch. Henry had decided that a goose would be just the ticket. I had gone back to acting by then and I was doing a television series called *Sally-Ann*, and my dresser happened to be German, so I thought, 'Perfect! Who better to know all about cooking a goose than a German?'

I asked for her advice. She said, 'It's very simple. You want to cook it upside down, and to put it on a very, very low heat for the longest time possible.'

On Christmas morning, Em, being five years old, woke up at sparrow-fart, at something like half past five, to open her stocking. We got up and watched while she opened her presents, and I made us a cup of tea. For some bizarre reason, which I shall never quite understand, when I went into the kitchen I thought, 'Now this is just the moment to put the goose on. I'll put it on very, very low – about gas mark a quarter.' And so I did. It was only about half past six – but it was a mammoth goose.

We now segue forward to half past ten that morning, when everybody is arriving for breakfast. I had a whole load of croissants and brioches, so I opened the oven door to put them in to warm up – and the goose was cooked. It was ready! It was crackling. It was the perfect goose – three hours early.

Beneath the bird was the biggest pan of goose grease you have ever seen in your life. My mother had said, 'That will be very useful. You can rub it on red flannel.' I poured it into huge plastic containers and put them in the freezer. (Nine months later we got home from somewhere and were tired and hungry I said, 'Don't worry, I'll defrost some home-made soup' and defrosted a bowl of goose grease. It was unspeakable. Useful on red flannel or not, I chucked the whole lot away.)

However, there we were, half past ten in the morning, Christmas goose cooked, everybody arriving for breakfast. So I took to the gin. By the time we got to lunch-time I had no idea what was going on. I served an entire Christmas lunch to twelve people and I have no recollection of any of it. There are photographs of me in a Christmas cracker hat, so I must have remained upright – but it is all a complete blank in my memory.

Emma learned to roller-skate on the Victorian tiles in the hall. As with all parenting, it's been some good, some bad, and thank goodness for that book, *The Good Enough Mother*, which brought such relief to us all. Not that one's children ever seem to think that good enough *is* good enough. I'm very conscious of the fact that I did many, many things wrong, but I did some things right.

She has been such joy and delight. One of the pleasures for me, when she was little and learning, was revisiting those things that I had loved as a child, reading all my old childhood books with her, playing silly games, building with Lego again, teaching her little songs, and that wonderful feeling when they show a bit of talent for something, of nurturing it and making things possible for her.

We lived in a street of many children, we were near all the parks, just round the corner from her little C. of E. primary school. By then I was back at work as an actor, and loving it again, so it was, for all of us, an entirely happy time.

12. The matter with Pete

By the time Emma had arrived and I was married to Henry, my two brothers had grown up into young men. Paul, after his apprenticeship in the garage, became a fully qualified mechanic and also a driving instructor. He taught people to drive HGV vehicles and he taught the army to drive their tanks. He now deals in parts for vintage and veteran cars. He married Gilly, and he has become a rather bluff, blustery man, with a heart of pure gold.

After taking the technical course at the Bristol Old Vic Theatre School, Pete had begun working backstage in the theatre, but by then things were beginning to go seriously wrong for him. He had a series of what were termed 'minor' breakdowns. Then they became more extreme. It was increasingly clear that he was suffering from some form of mental disorder. When he was twenty-two my parents, who had borne the brunt of all his mood-swings and unhappiness, very reluctantly had him admitted to a very bleak mental hospital called Barrow Gurney. Every city has its Barrow Gurney, and there have even been songs written about ours. It's less bleak now, but it was awful then.

After more than five years of nobody knowing what the matter was as he had grown increasingly disturbed, the hospital now diagnosed Pete as being schizophrenic. In many ways giving it a name – even such a name – was a relief. When you know your enemy's name, you can marshal your forces. It wasn't Pete who was acting in this strange way, not the real Pete; it was an illness, a chemical imbalance in the brain, and it could be controlled by medication. But at first, beyond knowing now what the name of the trouble was, there was no real help for my parents, or for Pete, in how to proceed; no one to talk to about it.

In the early 1970s, at the time that he was diagnosed, the National Schizophrenia Fellowship was first starting, but we didn't hear about it then. Today when someone is diagnosed – and of course the earlier the diagnosis the better the prognosis, particularly with young people – they can telephone this organisation and immediately be put in touch with a good psychiatrist, if necessary, and a support group including families who have been through it. It makes an enormous difference to carers who are learning to cope.

I am ashamed to say that at first we – or at any rate I – reacted like many families do on discovering that a family member has a mental illness. I didn't tell anybody but my closest, most trusted friends. I was afraid that if people knew about it, and if I were to be at all volatile or extravagant in my way of expressing emotion – whether anger or joy or love – they would start to wonder whether I wasn't similarly affected. It is terrible to have to admit this now, because it is simply the worst way to react. People with any form of mental illness have enough to cope with without being regarded as secret objects of shame by the people who love them.

The way schizophrenia had manifested itself in Peter – for there are many and various manifestations – was first a withdrawal, then a lack of caring about what he ate, what he wore, then not making sense in what he said and becoming hyperactive. He would walk around Bath very fast. He started to hear voices and see visions. His voices were often religious, and told him that he had to be at a certain place at a certain time, in order to save the world. He would get up, and have to make very quickly for wherever he had to be by nine o'clock that morning so that the world would not perish. Once he was told that he must go and stand on a hill outside Bath and watch the sunrise. He would see spacemen, angels. He would see Christ. He would have no sleep for days and nights at a time, so that he became absolutely frantic with exhaustion, but had no idea himself that there was anything abnormal about what he was doing. He was locked into his own internal world.

Gradually we started to find out more about the condition, and how we could help him. I find it distressing that so many people assume that if someone is schizophrenic they must be paranoid-schizophrenic, which means they are going to be violent and dangerous. This is absolutely not true.

Pete's form of schizophrenia is called 'benign' because he is never, ever violent, and never hurts anybody. Of course it is not benign for him. If he were ever to be a danger to anyone, it would be only to himself, although that has never happened, apart from the occasion when he felt he wanted to change all the furniture in his room. He got a Stanley knife and cut his chairs and carpet into shreds and put them outside to be collected by the binmen, with no thought at all about how he was going to replace them.

One of the most important stages along the schizophrenia sufferer's journey is to take his medication. In order to do that he has to recognise and accept the fact that he is schizophrenic. Unfortunately, the medication can have unpleasant side effects. Even if you have reached the stage of admitting to yourself that you are ill, taking the drug sometimes makes life very difficult. Either you don't get the normal highs and lows, and life is very bland, or there are physical effects, like twitching. In Pete's case, the worst time came when he was put on two kinds of medication, the one designed to counteract the side effects of the other. Unfortunately, the side effect of the second drug was to make it impossible for him to play his guitar – the one great solace and pleasure in his troubled life. For nearly five years he had to live without recourse to the only activity that made life bearable for him, playing the blues on his guitar. Can you imagine the sadness of that?

So Peter, like many other sufferers, has had his times of deliberately coming off the drugs. And because once a certain amount of medication has gone into your system, you can stop for maybe three or four months, with enough of the drug remaining in the system to keep you apparently OK, you can even kid yourself that you don't really need the drugs at all. Then, of course, the illness starts again.

In a recent episode, it was not that Pete had come off the drugs, but he had asked to change his medication. That's another thing that angers me – one of the most effective drugs is also one of the most expensive. When I say most expensive – rather than costing roughly £12 a year to treat someone, it costs roughly £120 a year, and apparently the National Health Service can't underwrite that in order to make someone's life worth living. I become speechless.

Anyway, at Pete's own request, they had changed his medication, because the side effects of the one he was on were giving him the shakes and having a very depressive effect. Pete is lucky, he has a good doctor and psychiatrist who look after him, and they listen to him. Even so, there was something not right about the new medication, and he recognised before they did the signs that meant he was losing his grip on reality and was about to go into a schizophrenic episode. He needed to be taken into hospital quickly, probably only for a couple of days, where he could be stabilised, and then he could go back home; so he presented himself at the hospital.

Instead of simply admitting him, the hospital telephoned my mother and told her they were going to section him. To section someone is a deep psychological blow. It is horrendous for the sufferer and for the family. She said, 'But you don't have to. He's not a danger either to himself or to anyone else.'

It turned out that the reason he would have to be sectioned was that there were not enough beds, and the only way they could give him a bed was to section him. A sectioning lasts for several months. Patients don't have to be in hospital all that time, but nevertheless it's like being under sentence, having a record. As if life wasn't tough enough for him.

So life hasn't ever been easy for Pete. He's fine now. He's on the best drugs ever. He looks well and happy. He lives in a wonderful place started by Richard Carr-Gomm, an amazing guy, a Quaker, a benefactor who has done an enormous amount for the old and the mentally ill by setting up sheltered houses all over the country. Pete's is a lovely, happy house, completely autonomous, on the outskirts of Bath, and he has many good friends there. He plays his blues guitar. He always tells people that he's schizophrenic when he meets them. People often think it means a split personality, like Jekyll and Hyde; Pete has a good sense of humour, and he knows all the old gags like, 'Oh yes? Where's your mate?' He knows many fellow-sufferers, and they all support each other; but some of his friends have committed suicide because they just couldn't cope with the sadness of their lives. It isn't easy.

One of the difficulties for a carer is to be able to see the person as separate from the illness, particularly when you are exhausted and things keep going wrong in the middle of the night. This is what my mother has had to live with. It is almost impossible to cope day in, day out. It has always been easier for me, because I wasn't with him all the time.

Historically, there has often been an attitude to mental illness which connects it with magic. In primitive societies, people suffering with forms of what we now call schizophrenia were thought of as holy fools, the wise women and men of the tribe. People would go to them for advice and to hear profound truths. They thought they were in touch with angels or spirits.

Through being Pete's sister, I too have learned a lot about love and about the limits to which one can go. It has been a strange process. Among the most important things he has taught me is that when he is in, or approaching, 'an episode', he has moments when he is not in complete touch with reality, and how not to be frightened of that; how to listen to him when he is hallucinating, and not confuse him or challenge him. So now, if for instance some old bag lady gets on the bus and sits next to me and starts to talk nonsense, I find it quite easy to enter into her reality.

That also helped me with my great-aunt Peg, who in her last years suffered a long time of complete befuddlement. I remember going down to see her one day when she was in that condition. She was very religious, and was especially devoted to the Virgin Mary. Indeed she eventually became a Roman Catholic. She had this very large picture of Mary with the Christ-child on her lap, and when Peg moved into her residential care home it was one of the things she wanted to take with her. So there it was on her wall; Peg was sitting in her armchair, and I was sitting beside her, and after we had been chatting for a while she suddenly looked up and said, 'They are evil people here, you know.'

I said, 'Do you mean the staff? The nurses, the people who look after you?'

'Yes. They're evil.'

'Why do you say that, darling? What have they done?'

'They want to steal Her,' she said, indicating the picture.

I thought very quickly, and realised there was no point in my saying, 'No, they don't. No, they're not,' because she was convinced that they were.

I said, 'Do you know what? I think that She is able to take care both of herself and of you. She won't allow that to happen. You know that the Virgin Mary would never allow them to take her picture away from you, don't you?'

Somehow that clicked, it was OK, and she stopped worrying. That was simple enough, but even so I would not have been able to do that if it hadn't been for Pete, and learning from him that when somebody gets confused, there is no point in arguing with them. They'll simply become more upset. What you have to do is look at the situation from their point of view and say, 'Right. Well, what are we going to do about this? How are we going to cope?'

If someone says they can see a big pink rabbit in the garden, you can say, 'I can't actually see it, but I'll try and see it – please tell me about it.' But don't say, 'No, there isn't.' And don't pretend to see it and say, 'Oh yes, so there is!' Because they'll know you are not being honest. You may enter their reality, but it must be from a place of honesty.

It won't happen in my lifetime, but I am quite passionate about trying to get people who don't come into everyday contact with someone with a mental problem to recognise that they are not dangerous, not to be steered clear of, not to be laughed at out of fear. We are beginning to learn how to behave towards those with physical disabilities – like not shouting at someone who is in a wheelchair, as if for some reason that makes them deaf as well. It will be a very long hard battle to reach the same place with the mentally ill, but one day I hope we'll win it. Schizophrenia so very often hits young, intelligent, interesting people.

I think in some ways the fact that, through me, Pete has talked very publicly about his illness on television and the radio, has helped him to be able to say to himself, 'I suffer from schizophrenia, so I will take my medication.'

I started to work for the NSF, National Schizophrenia Fellowship, as soon as I heard about it. What we believe would be most helpful would be for more people in the public eye who have any form of mental illness in their family to come forward and say so. We recognise that it can be difficult, because if the sufferers themselves do not want you to, then of course you mustn't. I had Pete's permission all the way along the line over 'coming out'; he's been absolutely for it. If only more people knew how valuable it can be.

I remember visiting a mental hospital in Poole. One of the patients I met was a young girl, and we started to talk. I said to her, 'What brought you here?'

'Oh,' she said, 'I suffer from the same thing as Spike Milligan.' It gave her dignity. It gave her the right to be a manic depressive, and not be ashamed of it. That is vital for the sufferers. What you see is the growth of confidence in who they are, and an ability to recognise that they have the illness, and not to be afraid. They don't have to deny it; they can learn to live with it. Pete, because he's a bloody good blues musician and a jolly good gardener, and because he's been seen on television, and has given major interviews in the newspapers, can feel it is acceptable. He can say, 'Yes, I am schizophrenic – I've talked to Mavis Nicholson about it on television. The *Daily Telegraph* did an article about me. I know about it.'

There's a wonderful place in Bristol called the Hope Centre, and a man there – a schizophrenic, a brilliant artist, a potter – has been enabled to follow his craft again, because he's regained his confidence. I have a friend in Northern Ireland who is a poet, and through his poetry he has regained his confidence. And all people who suffer from schizophrenia, unless it is very, very extreme, can be helped to regain their self-respect. Even if they only manage something that to our eyes is incredibly simple, like being able to sort cards in a filing system, confidence comes with any kind of achievement. Unfortunately, even when people have recovered to the point where their schizophrenia can be coped with – try getting a job. You just try. You can't. There are jobs that they could do, but they're not allowed to, because there is still such a stigma attached. We must try and get rid of this idea that if you admit on your application form that you have suffered at some time in your life with a form of mental illness, that you are going to turn out to be a mad axeman.

We can't change the person who suffers. All we can do is walk with them to wherever they are going. Sometimes, when the illness is very severe, it is almost impossible to see the person as separate from the illness, but you have to keep on trying. All this makes me sound like an awful know-it-all and goody-goody, but I don't know it all, and I have sometimes coped with it extremely badly; lost my temper with Pete and got upset and crotchety with my Mum. So I do know only too well what it feels like to get it wrong. I wouldn't want you to think, 'There she goes, Mrs Perfect.' It's really not like that at all.

Perhaps the most important thing of all that I've learned from Pete is the importance of recognising the uniqueness of each individual human being. When you suffer from something like schizophrenia, there is this feeling that you don't have anything to offer. You are just someone who is mentally ill. What work can you do? What right have you got to even be alive? For me to be courageous might require me to take on a challenging new role, or climb a high mountain. In hyper mood, off his medication, Pete could fly up any mountain. For Peter, courage is staying on his medication and putting one foot in front of the other, day after day after day.

Interval

When a person has arrived at a stage in life when he accepts the inevitable with equanimity, when he's tasted good and bad to the full, and has carved out for himself alongside his external life an inner, more real, and not fortuitous existence, then it seems that life has not been empty and worthless.

Hermann Hesse

I know we're only pretending that this book is a play about my life, that I am the actor and you are the audience, and that this is the interval between the two acts, but it is quite a useful device, because I can use this space to answer some of the questions that might have entered your minds since you began reading.

For instance, you might want to ask why I am writing my autobiography in two acts now when, with any luck, a third act is still ahead of me, waiting to be lived?

The simple answer is – I was asked to do it, and although I was very surprised by the idea at first, I can never say 'No' to a new challenge, even when I haven't the first idea how to go about it. Somebody at Hodder and Stoughton saw me on a television programme in which I talked about my life, in particular about my inner life, my spiritual journey so far, and I suppose they thought that 'I had a book in me'. I thought that probably about three and a half chapters was more the mark, but a challenge is a challenge, so here we all are.

I find as I write that I can now look back at her, at young Steph, with affection and understanding. I look at the bad things I did, the good things I did, the shyness, the rebellion, and I see it all with such a feeling of, 'Oh, dear heart, how could you have done that? Well, I do so understand.' I find I have compassion for my younger self, even for the things I did which were not very nice. I understand why, and forgive her.

The odd thing about writing this book has been discovering how unimportant the actual external events of my life seem now, as I look through the old scrapbooks sitting here, full of photographs of all the early years, when I was growing up, working in rep, living, learning, falling in and out of love, playing parts I loved and parts I hated. My external life was very busy. I did it all, and I know I did it – here are the photographs that prove it – but now it almost seems as if I was only marking time. I wasn't, of course, because I was learning lots of lessons and it was an essential part of my growing, but the details seem to me to be unimportant now. It feels almost as if my inner life, my real life, didn't begin until I had hit rock bottom, and thought I had lost it all.

I wasn't without my moments of gravitas, however, even in my early years. When I was fifteen, staying with Great-Aunt Peg at Croyde, I remember sitting on the cliffs at Baggy Point, which now belongs to the National Trust, overlooking the turbulent Atlantic Ocean as it pounds in on the beach. There are great rocks, and guillemots and kittiwakes and seals, and it's a wild and windy place. I used to sit there for hours in the desolate time of being fifteen. On this day I must have fallen into a sort of trance, because I sat there motionless for over two hours and a phrase came to me that I've never forgotten. I don't think I really understood it at the time: *The tall dark column of my being dissolves, and I am nothing and the universe.*

To be honest, I'm not sure that I quite understand it, even now. It's to do with being part of no less than everything, and yet remembering how small you are, but also how big you are. It came from deep in my unconscious mind.

Your next question might well be, so are you now a Christian?

On that original television interview about my life, *Sweet Inspiration*, Alan Titchmarsh asked me how I pictured God, and I heard myself saying, 'God is the bend in the river.' I'd never consciously thought that before, but as soon as I heard myself say it, I knew it was true. Even when I was a little child being taken to church, I never had the traditional idea of God as an old man with a white beard up in the sky. Behind the sand-dunes in North Devon there was a stream, with a little wooden bridge over it. Great-Aunt Peg used to take me there on walks, and when I was old enough I would go on my own. The stream of water came from sunlight, curved into the dark under the bridge, and then curved out to light again. When I was nine and we moved to South Gloucestershire we had a river at the bottom of the garden, and again there was a wonderful bend in it, where it went from light into darkness and through to light again. At some deep level, that has been how I have always thought of God – the bend in the river, the place where light becomes dark and darkness light.

Up until the point that we've reached in my story, the 'wilderness years' as I've called them, and all through that very dark period of my life, I had utterly rejected Christianity, and would have described myself, like my husband, Henry, as an atheist. However, I think some part of me had never stopped being in a secret dialogue with God, and when I started to come through that bleak time, for some reason, perhaps loneliness, I also began to take the first faltering steps of the journey I am still on, the long search to rediscover what I was born knowing, and forgot, the search for spiritual enlightenment. As Laurens van der Post wrote:

Called or not called, God is always there. Known or not known, sought or rejected, this master pattern theologians call God, night and day is there, in the collective unconscious of us all, calling us to live and be our whole selves.

That still doesn't answer your question about whether or not I am a Christian. In the beginning I didn't really think of returning to Christianity, and my search led me to draw thoughts and ideas from many wells, in the Upanishads, the *Bhagavadgita*, the Koran, and in the teachings of the Buddha, Black Elk, Lao Tse . . . I have worshipped in Hindu temples and celebrated Christmas with followers of Shiva. Nobody can disentangle the threads of a tapestry that has so many different colours in it. Nevertheless, as the journey has gone on, I have found myself more and more drawn back to Christianity, to following Carl Jung's advice to all his patients – return to the faith of your childhood, where all your myths are formed. Then the discovery of the Christian mystics and visionaries, the writings of Julian of Norwich, Hildegard of Bingen, and Meister Eckhart opened a door for me that made it possible for me to return without fear to a religion I had once found judgmental and stultifying.

And what happened to my beloved Great-Aunt Peg, after we all left Devon?

She stayed on, retiring from work, but taking an active part in village life. She wrote and directed the pantomimes for many years and was involved in the church. She had always loved church life and been a faithful attender, and at length became a devout Roman Catholic. We often used to go and stay with her, and she would come to visit us. She eventually had to move into a home, where she lived until her death, aged ninety-six. Her great, strong heart wouldn't let her body die and, because she was no longer compos mentis in her last two years, what I saw was like a little, empty shell. I still loved her, and somewhere in there was the spirit of the Peg I knew but I just couldn't find it. I didn't visit her more than four or five times a year. I often felt guilty about that, because I owe her a great deal. She gave me unconditional love; she taught me a generosity both with things and of spirit; she often used to say 'There are no pockets in a shroud.' She was my godmother, literally; my prayer book and christening things were from her, but in a deeper and wider sense, too, she gave me my grounding in God.

I have recently made a great new friend in James Roose-Evans, the theatre director who founded Hampstead Theatre Club, who is also a non-stipendiary Anglican priest. I have told him about Peg, how I tried to talk to her and just hoped and prayed that something was going in, so I kept going and talking, if not as often as I should have. He has often sat with people who are dying, and many times has spiritually aided the passage of someone between here and there, and he believes that it does make a difference, and that it is worthwhile.

When I used to visit Peg, towards the end, I would reminisce about when I was a child, and about when she was a child. Many times I said thank you for things she did, and for the times we had together. Very often I prayed. Perhaps it does go in. Who knows? Who knows?

Another important turning-point for me came when I took part in a drama-documentary on Channel 4 about the friendship between a Poor Clare nun from Australia called Sister Angela, and Helen Joseph, the great anti-apartheid campaigner. Sister Angela had read a book by Helen Joseph, and had written to her saying, 'You are under house arrest by an outside force, I am under house arrest by my own volition. I think we have a lot in common.' And they started to write to each other. They eventually met, in South Africa, but only twice before Helen Joseph died. Channel 4 made a programme about them with Phyllis Calvert reading Helen Joseph's letters and me reading Sister Angela's, combined with clips of actual newsreel of both of them.

They were very moving, beautiful letters between two extraordinary women. Helen Joseph died quite soon afterwards, but I had a short correspondence with her through this, and I also began a correspondence with Sister Angela, which has led to her becoming a supportive and wise spiritual adviser to me, even though at a very long distance.

When she was young, Angela was a talented sculptor about to have her first international exhibition, and about to get married, when she suddenly realised that she was supposed to do neither of these. She was supposed to become a Poor Clare. She's now seventy, and this was in her late twenties, so a long time ago. As there were several antipodean nuns at the mother house, she decided that she wanted to start a Poor Clare house in Australia, and she went out with two other Australian sisters. In the bush they made their own bricks, they scrounged wood from skips for windows and doors, and they built their own monastery, which I have visited.

I also started going to St James's Church, Piccadilly. I happened to read a translation of Meister Eckhart by Matthew Fox, and found a leaflet inside about creation-centred spirituality, which attracted me very much, and its London home is at St James's.

Creation-centred Christianity is to do with original blessing rather than original sin. It is about love, not about judgment and 'thou shalt not . . .' At St James's, under the aegis of Donald Reeves, through the recognition of other belief systems, through the spontaneity of the services and worship of a God not defined, not tagged, not made smaller by gender – all things which I had rejected in the Christianity that I had been brought up in – I have now discovered people who do not see Christianity in those terms, and I have found that there are people all over the world who never have, who are eclectic Christians, like me.

Sister Angela is one. She was one of the first women to be priested in Australia, and when she takes a service, she talks as much about her as him, when she talks of God. One of the lovely things I remember Sister Angela saying before I met her, on one of the pieces of film about her, was how, walking through the bush one day, she saw a bird floating in the sky overhead – I have a feeling it was an eagle – and it was simply enjoying itself, playing on the thermals. It wasn't seeking food, going anywhere, it was simply being.

I think we've forgotten that art of simply being. The old Protestant work ethic disapproves of it; you have to be up and at it, you only get out what you put in, make every second count, sixty seconds' worth of distance run and you'll be a man, my son . . . Utter tosh! The art of living includes the art of being and of learning to let things be. Lie on a little bit of a raft on the ocean and allow it to take you where it will. It's like truly praying that most courageous prayer of all, 'Thy will, not mine, be done.'

I sometimes think that is the most difficult thing, and the most important thing – to learn how, and be willing, to live in a state of not knowing. Human beings like certainty, because we feel so helpless and afraid. When we're born, we are entirely reliant for many years on our parents and even as adults we are still at the mercy of the world around us, so we cling to certainties and safety nets.

The nomad has no home, but he carries his familiar things with him, his household gods, his rugs, his cooking pot and his tent. When he stops for the night, there they are. He needs those things. We need them, too. We must just learn to whittle down our things to the cooking pot, the tent and the rug, metaphorically, and allow everything else to be a question mark. It makes life unbelievably exciting.

As you go back to your seats for Act Two, I would like to read you part of a poem by Christopher Fry, which I have quoted often in my life, and which I always keep by me, because it is so much a clarion call for today:

The human heart can go the lengths of God
Dark and cold we may be, but this is no winter now.
The misery of centuries, breaks, cracks, begins to move
The thunder is the thunder of the floes, the thaw, the
flood, the upstart spring.
Thank God our time is now when wrong comes up to
face us everywhere
Never to leave us till we take the longest stride of soul
man ever took.
Affairs are now soul size.
The enterprise is exploration into God.
Where are you making for? It takes so many thousand
years to wake,
But will you wake
For pity's sake?

Christopher Fry

Act Two

But will you wake,
For pity's sake?

Later, the same life

14. A time to dance

Well into my twenties, I was still so frightened of the dark that before I was married, if I had to spend a night somewhere on my own, I would have to stay with friends. I thought there were people at the windows, trying to get in, and I was convinced that every sound was something going to attack me. It was completely irrational, but you can't argue with irrationality. I was just absolutely terrified.

The turning-point came when Emma was two years old. In 1975, with my stepfather's kind help, we bought a small house in Bath. It was one of a group of lovely Georgian houses, built by the workers who were building Royal York Crescent, and very nearly everything else in Bath. Henry still had to spend most of the week in London, where we kept on the flat because the rent was very low, and he would come down at weekends. I was faced with the problem that I was going to have to be in this house on my own all week, with only a little child for company.

I was never a great taker of medicines, and one aspirin is usually enough to send me to sleep, so that first night, when Emma was asleep, I put out two aspirins beside the bed, ready to knock myself out, and decided I would just lie in the bed in the dark. And – this is going to sound so fanciful – the house actually cured me; it was so friendly, and so unthreatening in every way, even with its garden at the back sloping right away into the countryside. Of course there were houses on either side, and of course there were people

117

around, but that hadn't helped in London.

The sounds of this little house didn't seem at all threatening. I felt that nothing bad could happen to us there – which again was irrational, but this irrationality, for some reason, was stronger than the irrationality of my fear – which had always been huge. I was so at ease, lying in bed in this house, that I fell asleep without taking the aspirin. It was a minor miracle for me.

I was beginning to feel at that time that perhaps I'd got through the worst. I'd come through the depression, the agoraphobia, the claustrophobia, I'd given up the business, everything had been hideous . . . Now it seemed to be a time when good things might be starting to happen again, like Nat and Rudi believing in me and giving me the teaching job, like Reggie's call, serendipitous happenings, coincidences of people and events, and now this losing my fear of the dark, was just one more, one of many.

Although becoming a teacher at the Vic School the year before had done an enormous amount for my morale, and had helped me to fall back in love with the business, I realised that I probably shouldn't be a teacher, and that I probably should start thinking of getting back into acting.

Just at that same time, Sam Walters at the Orange Tree Theatre in Richmond was putting on a new play and was trying to cast it. He needed someone to play the lead, a character in her early thirties and rather plump. He was having some difficulty finding the right actor. Somebody who had known me, but didn't know that I'd given up the business, suggested my name. Sam tried to contact me, and was told by my previous agent that I wasn't working any more.

And that would have been that, had he not, one morning, been standing *outside* the Orange Tree. Now that is a thing which Sam very rarely does. He's not an outdoor person, Sam. But that morning there he was, standing outside the old Orange Tree pub, when someone else I knew, who didn't live in Richmond but who happened to be there that morning, happened to know Sam and happened to be passing the Orange Tree at that moment.

'Hi, Sam! How are you doing?'

'Fine.'

'What are you doing at the moment?'

'I'm trying to cast a new play by David Cregan.'

'Who are you looking for?'

'I think I'm going to have to cast somebody who is not quite right, because I can't find anybody who is. Somebody suggested an actress I don't know, called Stephanie Cole, but I can't find her, and anyway, I think she's given up the business.'

And my friend said, 'I've got her telephone number. Do you want it?'

I was living in our small house down in Bath. It was a blessed little house, really, as you've heard. Only good things happened there. So Sam telephoned me in Bath, and I thought, 'Yes!' And was excited. For the first time in nearly five years, I was excited by the idea of work.

I went for the interview and I got the job, and I did it. It was a lovely play called *Tina* and I played the eponymous heroine. Lots of casting directors came, from television and the theatre, and suddenly they were all saying, 'Why haven't we seen Stephanie Cole before? Why haven't we used her before?' And work started to tumble into my lap. I was only three years older. I was the same old Steph that had been working in the business now for fifteen years – but joy, oh joy, my time had come.

There has been a lot of work ever since, and a lot of friends. The friends have been the important thing. There were lots and lots of television parts, and also a fair amount of good theatre work to do, and it was wonderful.

In 1979 I went up to Liverpool Everyman. Em, who would have been about seven, came up with me. I was in *Funny Peculiar* by Mike Stott. I was happy to be asked, because I wanted very much to be part of the Liverpool scene of that time – working with Willie Russell, Alan Dosser and Alan Bleasdale.

Six months later, it paid off, because I was asked to do *Rose*, by Andrew Davies, with Glenda Jackson at the Duke of York's Theatre. It was directed by Alan Dosser, and was a big hit. I played a gimlet-eyed, tight-lipped headmistress, and Glenda was a modern young teacher trying to bring humanity into the classroom.

It was a comedy, basically the old story of the individual who tries to break through the brick walls of an institution, foolishly imagining they are made of cardboard, while at the same time trying to paper over the gaping holes in her marriage, and who winds up screaming, 'I can't fight the system. I am the system.' Andrew Davies has a brilliant eye for detail and it was a wonderfully witty, well-written play. We sold out for the whole of the six months.

Even in a hit play, the audience is unpredictable. Some conversations overheard during the run:

German lady: This is the worst play I have ever seen.
Lady (on hearing she'd booked the royal box): But I haven't done my hair!
Another lady: Well, I've seen her films, but a play . . .
New Zealand lady: It's all very well, but I don't know how it will go down back home.
American lady: You know the man who played the husband? Well, would he have travelled on the underground? Because the main thing I noticed was the plaster on his finger.

For me, it was really special. *Rose* was the first play to give me a really good part in the West End. Apart from making several more lifelong friendships, *Rose* also gave me the opportunity to learn to play bridge. Over the years since then, whenever I worked in Manchester I would stay with Di Davies and we would play. She had learned while in *Coronation Street*, so she always asked Doris Speed to be one of the foursome. In spite of many years' playing, Doris had never quite mastered the rules. One night she and I were partners, when not a decent card came our way. Then I picked up the hand from heaven – a ton of points. I opened the bidding with 'two clubs', which is a conventional call, meaning you have an enormous hand.

Me: Two clubs.
Di: Pass.
Doris (my partner): Oh, no, no. No bid.
Me (louder): I did say *two clubs*, Doris . . . (hint, hint).
Doris: Oh, no. I can't, dear. Pass.

Di's partner passed. Di led something, and Doris laid down her hand as Dummy. Between us, we had every single point in the pack.

'Doris!' I wailed.

'As you see, dear,' she said, 'I have very few clubs.' So we opened another bottle of wine.

In January 1981, I went to the Old Vic Theatre, London, to do the Restoration play, *The Relapse*, by Sir John Vanbrugh. Our production became chiefly renowned for the number of disasters that we had to contend with. It was a big cast and the director decided that it should be played in its entirety, which was a test for theatre-goers, because it runs for four hours. We included a huge masque in the middle, with music by Carl Davis.

Halfway through rehearsal we lost our leading lady, an American who felt, undoubtedly correctly, that she had been miscast and couldn't manage such an English piece, so she walked. Her replacement, Celia Foxe, only had about ten days' rehearsal.

The day before we were due to open, we all amassed on stage for the costume parade. You stand there thinking, 'I *can't* play the part in this – I actually can't breathe and I can't walk and I can't move' – and the costume designer says, 'Looks lovely. Next.'

So anyway, there we were, Monday morning, all in our costumes, John Nettles wondrous in his extravagant finery as Foppington, and there were so many of us in the enormous cast that nobody noticed that one of us was missing. These were still the days of telegrams. The director suddenly came on stage waving a piece of paper and said, 'I don't quite know how to tell you this – I suppose I'd better just read it. It says: "Can't cope. Have gone. Don't try and find me. So sorry. Love. B." And it was sent from Heathrow.'

It was our leading man. Lovelace must be the biggest part in the English language when the piece is played in its entirety, even longer than Hamlet. The actor playing him had flown off to Canada that morning, and we were due to open the next night.

The theatre rang up Michael Ladkin, who is my agent now, because Richard Kay, one of his clients, now sadly dead, had played Lovelace at the National about seven years before. Michael telephoned Richard at home later that Monday morning, and said, 'Richard, er, listen, er, the Old Vic would like you to, er, do Lovelace again. Do you think you could do it?'

Richard said, 'Love to. When do we start rehearsing, and how many weeks have we got?'

Michael said, 'You rehearse all today and you go on tomorrow night.'

And bless his heart, Richard did it, and was absolutely brilliant.

Unfortunately, however, our troubles were not yet at an end. On the first night, an older actor, who was playing several different parts, with many costume changes, fell very ill with flu which became pneumonia, and his doctor said he wouldn't be responsible if the actor went on. So our assistant director, who was roughly twenty-one years old at the time, went on and played all the parts, in his overcoat and holding the script!

The critics were remarkably kind. We toured it to Brighton and Bath (where I saw the famous ghost of the butterfly, which means you will come back there one day, and fifteen years later I did). We didn't do very good business, but we all rather enjoyed ourselves.

As well as the theatre, from 1976 I was doing a lot of television; all sorts of things – I can't remember a lot of it. Looking through my mother's old scrapbooks again, I see I did a couple of episodes of *Lillie* and was in the original *Just William*, with Diana Fairfax playing Mrs Brown, and the glorious Diana Dors as Mrs Bott. And I was in twelve episodes of *Emmerdale*. I'd forgotten all this.

I do remember being in a couple of episodes of a sitcom called *The Fosters*, with Norman Beaton, Isobel Lucas, Carmen Munro and a sixteen-year-old Lenny Henry. He was astonishing, quite, quite astonishing, so I expect everybody told him the same thing, but I do remember saying to him, 'You are a quite wonderful actor. You're going to be a most enormous star.'

I was in a series called *Sally-Ann* about the Salvation Army. It was the first time I'd done a whole series on television. People often say, 'When you play different parts, does it affect the way you are in everyday life?' Well, all I can say is that Emma and Henry both thought that I had become a saint during the six months I was doing *Sally-Ann*, I was so easy-going.

Then there was *One Day at a Time* by Dennis Cannon, a play about alcoholics; and I was in *Betsy* with Frank Finlay, in which I played Mrs Balcombe, Betsy's mum.

In the seventies, I did a half-hour television show by Willis Hall, called *Christmas Spirits*, starring Elaine Stritch. There were four of us in the cast: Norma West, Ben Aris, Elaine and me. Elaine was only drinking red wine, in the mistaken belief that it was non-alcoholic. We had a week's filming, and there was about twenty minutes to do in the studio, for which we were given three days on a huge set. We all sat and asked Elaine questions about her early life, and she told me about Josh Logan taking her for a horse-and-carriage drive round Central Park, and she sang her songs to me, and I really enjoyed myself. Unfortunately, things went rather badly awry on the set, and we had to go back and remount the whole thing.

Fairly recently I worked again with Willis, in two series of a very funny children's drama called *The Return of the Antelope*. I was the sister of the villain, played by Paul Chapman, whom I have known since Lincoln days. The basic premise was that some Lilliputians, a hundred years after Gulliver, had set sail in a boat and been washed up on the shores of Victorian England. Paul and I were always having to put on disguises – I've got a picture in my guest loo of me as a man and Paul as a woman.

The first time I was ever in anything by Alan Bennett was in 1978. It was a play called *Afternoon Off*. Stephen Frears directed, and there was a very starry cast: Anna Massey, Richard Griffiths, Thora Hird, Peter Postlethwaite and Elizabeth Spriggs. It was produced by Innes Lloyd, who ten years later was to give me the tremendous opportunity of being one of the six actors to play the extraordinary series of monologues by Alan Bennett, *Talking Heads*.

My television parts were gradually beginning to get bigger and bigger. In 1981 I was in a play by Thomas Ellice, from a novel by Robert T. S. Downs, called *Going Gently*. It was a bitter-sweet piece about two men in hospital, both dying of cancer, with Judi Dench, Fulton Mackay, Peter Attard and Norman Wisdom, whose wife I played. Again, Stephen Frears directed. It was an important piece of work, a first-class production, and another turning-point for me. That was through Innes Lloyd again.

Innes was a maverick. I adored him. He trusted people, and entrusted them with things. For instance, after *Going Gently*, the next play I did for him was *Amy*, about Amy Johnson. Nat Crosby, a brilliant film cameraman, had always wanted to direct, so Innes asked him to direct it. Innes showed such belief in people, including me. He died not long ago. British television is immeasurably the poorer.

I was nearly always playing older than myself, and everyone said the same thing as Daphne Heard, who had taught me at the Vic School, had said to me then, 'Stephanie darling, you'll never get anywhere until you're fifty.' At the age of sixteen and a half my heart sank. She was wrong – but only by ten years. I didn't really catch the public eye in any big way until I was nearly forty. In 1981, while I was doing *Amy*, I had the interview for *Tenko*.

Tenko had been created by Lavinia Warner, and the scripts were being written by two women, Jill Hyem and Ann Valerie. Ann, a wonderful eccentric, had written an episode of *Angels* that I'd been in a couple of years before, in which I'd played a completely loopy motorcycle-riding psychiatrist, and we'd become friends through this. She telephoned me and said, 'Steph, I've just written this series with Jill Hyem, and I think you're exactly right for the nun in it. Make sure you go up for it.'

They did see me for the nun but as soon as I walked in, Pennant Roberts, who was directing the first six episodes, and Ken Riddington, the producer, said, 'Can you read this other part?' which was the role of Dr Beatrice Mason. I did so, and then Pennant explained to me that the series was set in a women's prison-camp in Malaya during the Second World War, where many Europeans were interned after the fall of Singapore, from 1942 until the surrender of Japan in 1945. It was going to explore the experiences of a mixed group of women surviving that ordeal.

He said, 'You will need to – I mean everybody will have to – lose weight during it. You won't have any difficulty with that?'

'No,' I lied. 'Actually I'm rather overweight at the moment because I've just been playing the Nurse in *The Relapse* at the Old Vic, and I had to put on some weight for that . . .' Well, that was true.

He looked at me and said, 'Well, but what are you

normally? About eight and a half stone?'

I'd not been eight and a half stone since I was twelve years old, but, 'Oh, yes. Well . . . Ye-es,' I said.

During the interview I was telling Pennant what I'd done, and he said he knew my work a little. 'Of course, I've seen you play Shakespeare.'

'*Have* you?' I asked, and went back over all the Shakespeare I'd done in various reps, wondering where on earth he would have seen me, and he kept saying, 'No. No. No.'

Eventually I said, 'Well, I've never done it anywhere else.'

He said, 'Yes, you have. You did it at Bristol.'

I said, 'Oh. Right. What? *The Tempest* or *Richard II?*' thinking he meant while I was an acting ASM at the Theatre Royal in my very first year in the professional theatre.

'No, no. Before that.'

'*Before* that!'

He had been a biology student at Bristol University when I was a student at the Vic School, and we used to do our plays in the university drama studio. We had done what we called *The Shakespeare Exercises* – excerpts from all of Shakespeare's plays over about two evenings – and he had seen them, and more than twenty years later, he remembered. Despite that – I got the job!

15. *Tenko gels*

In 1980, the BBC had just had the biggest bummer of all time, *The Borgias*, so they needed a hit, but they certainly didn't expect *Tenko* to be it. With its comparatively tiny budget, unglamorous characters and grim storylines, it didn't sound likely to be much of a winning formula, but in the early eighties three series of *Tenko* had up to fourteen million viewers a week hooked.

It should have taught the suits something, but do you think it did? We were the BBC's biggest hit show, but those in charge found it almost impossible to accept that a series about women in Japanese prison-camps, hard-hitting and pulling no punches, which was also not sentimental, could actually win the hearts and minds of the nation. The story was simply about strong women, wives and mothers, real women; there were no daring escapes, no heroics, just a realistic portrait of how they survived an appalling ordeal. After the second series, the Beeb was actually going to axe it, but fortunately Michael Grade came along and said, 'You've got to be out of your minds. You must do more.' And thankfully, they did.

I don't think that beforehand they had had any idea or even a hope that *Tenko* was going to be such a hit. To be honest, I don't think any of us did. We were just glad to know that we would be working with a good director, doing twelve one-hour episodes with well-written scripts.

I had cut it a bit fine, getting to the first read-through,

which is very unlike me. I wasn't exactly late, but I arrived, uncharacteristically, at the last minute. I walked into the room, and I must have been frowning slightly because I was feeling tense, and they were all already sitting round the table.

Apparently Patricia Lawrence turned to Ann Bell and said, 'Oh dear, this isn't going to be a load of laughs.'

But within seconds we all realised that she was quite wrong, and it *was* going to be a load of laughs. Particularly for Patti, Ann and I, and for Roni Roberts, Lou Jamieson and, well, everybody actually – we all did an awful lot of laughing.

We had all had quite a few reservations about the fact that it was to be an almost entirely female cast. The only experience I had had of being with all women was at boarding-school, which, as I think I've made pretty clear, I absolutely hated. There were to be three Japanese actors – Eiji Kusuhara, Takashi Kawahara and Takahira Oba – as well as Burt Kwouk and a basic cast of twelve European women, with other women coming in at later stages. I thought, and I think we all probably thought, 'Oh, my God!' The idea of being incarcerated in a television series with virtually all women rather appalled me.

Patti Lawrence played the part that I had originally thought I was going for, Sister Ulrika, the formidable leader of the Dutch contingent in the old camp before the British arrived, after which they all had to live together in the new camp. Ann Bell played Marion Jefferson, wife of a colonel, who had been resident in Singapore. Her character had leadership thrust upon her. Jean Anderson was Joss Holbrook, the rebel at the new camp, an Oxford graduate and suffragette who lived in Bloomsbury in the 1920s, who had been running a school in Kuala Lumpur before the war. Roni Roberts was Dorothy Bennett, who loses both husband and child and becomes fatalistic. Stephanie Beacham was Rose Millar, a 'man's' woman, who saw the other women only as competition. And Stephanie Cole was

Dr Beatrice Mason, on the surface a very tough person, but inside, very vulnerable. I had no trouble at all in identifying with Dr Bea.

We became the '*Tenko* gels'. Everybody from *Tenko* is a *Tenko* girl and will be for the rest of their lives, with Burt Kwouk popping in and out as an honorary *Tenko* girl, and Pennant Roberts, the director, as our sultan.

Ken Riddington, the producer, was not very good in the heat, which was terrible for him on *Tenko*. He always wore white gloves so that the sun couldn't give him a rash. He has rather a solemn, wrinkled face that bursts into a brilliant smile that lights up his entire face. Poor bugger, it must have been terrifying for him at the beginning. At the first rehearsal he had to make a little speech. I think there might have been a little bit of the male chauvinist piggy in Ken. He wasn't at all at ease about having to address all these women, particularly in view of what he had to say, which was clearly all but killing him. The way he put it was this; 'I have to ask you not to shave under your arms, and not to shave your legs ... if your husbands and partners don't mind.'

After a stunned pause, an Irish actress, Jeananne Crowley, in a voice whose indignation sounded all the greater for its brogue, said in ringing tones, 'Why should we ask our partners or husbands – why should we ask any man – if we want to shave a part of our body or not to shave it?'

Poor old Ken stood there, white and shaking, and in that second was clearly wondering if it had been such a good idea to have agreed to produce this female series. It was a defining moment, and an object-lesson for a lot of the men who were about to work with us.

It was interesting to see the ones who didn't have a problem. Burt coped gloriously, because Burt loves women; and most of the crew were fine, although there were one or two who found it difficult. We were all vocal, feisty women, and we knew what was what. Our first director, Pennant Roberts, had no problem at all. We called him 'the Sultan' because we believed that in a previous life he had treated women appallingly, so as a punishment, he had to have all these women constantly around him, and be nice to them. He was wonderful. He loves women; and besides, he was the one who had chosen us all, so we had a great deal to be thankful to him for, our Sultan Penn.

We worked very closely with the Imperial War Museum, who opened all their archives to us. We saw film clips nobody had ever seen before, of life before the fall of Singapore, and of when it was relieved. The Imperial War Museum were wonderfully helpful throughout, and whenever there was any official function to do with that period of history, we were always invited, so we met very many of the survivors – men and women – some of whom had been children in the camps.

It was not for nothing that our army over there was called 'the forgotten army'. Nobody in the British Isles knew what they were going through; there weren't even rumours about them, as there were about the concentration camps in Europe. It was simply never talked about, never publicised, because it was so shameful. It wasn't just the defeat, it was that the Churchill government had had to turn its back on our own women and children; the men too, of course, but it was considered particularly shameful to turn one's back on the women and children.

When the first survivors were shipped back, on American ships, to England, they docked in Liverpool, on a cold, grey November morning. They were coming home, having undergone this horrendous experience. There was *nobody* on the quayside to greet them. Their relatives had not been told. The amount of counselling or advice any of the survivors had was minimal; they were simply expected to pick their lives up again. Not everybody could.

I think for many people who had actually been there, the showing of *Tenko* was quite cathartic. One of Henry's sisters had been interned, with her husband, in the Philippines, and they had never, ever spoken about their experience to anyone. With the showing of *Tenko*, they started to talk about it.

Whenever I met survivors and talked to them I always trod very carefully, because I was aware that I was encroaching on incredibly sensitive areas, but I would always ask, 'What is your abiding memory?' And the abiding memory of every single one of them, without exception, was – they would put it in different words but it was always the same thing – the laughter and the humour. I would say, 'Don't you remember the appalling cruelty, the hunger, the friends you lost?' And they would say, 'Yes, of course we remember that. We will never forget that. But what we also remember is the camaraderie and the laughs.'

It is understandable. It isn't that they remember it *with* laughter. What they remember is that, in these hideous conditions, amid the torture and the starvation and what must sometimes have been near despair, the way in which they dealt with it, coped with it, was through laughter. It seems to me that that is what we all do, what all human beings do. That's why I get very cross when people don't understand when, for instance, we try to deal with serious subjects in sitcoms, that one of the most important ways of helping people to cope with pain can be through laughter. Concentration camp survivors make jokes. It's the human way of making a dreadful experience smaller, so that it is not so huge that we blow apart with the horror of it.

We had a wonderful adviser called Molly Smith, who had been in the camps as a young girl. When we arrived for the first day at the first location, in Dorset, we found that they had created an exact replica of a Japanese prison-camp. All the technicians were wandering about, setting things up. People were trying on their costumes. Members of the cast were mainly just wandering around, getting used to the camp, talking to each other. A few of us were sitting with Molly on the steps of the *pendopo*, a covered area in the middle of the compound where it was shaded from the hot

131

sun, where the women would have sat in the actual camp. So Molly was sitting in the Dorset sunshine, surrounded by an exact replica of what she had been surrounded by when she was a young girl, with a group of women, talking about women's things – we weren't talking about Molly's experiences, just passing the time together. Three extras – young Chinese waiters from the local Bournemouth restaurants – wearing their costumes as Japanese guards, came into the compound and silently walked passed us. As they came into her peripheral vision, Molly leapt to her feet and bowed. It was a purely instinctive reaction. It was shiver-making. If you needed to know what it was like – that told you everything.

So we learned a huge amount about a part of our history that isn't often told, about how human beings survive in the worst circumstances, and finally about the glory of being with a group of women, all being utterly supportive and full of humour. We all went through our own personal dramas during this time – births, marriages and deaths. Lou Jamieson had her first baby during *Tenko*. Ann Bell lost her mother. I lost my stepfather. I also began to move towards separating from Henry during the years of filming. Between us, the women covered the water front in human experience, and we were all constantly there for each other.

Women have a shorthand. You'd come into a rehearsal and they'd say, 'How are you doing?'

And you could say, 'The freezer got unplugged, the washing-machine flooded, my daughter didn't want to go to school, she had a temperature, she said, my husband was too busy to do a bit of shopping, I feel rotten.' And everybody knew exactly how it was.

In one episode during the first series, Renée Asherson had to start to sing the first line of Blake's 'Jerusalem', and I had to take up the song, stand and sing, unaccompanied, very loudly, the whole of 'Jerusalem', surrounded by all the other women in the camp and all the guards and all the television crew. This is what I wrote in my diary at the time:

The first thing after 'Hallo' that the director says when introduced to me is, 'You can sing, can't you?' This question crops up with increasing regularity over the next few weeks. Several days before we are due to shoot the scene, it changes to, 'You are practising, aren't you?' Come the day, at about half past five, at the end of a hot, dusty day, with about eight hours of grit in my throat, I have to walk, surrounded by roughly one hundred and twenty people and cameras and sightseers crowding the wire, across a hundred yards of sand, without looking hit a mark the size of a peach stone at a precise moment and sing in a loud clear voice, in a key chosen by someone else, without one single rehearsal, the whole of 'Jerusalem'. It was my actor's nightmare come true.

I'm happy and proud to say that I pulled it off.

Tenko opened the world for me. It made travel possible and made me fall in love with actually travelling, which I had never been before. There had been two weeks' filming in Singapore for the first series, that I hadn't been involved in; I was only in the Dorset camp scenes. For the second series, though, we had four weeks' filming in Malaysia, sometimes in jungles and wading through swamps and rivers. We flew into Kuala Lumpur, had a few days there, then flew in a tiny little Focker Friendship plane over the hills to the east coast. In those days the east coast had not yet been discovered by the tourist trade, and oil had only just been found in the South China Sea. You landed on an airstrip that ran into the sea near Kuala Trengganu. As you came down past a small hut – which turned out to be the entire airport building – you felt you must land in the sea. For someone who had been afraid of flying as I was, it should have been terrifying, but because of the self-hypnosis I had done, I found it exhilarating.

In those days there was only one Western-style hotel there, a Hyatt, which was in Kuantan; and a new Malaysian-style hotel had just been built in Dungun, near Trengganu, along the lines of the *agongs'* houses. I think I am right in saying that there are seven *agongs*, rulers of the different districts making up Malaysia, and every seven years one of them is elected to become overall ruler, king of Malaysia. The houses in which they lived used to be the most beautifully carved wooden houses on stilts, with a little wooden staircase on the outside to each floor.

The hotel rooms didn't have air-conditioning, but huge ceiling fans. There were great wooden windows with wooden shutters, and the bathrooms had wooden tubs in the corner that you climbed into and stood or sat in. The windows opened out on to palm trees and beyond was the South China Sea. We were the first guests ever to stay there. I'm sure it does a roaring tourist trade now, and it deserves to, because it's a beautiful place.

But when we were there it had only just opened. It was run by an Indian, and there was a very willing Malay staff, but it was not quite as efficient as . . . well, it really wasn't efficient at all. But they were all enthusiastic and we had the most wonderful food: breakfast was slices of mango, papaya, melon and tiny bananas and in the evenings there were deliciously exotic Malay meals. Some of us even developed a taste for durian ice cream – quite an accomplishment as many Europeans can't get past the smell of bad drains of the durian fruit to try anything of that pungent flavour.

Malaysia is predominantly Muslim, and the rise of Islam became very apparent over the five years that we were making *Tenko*. When we first went out we were aware that it was a Muslim country, but there were also many Hindu temples, and Chinese temples, both Buddhist and Taoist. But as time went by we saw more and more women with the veil, and became increasingly aware that we must keep ourselves covered or evoke tremendous anger.

Singapore is in effect a dictatorship, but it is a place where cultures meet and live together in reasonable harmony with all the big temples of the world's great religions standing cheek by jowl with each other. You could sit in at a Buddhist or Hindu or Taoist ceremony. The only ones we were a little bit wary of were the Muslim ones, but we did go and sit up in the gallery, modestly covered of course, and we were made to feel welcome.

We filmed on the east coast near a tiny little *kampong*, a village in the middle of the jungle. It was amazing to see bananas and kapok growing on trees, little huts on stilts by the river, a couple of rather thin dogs scratching themselves, a lady sitting on the steps of her hut, surrounded by children. She looked to me at least ninety-eight, so lined and wizened was she. She was actually the mother of the children, the youngest of whom was a baby, so she can't have been more than in her late thirties. In some ways it looked idyllic but, bloody hell! It's a hard life.

We had Polaroid cameras, which are used all the time for continuity on film and television. The villagers had never seen photographs of themselves, so we took them, of the children particularly, and when we gave them to them they were received with much delighted laughter and surprise. They always offered us tremendous warmth and hospitality, and we had the joy of communicating with gestures and mime with people whose lives were utterly different from ours.

We were in Kuala Lumpur for a few days, and some of us – Stepha B., Ann, Roni, Patti and myself – were going for a walk early one Sunday morning through the deserted streets of Kuala Lumpur, when suddenly a car screeched to a halt in front of us. A young man leapt out of the car, ran across the pavement and started banging and hammering on a door. There was a little two-and-a-half-year-old child in the back of the car, and in the front was the child's mother, presumably the wife of this young man, and she was in the middle of actually giving birth. Most of us had had children, so we ran to help her. She gave birth half in the car, half on the pavement, aided only by five actresses from *Tenko*. Before it was fully delivered a midwife arrived and took her off to hospital. And that was that. We never even found out what sex the baby was, but somewhere in Kuala Lumpur there's a little boy or a little girl that should by rights be called Tenko.

When I first came to *Tenko*, I was nominally a Buddhist, but I was still searching, and I think these beliefs were perhaps already fading. I was becoming aware that it was not quite right for me, although I was still a vegetarian. When we were doing the second series, in the middle of the four weeks' filming in Malaysia we had a day off – Glory! Hallelujah! My best friend, Roni, and I had heard about some vast caves in huge limestone outcrops about fifty kilometres to the south of where we were staying. Everybody else was going to the markets to shop, but Roni and I decided that we would borrow a unit car and drive down to see the caves. In the innermost one there was said to be a huge statue of the Buddha, the carving of which had been the lifetime's work of a hermit Buddhist monk. We thought it would feed our spirit to visit this. Roni wasn't actually a Buddhist herself, but she was interested, and we had all talked a lot about the inner journeys we were on. Roni and I thought of this trip as part of our spiritual quest.

We drove down, through rubber and oil-palm plantations until, through the trees some miles ahead, we saw a towering limestone outcrop. We carried on towards it, drove through a little *kampong*, and eventually, three miles further on, suddenly there we were, among the trees at the base of a great limestone pinnacle. It was almost as if it erupted out of nowhere – for miles around the land was absolutely flat.

We got out of the car and were immediately besieged by mosquitoes as we started to climb up the stone steps. They were very, very steep, and there had recently been a short shower, so they were slippery. We climbed and we climbed and we climbed. And we climbed and we climbed. And there was nothing. Just vegetation and birds, but no huts, no houses, no people around. And we climbed. Suddenly we glimpsed through the trees above us a little flash of yellow. 'Aha!' we thought.

We reached a rock platform, little more than a ledge, on which there was a small lean-to hut, over which saffron robes were hanging out to dry. And there, sitting in a corner, smoking a cigarette, was a Buddhist monk, living alone in great simplicity on this rocky ledge with almost no material possessions, except an enormous pile of packets of Marlboro cigarettes.

(When you set out on these spiritual journeys, if there is any danger of you becoming overly pious and otherworldly, God always sends a little something to kick you up the butt and say, 'It ain't like that, sister! You are human beings. You have bodies.' I love that.)

We greeted the monk and made the sign of the *Namaste*, touching the head and the heart, ending with the hands in prayer, which means 'God be with you'. It's a lovely greeting, a form of respect to the other person.

We explained to the monk in sign language that we wanted to go and see the cave. He indicated that it would be a good idea if we gave him a little something to keep him going in Marlboro cigarettes, which we duly did. He waved us off in a fairly desultory way, and we continued on up the steps.

And we climbed and we climbed and we climbed. We noticed bats flying round our heads, so we knew we must be getting nearer. A little bit higher, and there was the mouth of the cave. We walked in, and it was like a great cathedral. Everywhere were stalactites and stalagmites. There were little carvings in niches in the rock, and bats and swifts flying about. Presumably there was a generator somewhere, although we never heard or saw it, because there was an electric wire with a light bulb hanging from it every few yards, which the monk must have turned on for our benefit.

As we walked deeper and deeper into the caves, there were more carvings, and then a huge puddle in which there was a giant turtle. They live to a very great age, and he was probably at least fifty, and would remain there for maybe another hundred years in this pool in the dark in the cave all on his own. We found that very sad and hard to bear.

At last we came to the great carving in the innermost cave, a huge Buddha lying on his side, with his head propped up on one hand and a beatific smile on his face. It was beautiful – except that someone had spray-painted on it: 'Kilroy was here.' Roni and I looked at this and burst out laughing. It was the same thing as the Marlboro cigarette-smoking monk – it burst our bubble; it was perfect.

Just as we were coming out, three boys appeared, about fifteen years old, who had obviously heard on some sort of grapevine that two white women were there – albeit cackling with laughter – and maybe a few pennies could be made through guiding them. So they started guiding us, and it became rather like in *A Passage to India*, when Adela Quested goes in to the Marabar Caves with Aziz. I became absolutely certain that these three young Malays were going to attack us, and that our bodies would be left to rot in the limestone caves of Malaysia . . .

I don't know where I got this idea from. Roni is far more intrepid than I am, and nearly fell over laughing when I told her what I'd been thinking. At all events, the boys guided us safely out, and that was the end of our spiritual pilgrimage. We went all the way back down the slippery stone steps, a descent of what must have been several hundred feet, waved good-bye to the monk and his Marlboros, and drove back to Kuantan.

For the third series of *Tenko*, we were in Singapore. One day Jean Anderson, Ann Bell, Roni and I decided that we would go up to Malaka, a famously exotic town. Stephanie Beacham, during the filming of the first series, had got to know the current king of Malaysia very well and had been taken everywhere; she had recommended a restaurant in Malaka to us. We borrowed a unit car and drove up there. Malaysian roads are notoriously difficult, so it took us a long time, many hours. However, it was worth it; we had a wonderful lunch at the restaurant, and then we set off to drive home.

It was completely dark on the way back, no street lights and people don't believe in putting lights on cars and bicycles in Malaysia – apparently it's better to trust to luck. Suddenly we saw bright lights on the hillside. It seemed to be some sort of fair, so we parked the car and walked across to a huge, sloping field, where we found a street theatre troupe in action, performing a comedy. There were stalls up and down the hill on either side, selling drinks and sweet-meats and paper kites. It was not for tourists, it was for the local villagers, who sat around on the grass watching the play, which was rather like an English pantomime, and it could go on for hours. We couldn't really understand what was going on, but we could see when it was funny. We sat down among a group of grannies and grandpas who beckoned us over. As always, we were shown their wonderful hospitality, a mixture of curiosity and kindness: do you have children, where do you come from, will you have something to eat? The children, particularly, were riveted by us. In the end we ourselves were such objects of interest that gradually – to the understandable annoyance of the actors – the audience had turned round and were watching us, instead of the play.

We got back to the hotel very late that night, because it really did take hours and hours on the Malaysian roads. Roni had driven us there, and I had driven back, with Jean and Ann sitting together in the back. Patti Lawrence had arrived in Singapore in the middle of that day and she was rather miffed that she had missed out on this magical outing. The five of us were sitting talking about it the next day, and Jean said, 'Oh, it was simply wonderful!' Then rather surprisingly she turned to Ann and exclaimed, 'Oh, Ann, I wish you'd been there!'

Ann said, 'Jean, I was. I sat in the back of the car, next to you, for roughly fourteen hours!'

Jean isn't at all dippy, but she had been so enthralled by the whole thing that she had simply forgotten that there had been anyone else with her.

We had had to bring several fake guns into the country with us, along with all the costumes and props. The equipment always travelled on Singapore Airlines, but for some reason we had to travel on Sabena. It would take us twenty-five hours to travel to Singapore; the equipment got there in a little over twelve.

When we arrived in Singapore, customs officials had gone through all our luggage and found the guns. Unfortunately, the production unit manager had forgotten to get clearance for them. 'Be prepared' was not his motto. He wore a woolly jumper all the time he was out there, ochre-coloured. How can anyone wear a pullover in Malaysia?

Anyway, he had forgotten, so we were all held up. What to do? Stepha B. said, 'Just a sec.' She went and made a telephone call to her good friend, the agong's aide-de-camp who rang through and got us clearance, and we were waved through. Thank heavens for friends in high places.

We all got thinner as the series went on. A slimming magazine came along and gave us a regime. We actually got down to below what was really safe. I was under nine stone, which for someone of five foot eight with size six and a half feet is crazy. But we did it. We had to be a bit careful, because we risked becoming ill and not being able to do the job, so we were monitored.

A rather odd thing arose out of the fact that when we were actually filming, and when we were recording in the studio, we were all made up to look like hell. There were no holds barred. We were filthy. Our hair was greased down; we were covered in water for sweat. In later episodes we were covered in terrible sores and streaked with ground-in dirt. However, we suddenly realised that we were all coming to rehearsals looking exceptionally good. We would all arrive in make-up, we were all using nail varnish and we wore mascara all the time. Our hair always shone. It was Patti who said, 'Hey, girls! Look at us! We look so good! Do you normally wear nail varnish and lipstick and mascara to a rehearsal?'

'No,' we all said.

'Interesting, isn't it?'

It was interesting. People always say that women dress up and want to look good because they want to be attractive to men, but this was nothing to do with that. It was to do with making ourselves feel good. It is depressing when you look like hell most of the time, so when you have the opportunity, you will do everything in your power to feel good by looking good.

I'm left with a great jumble of *Tenko* snapshots – so many memories of moments during the filming in Singapore and Malaysia. Exotic scenes all mixed up with pictures of the canteen at the BBC Television Centre in London: of warm, dusty days in the sandpit in Dorset and wet, shivering days in the sandpit in Dorset . . .

Wading through swamps and finding leeches on our legs; going for a pee among the palm trees and being bitten by giant red ants, the cry of monkeys overhead; the baby oil we had to cover ourselves with to look like sweat, until we came out in a rash and discovered we were all allergic to it . . .

Jo Hole playing guitar; Annie Queensberry beating all-comers at scrabble; Stepha B. making rags look glamorous. Renée Asherson losing so many pairs of sunglasses she gave up bothering to take off the price labels; Brian Rix losing his trousers in the hotel foyer while visiting his wife, Elspet Gray, during filming. Emily Bolton looking like a fashion plate even on the worst day; Claire Oberman running miles every morning come rain or shine; listening to tales of Burt's childhood. Liz Chambers trying to keep a straight face while bemoaning the death of her character's canary; producer Ken reading in for a new character – so badly that he became known as 'Madge' for ever afterwards . . .

Swimming in the South China Sea, and then in the most

luxurious pool in Singapore during a tropical storm; swimming in Studland Bay in Dorset. The exotic birds in Jurong Bird Park; the Laurence Whistler windows in the little church in Morton; visiting the *kampongs* on the island of Singapore; being shown around the cemetery of Changi camp by a Singaporean survivor . . .

Feasts in the warm night air in Newton Circus; eating off banana leaves with our fingers in the Indian quarter; salads in the BBC canteen while we slimmed; Chinese buns on the grass as we sat watching the street theatre; learning a little Japanese from Eiji, Takahura and Takashi, and them taking us all for a Japanese feast in Covent Garden; an invitation to share lunch with the owners of a tiny shop in Malaysia selling flip-flop sandals made out of old car tyres . . .

Getting stuck in the thirtieth floor of a half-built high-rise in the mother and father of a tropical storm because the lift jammed; taking turns cuddling and singing to Harry, Lou's first-born and the first *Tenko* baby. Roni wearing six bamboo sola topees, the only way to carry them home; Patti almost denied a seat on a return flight, her hand luggage weighing more than all of ours put together . . .

We were all very sad when *Tenko* came to an end, of course we were, but we knew it couldn't go any further. All the stories had been told. The final section we did was a two-hour film called *Tenko Reunion* which was set five years on in the women's lives. For this, some of us, Ann Bell and myself and a couple of others, had to be shot leaving Southampton in a liner, waving to the shore. They got us on board this vast cruise liner, and it set sail. What we had forgotten was that we would have to get off again. It takes ten miles to stop a liner, and we hadn't thought of this. After the shots had been done from the quay, the director said, 'Right, we're going to get you off now.'

We had to go through the bowels of the ship – and I'm here to tell you I would think twice about eating on a cruise liner – we went through this door, that door, then another, all air-locked, and then there we were, all the way down, just above the waterline. Now from the shore it probably looked as though the ship was moving very slowly and majestically out of port. But we were standing at an open door, just above sea level, looking at a great churning, thundering white mass of water, and we knew we were going hellishly fast. Alongside came a little tug, and we had to climb down a rope-ladder and then jump across. We were all wearing life-jackets, but it was more than a bit scary.

At the end of filming we had a tremendous party. It didn't feel like an ending in a way, because we've all gone on seeing one another ever since; the links were too strong to ever die. But it would never again be on that daily basis which had brought us all so close.

Because I'd been Equity deputy all the way through, and had fought a few battles on everybody's behalf, they presented me with a huge parcel. All the way through Beatrice Mason, my character, had had what she called her 'Huddy's box' – a big Hudson's soap box that she carried with her everywhere, tied up with a piece of string. In it she had all her medicines, what few there were. So I used to take advantage of it. I was the one with the travelling chair, the comb, the mirror and the sweeties when we were filming. My 'Huddy's' went everywhere.

This was what they gave me, when it was all over. In it they had placed the coconut shell that had been my eating bowl, the two pieces of wood that were my chopsticks, the dress that I wore all the way through, a Red Cross newspaper, some bits of medicine. All the props I'd had as Beatrice were beautifully wrapped up and placed in my Huddy's box.

The powers that be just never got into it. They have never repeated this BAFTA-winning series, except on the fiftieth anniversary of VJ day, when they re-showed one episode, the release of all the women from the camp.

The character of Sister Ulrika, played by my dearest friend,

Patti Lawrence, left halfway through the third series – although she did come back into it for the *Tenko Reunion* – but her final scene in the third series, when she was saying good-bye, was between her and my character, Beatrice. And it was very odd, because Patti and I found we couldn't do it. We were so upset by it. Eventually we pulled ourselves together, and said, 'We can only do this once.' We were on the set in Dorset, in the camp, and we did this farewell scene just as the daylight was dying.

Patti died in 1993. When I got the news, I was sitting with Roni and Lou and Ann. We cried and we remembered and we talked about her all evening. Then we played the video of that farewell episode from *Tenko*.

Getting the part in *Tenko* was probably the most significant turning-point in my life – not just in my career, in my whole life – professional, emotional and spiritual. Far the most important thing about it was working with all those wonderful women, pooling all our life-histories, everything we'd all gone through, and continued to go through as we worked together, from Jean Anderson, who is now coming up for ninety, down to the youngest, Cindy Shelley. All of us talked about our life's experiences, our relationships with fathers and mothers and lovers and husbands and children, pooling all of this. It was the best experience, the beginning of many lifelong friendships; and it was the time when I really began to see the wood for the trees about myself.

16. Emma

My stepfather, Colin, had always had a very close, loving relationship with Emma. They adored each other. Then when she was eight, he had the first of a series of strokes. He became, as many stroke victims do, rather childish, and sometimes unpleasant.

My mother was amazingly patient with him, because he really was very difficult to deal with. The sweet and gentle man disappeared. I know this often happens, and what appears is not the essential person; it is the stroke that you are dealing with. I didn't know enough, to my shame; I was in my thirties and I should have done, but I was often irritable and impatient with him.

Emma was the one person, after his stroke, with whom he would always be sweet and gentle. She was endlessly patient and loving. Right up to the end of his life he grew tomatoes in a little greenhouse, and they would go down together to pick the tomatoes and sit and talk, and it was a delight to see them together.

When he was in hospital just before he died, I asked Emma if she wanted to visit him, and she said, 'Yes.' I warned her that he would be not quite as she remembered him. When we arrived he was asleep. I sat down with Em beside the bed, held his hand and said, 'Hallo, Dad. It's Teff.' He opened his eyes, saw Emma, and immediately brushed me aside and started to talk to her.

The grown-up part of me understood, because she was

incredibly important to him, and he to her. He adored her, and he knew he might never see her again. In fact, he never did. So the grown-up part of me absolutely understood, but the child in me was devastated. That is pretty pathetic, but I fear that's how it was.

I hadn't been to many funerals of people I was close to before. When we buried Colin, my mother and I sat together in the first car, and as we were following the hearse travelling slowly from Keynsham to Bath Crematorium, I understood for the first time why this was essential, the very, very slow progress. You have to do it in nature's time. I understood it profoundly, in my body. I understand all sorts of things intellectually, but it means nothing until I 'get it' in my body.

Emma's grief was huge when Colin died, but she hardly showed it. She cried, but I don't think any of us knew the extent of it, and it wasn't until Henry and I split up a few years later, with her grief over that, that her grief at my father's death came out. That's her story, and I wouldn't presume to tell it, because she has her own inner journey, but I do know that much was released then: the anger and the sense of loss.

My mother had never been at all dogmatic about what I did or didn't believe in the matter of religion, and I wanted to be the same with Emma, to let her find out about things in her own way, and value for herself the things she learned at school and from the world around her. She has never been christened. Whatever decisions she made for herself in her own time were fine with me.

She went to a little C. of E. primary school close to where we lived in Belsize Park, not for religious reasons, but simply because it was the nearest and the best school. There she was introduced to church ritual at times like harvest festival and Easter, so those have been part of her upbringing. Her Dad was and still is an atheist, but because he was also a musician, he loved hymns. We would often, when she was little, have singsongs around the piano, and sometimes they would include hymns, particularly when I was doing the Salvation Army series, because I had the song book with all its catchy tunes. When, later, I started my own long spiritual search, Em and I often talked about life and death, doubt and faith, so although nothing has ever been imposed on her, equally it has never been a taboo subject.

Emma came home one day when she was about nine and declared that she was a vegetarian. She had been taken by the school to Guildford Market and had seen the rabbits hanging up and the chickens, with all their fur and feathers, and suddenly the reality of eating meat was brought home to her, and she was appalled by it. I'd been verging on the vegetarian myself for some years, so I thought, 'Come on then. Let's go for it. We'll do it.' So we both did. Unfortunately Henry was unable to eat potatoes or vegetables of any sort. He would eat only fruit, and meat. So family meals became peculiar occasions; we each just had a bit of everything. Having loved giving big dinner parties, I started finding it more and more difficult to cook at all. I began to dread going into the kitchen.

When Emma was coming to the end of her primary education and it was time to go to secondary school, we asked her where she wanted to go, because it seemed perfectly clear to us that at eleven she was quite capable of knowing what she wanted. She came round with us and saw all the schools. She didn't want to go to Hampstead School, because it was so big she found it terrifying. She didn't fancy Quintin Kynaston because we felt there was an atmosphere of violence there at the time. She didn't want a school with a uniform but, amazingly enough, having been to a mixed primary, she did want to go to an all girls school. Eventually we picked Camden School for Girls which had not long before gone comprehensive, one of the last to do so.

We applied there, but it was very oversubscribed and we were turned down. We went to appeal, and I had to go for an interview. The interview board consisted of someone from the education committee, someone from the board of governors and an independent member. The headmistress was there as an observer.

They'd obviously got me down as a Hampstead 'trendy' Mum. We talked a little about our family background and then about Emma. She was keen on Latin, and the headmistress was a classicist, so that was a good start. Then they asked, 'What does your daughter want to be?' I thought I might as well be absolutely truthful, as there was nothing to be gained from making up a great story about her being academically brilliant and likely to win the next Nobel Peace Prize for the school. I said, 'Well, just at this moment she's very keen on owning and running her own sweet shop.'

It got a laugh, but I said, 'I'm being absolutely serious. At the moment, that is what she wants to do. I jolly well hope that when she gets to eighteen that's not what she wants to do. On the other hand, if it is, good on her.'

Something I said must have been right, because she got a place. We believed in the comprehensive system, but I now think that we may have sacrificed our daughter on the altar of our ideals. When she first went to Camden it was run by a wonderful headmistress called Mrs Handley, but unfortunately she left a couple of years later, and after that it started to be not so good and Emma was not as happy there as she might have been.

However, she's a determined person, my daughter. She did very well in her GCSEs, particularly in Latin and English, her favourite subjects, and the only one she didn't pass was maths. I said, 'Well, darling, it doesn't really matter.' But she retook it twice, and on the third time she passed. She was not going to be beaten.

When she came to her A levels, she chose what were for her three perfectly ludicrous subjects. I can't even remember what they were – something like biology, psychology and geography – for none of which had she ever shown the slightest aptitude. She failed quite gloriously in all three, more than failed – she got three Us, which means unmark-able, or unclassifiable. We didn't mind at all. I rather enjoyed it – an excellent way to rebel.

She didn't quite know what she wanted to do after she left school. She thought at one time that she might like to be a nursery nurse, because she has always been very good with children, but although she looked into it, it didn't seem quite right for her. Then one day she said, 'Mum, I've decided what I want to do. I want to work backstage in the theatre.'

It was like the sun coming out. I thought, 'Of course! She's very good with people. Very practical. Slightly bossy. (I wonder where she gets that from?) Perfect!'

It all fitted. She was still quite young, but she went for an interview with the Vic School, and they said, 'Go out into the world and have a few corners knocked off. Then come back and see us.'

So she spent a year working in some of the best fringe theatres, the Orange Tree and the King's Head in Islington among them. Then she went over to America, and got some experience in Summer Stock – professional theatres in America that do perform a repertoire of plays each summer. This way Em had the most wonderful basic training, doing anything and everything, and working day and night for nearly a year. She met lots of people and learned about her profession.

Finally, she went to the Vic school for two years, and she's been in the business ever since. She has earned a good reputation, and she's building up an impressive body of work, and she has fun. She doesn't have the same name as me, and she has found her own niche, entirely on her own merits.

My image of myself as a mother has changed over the years. I started out thinking, 'Here is this tiny thing, completely reliant on me. What do I do?' When Emma was little I suffered terribly from guilt, always trying to be the perfect mother, wife and actress. It is impossible.

Emma is twenty-four now and we've been through a lot together. I've learned more from her about myself, and about how to cope with other people, than from anybody or anything else in my life. There have been some rough times, but through them all we have always talked to each other. I'm more forgiving of myself now. You look back on your own childhood and try to avoid your parents' mistakes, and to copy their virtues.

After that, it's up to fate, and the child.

17. Hope

It all started with a telephone call from Lou Jamieson, one of the close-knit group of *Tenko* girls. It was 1989. The Iron Curtain had collapsed and the truth about what was going on in various East European countries was emerging. The stories coming out of Romania were horrendous, particularly what was being discovered about the orphanages. Lou, who always has her charger saddled, had started a charity called HOPE, which had adopted an orphanage, and was supplying it with medicines, clothes, equipment, anything that was needed. Several lorries had already made the journey, and Lou had been given a large Dormobile, which she was having serviced, and the plan was to drive it to the orphanage packed with medicines, etc., and leave it there for them to use. The drivers would make their own way home.

My best friend Roni and I were having coffee together and chatting about this and, I don't know which of us said it first, but the idea came – *we* would take it to Romania for Lou. We both had some free weeks and then would be coming back to work – a rare event in an actor's life – so the timing seemed God-sent. Lou was delighted and everything went into top gear.

We had to get all the various visas, and we could only get Romanian maps from the Romanian Tourist Board, whose office was to be found in a tiny room at the top of a tumbledown house between Baker Street and Marylebone

High Street. We had to ring the bell several times. Once we were admitted, the man who looked after us tried to be very helpful, but he was ill-equipped. His maps were few and rather out of date, so we just took what he could find.

When I was a child, I was fascinated by maps from a very early age. I can remember poring over the wartime maps they had printed on canvas, planning imaginary journeys; for some reason, in my dreams I was always travelling through Switzerland, on a train, among great mountains covered in snow. It seemed the height of glamour to me. We sometimes went by train to London, and I used to get very excited even about those journeys, the smell of egg sandwiches that trains always seemed to have during the war, and the darkness – because of the black out the blinds were always kept pulled down.

In 1989 the RAC planned the route across Europe for us. We acquired more and more maps which Roni and I pored over for hours, and I felt as excited as a child again. We planned stopovers in Vienna and Budapest and discussed at length what we should take. It had to be minimal; we would be getting the train from the orphanage back to Bucharest, and then a flight home. We reckoned we would need strong boots, good cold- and wet-weather anoraks, warm jumpers, possibly thermals, and something a bit more glamorous for Vienna. To satisfy Roni's trekker spirit, we took a Swiss Army penknife. I bought my first bumbag to carry all my valuables close to me.

Arrangements had to be made for us to be met at the border; it was too dangerous to travel without someone in the know who spoke the language. The countryside was full of latter-day highwaymen, which was not as romantic as it sounds, because they were prepared to ambush and make off with any foreign aid.

I began to get more and more thrilled at the prospect of the venture. It seemed fitting to be taking much-needed things to the orphanage. The memory of the day that I had gone with my parents to find my brothers was in my mind all the time. The emotions I had felt at eleven I still feel even now, and I had always promised myself that if ever I were able to, I would adopt a child.

When Emma was about four Hen and I had tried for another child, and failed. We had then applied and been accepted as adoptive parents, and I had felt I could at last fulfil that promise. The telephone had rung one day, and our social worker had said that there was a baby who needed a home, and she thought that we were the right parents. Then Henry suddenly decided he couldn't cope with another child. We talked it over for some days, but Henry was adamant and I knew that I couldn't do it on my own. I have always believed that things happen for a reason and that, however painful at the time, it is finally best to 'let go and let God'; which is not to say that the battle I wage beforehand is not sometimes fierce.

The day for Roni's and my big adventure came, and we travelled down to Kent to Lou's house, snuggling just below Toad's Rock outside Tunbridge Wells. There was the Dormobile, packed to the roof. We received our last-minute briefing from Lou over a great meal and wine: what to do at the border, how to recognise our guide, where to get hold of a train timetable, and messages for everyone at the orphanage. Lou had some wonderful photographs of the beautiful painted churches and monasteries of Romania that had somehow survived the terrible regime, and I found it hard to sleep, with the mixture of excitement and fear.

The morning of our departure was cold and misty – hooray for the boots and duvet jackets! We got in the van and I felt like Marco Polo. Roni was driving the first lap to Dover and, as we got on our way, the engine note gave us both a tiny hint of apprehension . . . but it had had a thorough service . . . and besides, it *had* to be okay if it was to be left for the orphanage to use – not much chance of spares in Romania if it went wrong.

We had to go through a special channel at Dover because

we were carrying syringes and medicines, but we had our Aid for Romania stickers on, and we were on the ferry in no time. The crossing was calm, the coffee strong and the croissants were delicious. We kept hugging ourselves and saying, 'What an adventure this will be!'

The first real hint of trouble came as we drove off the ferry. The engine sounded sicker, and the gears started to be a bit sticky. But customs whizzed us through and off we set along the French roads. If you are a travel addict, as I am, you will know that the mere fact of driving on the other side of the road is a thrill, and the frankly rather flat and boring countryside of northern France seemed glorious as we bumped along.

Our route had been planned to take us to Brussels, but long before we reached the Belgian border we knew that all was very far from well with the vehicle. Now the brakes had joined the gears in malfunctioning and I decided we needed the AA. I went into the little booth which was the border control, spilled out our difficulties and problems, and asked if we could use the telephone.

My story, or the way I told it, was obviously excruciatingly boring, because the border guard told me, barely stifling a yawn, that no, I couldn't use the telephone; no, she didn't know where the nearest public telephone box was, and as for a garage, who knew?

I got back in the van, and we agreed that somehow we must get to Brussels. Roni took the wheel, and I held the van in gear as we jerked along, praying very hard. We were praying even harder by the time we reached the outskirts of the city. The traffic was very busy and we had to navigate our way with a van whose behaviour was becoming more erratic by the minute. As we drove through one of the many tunnels, one that had a very steep gradient, I was both holding the gear-lever in place and hanging on to the handbrake every time we stopped. Then the engine began to stall.

Our prayers became louder and louder, and my swearing took on a colourful turn, but somehow we made it into the centre of the city and spotted a rather nice-looking hotel. 'Bugger the expense,' I shrieked, 'it's our salvation, our oasis, our refuge!'

The Dormobile was by now ready to receive the last rites, and we parked it, not prettily, but reasonably safely. Hoping that no Belgian thieves would break into it and make off with the drugs, we dragged ourselves into the smart hotel, looking like two very old hippies. They were obviously used to scruffy *Anglaises* and – joy! – there was a room. We called England, found a garage who would have a look at the van in the morning, bathed, and then decided to hit Brussels. We ate and drank like royalty and I was feeling wonderfully optimistic by the time my head hit the pillow.

The next morning we managed to bump start our dying vehicle and nursed it along to the garage. The mechanics' faces dropped as we drove in, but they said to leave it with them, and they would do their best to get us and the Dormobile to Romania.

We took a stroll round the centre of the city, with a glance at the Mannekin Pis, me boring Roni with stories of my last visit to Brussels, when I was fifteen, the year of Sputnik and l'Atomium at the first ever post-war World Fair, one of my few trips abroad in my youth. I had been taken to the great theatre in Brussels, where Madeleine Renault and Jean-Louis Barrault were playing *Le Misanthrope*, and where I had disgraced myself by falling sound asleep, because it didn't start until nine o'clock.

When it was time to collect our van and be on the road, one look at the mechanic's face said it all. Even my French stretched to, 'The gears have gone. The brakes have gone. The big end has gone, and there is no way this would ever have reached Vienna, let alone Romania!'

We had to get the vehicle sealed officially and make arrangements for someone from HOPE to come over from England to empty the van and take the contents to the orphanage by some other transport. Then we had to get ourselves back home.

Our great adventure had been a fiasco. We both felt furious that the English garage should have been so uncaring as to say that they had, out of the kindness of their hearts, made the van fit not only to drive to Romania, but also to be given for the use of the children – a great gift that would have turned out to be. I also found myself feeling angry and frustrated that yet again I had been unable to do something to heal the wound of all those years ago – the memory of collecting the twins from the orphanage – and thwarted in my wish to honour my promise to myself.

We got a flight home and had a debrief with Lou and her husband Martin in the restaurant at Heathrow, replete with many tears and some recriminations. The contents of the van were eventually taken to the orphanage in a new van that someone donated and which, as far as I know, is still in service. Our friendship was not hurt. Lou and Roni and I are always able to step into one another's moccasins, to know what it feels like, and that speeds the healing.

18. Group therapy

For many years Hen and I had a very happy marriage. Nevertheless, it slowly became apparent that I was the strong one, that he was the one who leant on me, and not the other way around. The years went by. Life went on. We worked, had holidays, moved house, lived in town, lived in the country, chose schools for Emma.

Then I went into *Tenko*, which seems to have been a turning-point in my life in so many ways, and the emotional imbalance between Hen and me became obvious and acute. I had felt that I had to become stronger and stronger and, because of that, he had become weaker and weaker, and it was a vicious circle. I certainly can't say why or how, but we were not a working partnership any more.

I thought it was all my fault, that I was not giving enough, loving enough, just not anything enough. During *Tenko*, through the friends I made there and because of the spiritual journey I had started on, I had begun to grow; nevertheless, I still imagined that because things were unhappy at home, it must be my fault. I went to my doctor and said that I thought I needed help. He put me in touch with a famous practice of group analysts.

I went twice a week at eight o'clock in the morning to a group run by an enchanting woman. There were about eight of us in the group. At first I found it very difficult, I didn't know what the rules were when I arrived. As in everything else in life, there are rules. There was a woman in the group who was training to be an analyst – and God help whoever came under her 'guidance'. A member of the group said to me, 'Now tell us about yourself.'

So I started to talk, 'Well, you know how it is when you . . .'

The trainee analyst jumped in with self-important aggression, 'Why can't you say "I"?'

'Sorry?'

'When you say something about yourself, use "I". Otherwise it's not about you.'

'Oh. Right. You mean, when I do so-and-so, I feel so-and-so?'

'That's better.'

What chiefly happened there was that I became so utterly riveted by other people's stories – I used to sob with them as they told their tales – that I hardly ever got round to talking about myself. Even when I did, I wasn't very good at it, because I didn't really know what was wrong.

I attended sessions for about three months, but I had a growing feeling that, being an actor and so used to working in groups, the solution to my problems didn't lie in communities or in groups, but that I did have a real problem with *myself*, and myself wasn't getting much of a look-in. All I really wanted was someone who could help Hen and me to get our marriage rebalanced.

This group practice had a very famous marriage counsellor, the most famous, let's call him R, at the mention of whose name even now I start spitting blood. I said to the therapist who was in charge of the group, 'I think I can persuade my husband to come along, because we both need help together. Do you think that R would see us?' She said she thought it would be a very good idea.

We had to wait a few weeks, and during that time I managed to persuade Hen, bless his heart, and he agreed that he would come along, so we made an appointment. R had a cancellation, and along we went.

I felt that because it was a place that I was used to walking into and Henry wasn't, I mustn't prepare what I was going to say in any way, but I must go in as innocent, as it were, as Henry was, to put us on an equal footing. We were shown in, and it was obvious that R was in a bad temper – nothing to do with us.

We all sat down, and he asked us for a little background information: how long had we been married, did we have children, had we been married before? Just a few basic facts, which we gave him. Then he said, 'Right. So what's the problem?' and he looked at Henry and said 'You first, what do you think the problem is?'

And Henry, who was sitting there puffing away on his pipe, said, 'Well, I don't know. I don't think there *is* anything wrong.'

Which was honest of him, because he didn't think there was anything wrong – except that there was, but he couldn't admit it even to himself. So then R turned to me and said, 'What do you think is wrong?'

I tried. I didn't know quite what it was or how to say it and, because I felt so disloyal to Hen, I burst into tears. I tried hard to put my feelings into words, and eventually I came up with this ludicrous explanation. I said, 'Well, I don't know how to explain it, but I'll tell you what it is. I'll come home after a very long, hard day's work, and Hen won't have been working, and I'll have asked him to run the Hoover over the sitting-room floor, and when I come home he hasn't done it, and there's tobacco all over the floor . . .'

After a very little further discussion, R turned to Henry and said, 'Your wife is a neurotic hysteric. I can't help her. You I can help. If you want to come back and see me, come back.'

And that was it. We left. Neither of us spoke. I have to say to Hen's credit, he was as upset as I was. The fact that apparently he was the guiltless party in R's eyes didn't matter a jot to him; he was just flabbergasted. And so was I.

We got into the car. I had always driven. Henry had a licence, but he hadn't driven for years and frankly I think he might have been a bit of a menace on the roads. We had with us in the car an answering machine which had gone wrong, which we were going on to take to a place on the North Circular; it was quite an early model, and we had to take it back to the factory for repair. When we got there, parking was rather difficult, so I said, 'Listen, Hen, I'll drop you here, you take it in and tell them what's wrong, and I'll sit in the car, just in case I need to move it.'

I sat there waiting, for about ten minutes. I remember it was quite a warm, sunny day. Suddenly there was a tap on my window. It was Henry, still holding the machine, and he was saying, 'It's no good. I can't explain to them. You come and do it.'

And I started to laugh, because this was exactly what was wrong with our marriage. I had driven us there, I had asked him to tell them what was wrong while I stayed with the car – a fair division of labour – and he couldn't. I don't doubt he wanted to. Just couldn't.

By the end of *Tenko*, I realised that nothing was going to work for Henry and me, and we began the business of separating. I've seen people harnessed together miserably in marriage. What's the point? It wouldn't work. End of story. We went to Relate marriage guidance, but only to help us split up.

We sold the house and split the proceeds absolutely down the middle. We didn't hate each other. We had no problems about the division of belongings or money. Neither of us had a thing about possessions, and we were both able to be generous.

Even so, like any two people splitting up, it was a long and painful process. Hen was very unhappy, I was very unhappy, our daughter was devastated. Em was fourteen when we told her, fifteen by the time it was all finally settled – a bloody age, but any age is bloody when your parents split up. What's to be done? It was bad for all of us. It was very bad for Emma.

It wasn't easy selling the house, finding and buying two

flats within walking distance, both of which had to be ground floor flats with gardens, because of the other family members – our four cats and a dog. I kept the cats: Scrappy, Missy, Treacle and Pudding (names chosen by Emma), two Siamese and two rescued moggies; and Henry had Whompie, our Cavalier King Charles spaniel.

There was one terrible moment for me when Emma came to me and said, 'I've decided I'm going to live with Dad.' I thought my world had come to an end. I couldn't show it, because she had every right to choose to live with her Dad. I said to her, 'OK darling, if that's your choice, that's absolutely fine, and you know you can come to me whenever you want to, and if you change your mind later, that will be fine too.'

I walked quickly out of the room, and waited until she went out. Roni and Patti were both away. As soon as Em had left the house, I picked up the telephone and called Lou. I was incoherent with grief. I don't think Lou even knew who it was for the first five minutes. Then she kept saying, 'It's OK, Steph. It's all right, darling, just tell me what's happened.' And I couldn't, for minutes. Eventually I spilled it all out, on and on and on, and she just listened. She was a mother herself by then, she had her baby son, Harry, and she understood. She listened and listened, and that helped get me through that first agony of grief.

Of course Emma knew I wouldn't walk away from her, and in the end, she chose to live with me after all. And that was it. We moved into the new flats, and life has gone on. Henry still lives round the corner from my home in North London and has a new lady in his life. We have always remained on good terms, and Em and he are very close. Recently he has been diagnosed with cerebellar ataxia, which handicaps him terribly, but he remains his old rather rueful self.

It was only through analysis, when I had to really look, that I rediscovered the many sunny days and the many happinesses in my own childhood. There was love, but for years I had remembered only the bleak and the bad times.

Emma had a very secure childhood. She had lots of friends and although she wasn't overindulged, nothing was ever lacking. My mother was an affectionate, not to say doting, grandmother and they have always been very close, as she was to Colin. Henry was a wonderful father for a little one to have. They still maintain a tremendous closeness and a sense of play and fun that they share.

She'll sometimes say, 'I'm like that because you did this, that and the other.'

And I say, 'Yup. But you're your own person; you have a choice. Don't waste your time blaming us.'

For a long time I blamed my own mother for all sorts of things, but I don't now. She did what she thought was best, just as I, with *my* daughter, have done what I thought was best. I have scars. My daughter has scars. It comes with the territory. Hopefully my daughter's scars are slightly fewer than my scars, which are certainly far fewer than my mother's scars, which are probably fewer than her mother's scars. So with a bit of luck, and effort, it gets better.

19. Talented dreamer

This is rather a mystical chapter about dreams and psycho-analysis and self-help groups, so if you aren't into those things, I should skip it if I were you.

All the time I was working on *Tenko*, I was beginning to go to work on myself, and I would reach sometimes minor, sometimes major moments of self-discovery. One small turning-point came about through doing 'the Mastery', a weekend course run at the now defunct Actors' Institute in London. The Mastery had been set up, in the first place, by actors for non-actors, to help them to be better able to express their feelings, but it had much more than that to teach along the way. The leader in the session I attended was an ex-actor called Mike Maynard, a wise and thoughtful man. The Mastery started in America – as you might guess. It was looked on with a good deal of scepticism and fear by some people, rather like EST – an American self-development workshop – in the seventies, but it wasn't anything like EST.

You went along for Friday evening, all day Saturday, Saturday evening, all day Sunday and Sunday evening, and you took part in what, for want of a better word, I would call 'exercises'. The one that taught me most was called the Three Corners. The corners were Anger, Love and Need. There would be three participants at a time, who would each choose which corner to go into first. While you were in your corner you would find all the ways you could to express whichever of the three emotions it was – Anger, Love or Need. Then you'd move on to another corner. Interestingly, the corner I first chose to go into was Need.

I discovered that anger always comes to an end. You get tired; expressions of hatred and anger cannot be kept going indefinitely. It is physically impossible. Love, on the other hand, you cannot stop; there is no end to it. You don't tire of it. Even when the demands of need also seem endless, you learn that anger is finite, and that love is infinite.

The other lesson I learned from the Mastery came at the end of the two-and-a-half-day session, when each of us had to write a critique of everybody else. There were forty of us, so everybody received thirty-nine comments, and quite a bit of time was set aside to write them; they were not to be just off-the-cuff comments. There followed a feedback session. I got mine, and thirty-eight of them were wonderful; glowing, generous, warm appreciations. But there was one which said – I can remember it almost exactly – 'You are a con artist. I don't believe a word you say. All your humour and love and joy in life is a lie.'

I read this, and it took precedence in importance over all the others. I said in my feedback session, 'I've discovered that the only critique that I have let in is this very hurtful, aggressive comment. I know it not to be true, but nevertheless it is the only one. I have not acknowledged – my body, my mind, my heart will not take in – any of the generous, kind, complimentary ones.' That, for me, was another small beginning, discovering that I still needed to learn how to accept praise, and how to let in love.

Through the Mastery I met someone who was to become a great friend, an American who had been an actor, and was training to be a therapist. Gay had been in analysis both in America and in Britain, and knew the whole scene.

I asked her advice about getting help for my marriage, which wasn't quite finished at this time, but was getting bleaker and bleaker. She recommended that I went to see a lady called Nina Colthart, then in her seventies, a very famous Freudian analyst, who fitted analysts with analysands. I spent a couple of hours with her, and she placed me with an analyst who was also an eclectic Freudian, and had worked with Winnicott. He had a great gentleness about him. I went to S for four years, three times a week. He helped me greatly, in a way the group therapy sessions never could, to cope all through the painful separation from Henry.

S hardly said anything. I would lie on a couch and we unpacked a lot of the childhood stuff, the memories of separation from my mother, a lot of the fantasy father stuff, but he did not see everything simply in terms of the Oedipus complex and similar psychological clichés. It was very liberating. After a while, whenever a pattern of behaviour emerged, I became able to recognise the pattern, and to make the choice between running the pattern in the same old way that was destructive to me, or reacting in a different way. Ultimately, I think, that's the main thing that analysis has to offer: freedom of choice.

I've always been a talented dreamer. That's not a boast, it's a standard phrase that is used for someone who dreams a good deal, in colour with sound and smell and touch, and who is able to remember the dreams. I always keep a notebook by my bed in which to jot down any big dreams.

I had a lovely dream at the beginning of my analysis. I was at a pool which was fed by clear, fresh water and in the middle of the pool was a stone, standing slightly proud of the water, which had a hollowed-out middle. There was a woman with long hair standing thigh-deep in this pool, and she was feeding into the water, into the hollowed-out stone, sweet-smelling oil, and this sweetness was feeding the well of a village further down.

I think now that it was a dream about the beginning of the feeding of the village that is me. That is something I was just beginning to do, with the help of others; to feed myself with nourishing attributes that had always been there, true qualities and gifts I had within me, but which I had not been able to see.

The minute you begin to work like this, in analysis, the dreams come thick and fast. The number and intensity of messages coming up from my unconscious mind was amazing. I had several very big dreams, by which I mean that they were dreams from the collective unconscious, as Jung would tell us. I had a series of dreams that were all set in a country that I didn't know. It had the biggest sky I have ever seen. The earth was dry red desert with mountains that reared up out of it. I dreamed of a people whom I had never seen, but they looked like Native Americans. They didn't wear feathers, but they had Mongoloid features. They appeared to live underground in caves in the red earth.

An important dream at this time was set in the caves in this red stone, deep down. I was on my own, walking along a tunnel. On either side there were people sitting, just quietly sitting, men, women and children. And behind them, on the wall, there were works of art that each had made – paintings, sculptures, collages. As I went deeper into the cave, the people became more and more obviously disabled. I reach the centre of the cave, at the end of the tunnel, and there were just two people. One was a very, very old woman, totally disfigured by age and by arthritis, a terrible sight; the other was a very young child, about eighteen months old, who also was badly disabled and disfigured, with a great gaping hole in its spine – I didn't know if it was a boy or a girl. But behind them, on the wall, were the most breathtaking paintings, far more beautiful than I have ever seen in the whole of my life. They were reflections of who those people really were.

It was like a lesson. You see a person, the outward show, somebody whose body or spirit has become so twisted and deformed, either by nature, or by experience, by pain, or by the injuries of life. They can be the most evil person, or appallingly physically disfigured, but somewhere inside them is great beauty, which is who they actually are. That's

Memento Mori, 1993: Me, the late Cyril Cusack, Michael Hordern, Maggie Smith, Maurice Denham, and Zoë Wanamaker

In India with Sundari and her co-workers

Vemkadesu

Dawn at Ayers Rock with Kerin Parfitt on route to New Zealand

The cast of *Tenko*, 1985: (back row) Liz Chambers, Me, Ann Bell, Elspet Gray, Jean Anderson, Claire Obermann, (front) Elizabeth Mickery, Veronica Roberts, Cindy Shelley, Emily Bolton, (inset) Patricia Lawrence

Me in *Tenko* with Patricia Lawrence, 1985

With Graham Crowden as Diana and Tom in *Waiting for God*, began in 1992

Playing Muriel in *Soldiering On*, one of Alan Bennett's *Talking Heads*, 1987

Playing the passionate woman in Kay Mellor's *A Passionate Woman*, 1994

Playing Peggy in BBC Television's *Keeping Mum*

Colin with Emma

Great Aunt Peg, 1994

Me, my mother and Emma,
1982

This Is Your Life with Michael Aspel

Me and Sister Angela on *This Is Your Life*

Family photo, 1992: (back row) Wigs, my mother June, Emma, Me, (front) Paul, my niece Alice, and Peter

Peter Birrel and me, 1997

what the dream said to me. It was a gift from my unconscious, or from my higher self, or from God – whatever you like to call it.

S interpreted all my dreams in an orthodox Freudian way, and he was very insightful and helpful, but I felt sure there was something more to it than that. I was doing quite a lot of reading at that time: Freud, Adler, Winnicott, Klein, Marion Milner, Alice Miller, many others and, of course, Jung. I read Jung's autobiography. In the middle there were some photographs and I was flicking through them when, to my astonishment, there was a photograph of my dream country. It was a photograph of the Pueblo Indians in Taos.

After four years, I began to feel that S and I had gone as far as we could go together. He seemed to concentrate on the personal, about which he was very good, but rather to ignore the spiritual dimension, which I felt was growing increasingly important to me. So, after a breathing-space, I found myself a Jungian analyst, a woman, and I went to her for the next two years.

After *Tenko* had finally finished, and Henry and I had made the final break, I felt I needed a holiday. I was talking about it with some friends who asked, 'Where will you go?' Without thinking, I said, 'I'll go to Taos.' The words just came out of my mouth. I thought, 'So that's where I'm to go.'

I flew into Albuquerque at night and checked myself into a motel near the airport. The next morning I drove out of Albuquerque in a big American hire car and as I travelled through the red ochre landscape, so familiar from my dreams, the car radio was playing Ry Cooder music, the perfect soundtrack. The road winds across the plain, and you see the mountains ahead of you, some flat-topped, some peaked; one is the sacred mountain of the Pueblo Indians. Then there is a long curve through Taos, and suddenly there was the Pueblo, just as I'd seen it in my dreams.

It was October, after the summer and before the skiing, a time of year when there were very few tourists. I spent all day there, day after day. I sat by the stream that runs down from the sacred mountain through the middle of the reservation, dividing the north from south. I ate honeyed bread baked in the beehive ovens. You have to leave in the evening, as the sun goes down. One evening I was about to leave when I heard the sound of drumming, and there was a young man and his friend, drumming and chanting, and they gestured to me to sit with them and I sat on the ground and listened.

I went back again the next day and the young man told me he was a university student, and in his vacations he made drums to sell to tourists. He only had two left. One which was finished had a butterfly on it, which is their symbol for transformation. There was another drum which he was just completing. I played the butterfly drum, and it was quite good. Then I played the unfinished drum, and I said, 'That's the one.' And he said, 'I made it for you.' He and I are the only people who have ever played or ever will play that drum. He made me a stick to play it with, covered in deerskin, and now they hang on the wall above a red ochre sandstone fireplace, like a Pueblo dwelling, which I have had built at home. Sometimes I still take down my drum and play it.

I stayed near the Pueblo Indians for two weeks. It was such a strange time, horse-riding up into the mountains on a Western saddle, and walking about among the people and in the landscape of my dreams. The odd thing is, I have never dreamed about them again.

It was while I was reading Jung, that the idea came to me that I should return to the religion of my childhood. Jung said that whenever he got a new analysand, he would always say to them, 'Go back to the religion of your childhood, because it is bred in the bone.'

For the first time I discovered the Christian mystics. I had no idea that Christianity had given rise to these extraordinary people, like Meister Eckhart – whom the Pope eventually excommunicated because he couldn't silence him any other way – and John of the Cross and Julian of Norwich. Reading their writings and the stories of their lives was my first step towards becoming a follower of Christ.

Many people thought my going into analysis odd, even some of my close friends. Some said, 'I couldn't do that! What do you want to do that for?' A lot of people are still afraid of it. It's the same old thing, anything to do with the mind, things you can't see, feel or touch, are deeply suspect as far as many human beings are concerned. But I find it all endlessly fascinating. I don't mean just navel-gazing, looking at my own subconscious. I find other people's psyches equally fascinating, and I feel it has all taught me to love and understand others much better, as a direct result of being taught how to love and understand and to forgive myself.

20. Noises on and noises off

Noises Off is a comedy by Michael Frayn, and has a play within a play. Just before I went into *Tenko* I was in it for a year at the Savoy Theatre, playing Dotty Otley. The cast included Hugh Paddick, Michael Cochrane and Chris Godwin. Chris is more than a friend who shares my love of poetry; he's like another brother, as we have virtually grown up together since we were first in rep at Canterbury when we were hopeful young seventeen-year-olds.

In *Noises Off*, the first act is a rehearsal that is going wrong of the play within the play, and the director, played by Chris, stands at the back of the auditorium, and joins in the action by coming down the aisle, shouting, 'No, no, no.' One night, about ten minutes in, while Chris was waiting in the auditorium for his cue, he heard this bit of whispered dialogue between two people in the audience, an American man and wife.

The wife said, 'Honey, how long has this play been on?'

'I don't know. Couple of years, maybe.'

'A couple of years! But they don't know their words . . .'

To which the husband replied, 'Hey, yeah, honey, but it's Monday.'

The second act is almost a mimed ballet, a movement sequence with no dialogue. The set swings round so, for the audience, 'backstage' is now on-stage and 'on-stage' is now backstage. So the play within the play is going on out of the audience's view and what they are seeing is what is going on

170

behind the scenes. During the course of this Dotty Otley, my character, is refusing to go on stage, and is threatened with a backstage fireman's axe by another character. This axe had a large wooden stave, and the business end, the head, was made of painted rubber, so it was perfectly safe. I would be crouching down, and the other actor had to come over with the axe, threaten me, and I would then rise and go on-stage. Unfortunately, one night she threatened, I rose, she brought the axe down, and instead of the rubber part, the wooden stave hit my head. Very, very hard. I saw stars. I carried on, feeling very peculiar.

I was aware that the laughter was diminishing somewhat, but didn't take much notice, because during the summer months the audience was often full of Japanese tourists, who must have been completely perplexed anyway, so if they didn't understand all the humour it was not altogether a surprise. It was a very energetic play, and a very hot summer, so we all used to sweat an enormous amount, and I was wearing a beret pulled over my head, which made me even hotter. I was rushing on and off, feeling groggier and groggier and sicker and sicker, and thinking, 'God, I'm sweating a lot!' I drew my hand across my forehead and saw not sweat, but blood, pouring down my face on to my costume. Then I passed out.

Chris Godwin and Hugh Paddick were on the stage, thinking that I was about to come on. When I didn't, they continued the rest of the scene, which was all in mime, exactly as if I was still there, because they didn't know what else to do. Had they been able to speak, of course, they could have made up some sort of dialogue to cover for me, but they couldn't, so they had to mime. What the audience made of it, I cannot think. Luckily I had passed out towards the end of the second act. The curtain came down, I was carried to the nearest dressing-room, and the word went out, 'Is there a doctor or nurse in the house?'

When ticket sales are slow, seats are often offered to local hospitals for the doctors and nurses. So, on the cry, 'Is there a doctor in the house?' almost the entire audience appeared backstage. Chris Godwin, Hugh Paddick, Mike Cochrane and I all kept large bottles of whisky in our dressing-rooms – mainly for visitors, of course – and we would usually have a shot together with the rest of the cast while winding down after the show. Doctors and nurses began to appear from the audience and they all agreed that I should go to casualty. As each one arrived, Chris, good host that he is, said, 'Have a drink.' And, of course, they all did. By the end of the interval we were wiped out of Scotch, and an audience of very merry doctors and nurses went back into the auditorium to see the third act, while I was carted off by ambulance to St Thomas's Hospital. Luckily I had an understudy, although I was a little bit concerned to pass her on the stairs as I was being carried out, with a script in her hands and her lips working, looking as though she were just learning the lines.

The next day was a matinee and I was allowed to take that off, but I had recovered enough to play the evening show. I thought that was the end of that, but it wasn't.

About a year later, I was at home, hearing a high-pitched whining sound. I thought, 'There's a light bulb going somewhere in this house.' I searched the entire house, but all the light bulbs were fine. Eventually I realised that it was my ears ringing. I went off to the doctor, who sent me to a specialist, who said, 'Tinnitus.' I told him that I'd had a bad blow to the head and concussion a year earlier and asked if that could have caused it. 'No,' he said, quite unequivocally.

Four years later I happened to hear a talk on the radio, where a specialist was saying that tinnitus could indeed be caused by a blow to the head. I took myself off to see another specialist, who said that it could easily have been, and most likely was, the cause in my case. Unfortunately, by then it was far too late for me to claim compensation.

I have tinnitus in both ears now. It's there all the time, and sometimes it is louder than at others, but usually I can switch off and not be aware of it. I've always been able to block out noise that I don't need to hear. I think it comes from the early days of rep, when I used to get home at night and learn the next part against the sound of the radio. One of the sadnesses of having tinnitus, the only thing that really upsets me about it, is that I've always loved silence – and it is permanently lost to me. The absolute silence of night, when the birds are asleep, there's no wind and it's very still, particularly in the country when it's utterly quiet, is the most wonderful deep silence – and I will never experience it again. There will always be noises off.

While we were making the first series of *Tenko*, in 1980/81, I was thrilled to be asked to play Mrs Featherstone, the Black Widow, in two series of *Open All Hours* starring Ronnie Barker, with David Jason and Lynda Barron. In fact, the first series of *Tenko* and the first series of *Open All Hours* were transmitted over the same period, and at one point during the second series of each I was working on both of them at once. In the morning I would be on floor 3 of the Acton 'Hilton', as the BBC rehearsal rooms are called, rehearsing *Open All Hours*, and on floor 5 in the afternoon, rehearsing *Tenko*.

I was so lucky to be in this wonderful drama and in this completely zany comedy, both at the same time, and it was then that I first started to be recognised in the street. When people ask, 'Do you mind people coming up to you in the street?' I always say, 'No, I never mind. Anybody recognising you from your work and saying they enjoyed it – it's lovely.'

But it does have its downside. When the two series, *Tenko* and *Open All Hours*, were being shown at the same time, I was out shopping one morning, and I noticed that there was a little old lady following me about and I could tell that she wanted to speak to me. She managed to corner me by the baked beans. Swiss Cottage, where I live, is where a great many Jewish refugees came to live both before and during the war, and she came up to me and said, in a pronounced mid-European accent, 'Excuse me. Excuse me. Are you ze lady from *Tenko*?'

I said that yes, I was.

She said, 'Oh! It is such a beautiful series. You are so lovely. It is so moving. It is so profound.'

I said, 'Thank you. That's very kind of you.'

She went on, 'Also, you are in zat thing with Ronnie Barker?'

I agreed that I was.

She shook her head sadly, 'Oh dear . . . Do you need ze money?'

It keeps your feet on the ground.

I was still able to do the odd character part, in episodes of shows like *Crown Court* and *Terry and June*. I played a dippy, drunk woman in a thing called *Room at the Bottom* with the director/producer David Reynolds, which some years later led to him giving me the part of Betty Sillitoe in the series *A Bit of a Do* written by the great David Nobbs, with a cast that included David Jason, Nicola Pagett, Gwen Taylor, Paul Chapman, Michael Jayston, Tim Wylton and David Thewlis. I played a warm-hearted, blonde drunk, and I found both Betty and her equally tiddly husband, a battery-chicken magnate (Tim Wylton), utterly endearing.

As we were all milling around for the first read-through, I was aware that David Reynolds was looking at me, and I could tell there was something he wanted to say to me. I kept catching his eye, and I just wished he'd come over and come out with it, whatever it was. Suddenly I flashed what it might be so that when eventually he did come up to me and said, 'Steph, I need to ask you a great favour . . .' I said, 'I know what you're going to ask me. You're going to ask me if I mind going blonde.'

He said, 'How did you know?'

I said, 'Because Betty has to be blonde. It's not in the script, but I know it. And can I just tell you, I have been waiting for twenty years for a good excuse to do it! I'll go blonde, honey, I'll go blonde!'

And I did. My natural hair colour was dark brown then, although I had begun to go grey during the five years I worked on *Tenko*. I always tell Ken Riddington that he and the BBC turned my hair grey.

I played Claree in *Steel Magnolias* at the Lyric, Shaftesbury Avenue for producer David Pugh, with Rosemary Harris, Maggie Steed, Jean Boht, Janine Duvitski and Joely Richardson, directed by Julia Mackenzie. Once again, I was in a group of half a dozen super women, and we had a glorious time. It ran to packed houses for six months.

There were two acts, and each act had two scenes in it. In the second act, between scene one and scene two, we all had terrifically big changes, with hardly more than a minute to do it in. I had to change my costume, my tights, my shoes, even my hair, almost literally everything. The only things I didn't change were my bra and knickers. My dresser and I, a wonderful lady called Barbara Toye who had been a cabaret singer, got the change down to twenty-eight seconds – which was phenomenal. Everyone else had big changes also. Two of them, Jean Boht and Janine Duvitski, had to change on stage – it was quicker, and there wasn't room in the wings for everybody. They both had to strip down quite a bit, and one fateful night I walked back on stage to be greeted by the sight of Janine, her head stuck inside her pregnancy padding, with almost nothing else on, and of Jean Boht, who in order to help her dresser had, in an excess of zeal, stripped off completely, totally starkers.

We had been running for some months, but a new ASM who had only just taken over the show thought that, because Maggie, Rosemary and I had gone back on stage, he could now take the curtain up. The curtain started to rise. For a terrible moment we all just froze with horror. It had got to knee height when we all shouted, 'Get that curtain down!' And it came back down, whoomp! Sighs of relief all round.

A lesson in what not to do when something does go wrong: do not try to be helpful. *Steel Magnolias* opens with Truvy and Annelle on stage, about to open their hairdressing salon, in the garage of Truvy's house – Mags Steed was Truvy and Janine was Annelle. I was the first character to come on from the outside world. Mags went to open the door to the salon, and it had stuck. The ASM came to me and said, 'Steph, the door's stuck. Go round the back.'

I said, 'OK.'

I still had a few minutes before my entrance, so I sat there thinking, 'Well, the audience are going to wonder why all of a sudden I'm coming through the house, rather than through the door.' Then I thought, 'Oh, I know what I'll do.' My cue came, and I walked to the door, which of course wouldn't open, and after rattling it I yelled through 'Hey, Truvy, Truvy, your door's stuck. Ah'm goin' round the back.'

'OK, Claree.'

What I had forgotten was that between me and the door at the back was an over life-size Father Christmas, with reindeer and sleigh, furniture, lights, rolls of carpet, two Christmas trees – and I had to get through it all. I stumbled about trying to get over and round all this stuff; I was taking some time so Mags and Janine started to improvise. Every now and then I felt it incumbent on me to shout out, 'Ah'm comin', Truvy. Ah'm a-comin'!' Eventually I reached the door from the house into the salon/garage. 'Ah'm just comin', Truvy.'

And I heard Maggie Steed, in exasperation, shout, 'Well, if yer comin', for God's sake come!' At which moment I burst through the door and for several minutes the dialogue took second place to our laughter.

Innes Lloyd was a tall, good-looking, clean-cut man, who always wore blazers and used to ride around on an old-fashioned sit-up-and-beg bicycle with a basket on the front. He was sweet and considerate, and would nurture talent, and I was one of the many people to whom he was wonderfully generous. He would never contact me through my agent; he always called me at home. Gradually, over the years, he would ask me to play bigger and bigger roles until, one day early in 1988, there was a phone call, 'Steph? I've got a script here which I think you might like. We'd like you to have a look at it. I'll bike it over to you now.'

Half an hour later there was a ring on the doorbell, and there was the messenger with a rather thin A4 envelope. I signed for it, took it through to the sitting-room, sat down and opened it. There was just a brief note on the front saying, 'Hope you like it. Love, Innes.' There was no indication of which part I should read. I opened it at the title page, and saw it was by Alan Bennett, a series called *Talking Heads*, and this episode was titled 'Soldiering on'. OK. I turned the page. There was still no indication of which part I was to read for but, nevertheless, I started to read. It begins with Muriel. She starts to speak, and she speaks through the first page, and she speaks through the second page, and I thought, 'She's got a lot. When do I come on?' And then I realised – it was a monologue.

I read it through twice. I wanted to do it more than I had ever wanted to do anything. I telephoned Innes immediately and said, 'It's wonderful. Wonderful.'

He said, 'Oh good. Come and have lunch with me and Alan, and meet Tristram Powell, who we want to direct it.'

I went along to meet them, supposing that this was to be the interview, when they would decide whether or not to offer it to me. So I was very nervous – so nervous I couldn't raise the glass to my lips. I could hardly eat. I think I managed a mouthful. They did nearly all the talking. Then Innes said, 'Well, I suppose really, the next thing is talking to costume and make-up.' And I realised – it had been mine all along.

There was a delay before I actually did it, because we did them back to back, two at a time, and I did mine at the same time as Maggie Smith did hers, in August 1988. So I had the script for six months, and I walked around with it in my handbag, and I learned it by osmosis, really, just reading and reading and reading it. Alan Bennett writes with such rhythm, such a natural style, that it's almost impossible to get it wrong.

It was a joy to do. It was one of the greatest gifts I have ever been given. The most wonderful script, and the opportunity to work in the most wonderful company. I owe that entirely to Innes.

21. Glittering prizes

I actually think 'Soldiering on' was the best-written and most subtle of the *Talking Heads* monologues. It was a beautiful play. It shoved me another eighty-five rungs up the professional ladder, because it was a serious piece of work on television, and I was up there with some Big Names, when I myself was not a big name, only a minor one. So it was a great act of trust and faith on the part of Innes, and of Alan.

There were six monologues and the six of us who performed them were Thora Hird, Alan Bennett himself, Maggie Smith, Patricia Routledge, Julie Walters and me. There was a tremendous response to them all, and I got the most wonderful, encouraging, generous feedback and accolades. The series was nominated for several awards as were all the actors, except me.

I then had a battle with myself getting to grips with the fact that I'd always considered myself to be completely non-competitive, and that, for me, awards were neither here nor there, and I didn't value them very highly . . . and that I now knew better. I minded terribly not being nominated. I remember sitting at home on my own – deliberately on my own, I didn't want to be with anybody else – watching the ceremony, hurling cushions at the screen, and going through what it felt like to have the biggest slap in the face ever. It hurt, but I survived.

My confidence in myself and my abilities, oddly enough,

was not rocked by that experience. I knew deep down that it was an OK piece of work, and I wasn't going to let this make me believe that it hadn't been. If I hadn't been through the earlier experience of losing my confidence, when I had been hit by depression and had given up, I don't think I could have weathered this with quite so much equanimity. It taught me two things. It made me face the fact that I was and am just as competitive as the next person – which I think within reason is perfectly healthy. Second, it made me look at the whole system of awards (in any area of life) and to put it in its proper context.

It is very nice to win an award, but it really does not make you 'best actor'. (Incidentally, if you are wondering why I always call myself an actor and not an actress, it's because to me it's the same sort of word as doctor – you don't call a female doctor a doctress, do you?) Anyway, you may happen, one year, to have been judged by a few people, to have given a performance which in their view is more interesting than someone else's. But the difference is infinitesimal and the judgments hardly universal. So many people don't win or are even ignored who are just as good. Award ceremonies are the most wonderful publicity for our business, and that is why they are there; let's not kid ourselves. But that is not to detract from the joy of winning, or from the fact that when you are at the ceremony you have to treat it with a certain respect, and not send the whole thing up. To do that is to be unkind to the people who have been nominated and insulting to the people who are watching, and overlooks the fact that even though it is mainly good publicity, it is also something more, it is a kind of thanksgiving for the pleasure and beauty that all art brings into the world. My experience helped me begin to get the whole thing into truer perspective.

Some years later I was given Best Comedy Actress for *Waiting for God*, and all the winners had to stand in a group to be photographed. I was standing next to a thrilled Des O'Connor, who had just been given the Lifetime

Achievement Award, and he said to me, 'Isn't it all exciting?' I said, 'Yeah. Well. It's OK.' He seemed quite shocked and hurt that I was sounding so lukewarm. Nowadays I wouldn't be so ungiving. It was mean of me not to go along with his obvious delight.

The Bennett monologue has clung to me. I've done it on BBC radio, and I've done it yet again in the West End. Ian McKellen, Sheila Hancock, Imelda Staunton and I did four of them; we gave five warmly received performances at the Haymarket, for Crusaid.

In 1995, a subsidiary of London Weekend Television decided to make a programme to honour four people in our profession by entering them into a 'Hall of Fame'. This was the first year, and they had decided to honour Jack Rosenthal, Lew Grade, Alan Whicker and Thora Hird. Each of the celebs being honoured were introduced by another celeb, who had to say a few words, introduce a series of film clips, and then bring the recipient on to the stage. They were to receive their award, speak for exactly four minutes, and then you would both go off. I was asked to introduce Thora, who I always enjoy working with. I was very honoured, because she is extremely talented and I'm very fond of her.

We all got there in the afternoon to rehearse our bits, although the people being honoured were not there until the evening, which was to be recorded in front of an audience 'as live', which meant it all had to be timed to the last second. I was given my little bit, and that was fine, and I knew what the film clips were. I said to Michael Hurll, who was organising the whole thing and whose production company was making the programme, 'Michael, have you actually told Thora how long she has to speak when she receives her award?'

He said, 'Oh, yes. It's just four minutes.'

I said, 'No, you misunderstand me, Michael. She really *does* know, does she, that she only has exactly four minutes?'

'Oh, yes. Don't worry.'

I said, 'Well, you do know, don't you, that Thora is a stranger to silence?'

'Don't worry about it, Steph. She knows.'

So I said, 'OK. If you're sure.'

The evening came, I did my piece, showed the film clips, and then I introduced Thora, going down into the audience to escort her on to the stage, and there she was in front of the mike. I had been told to stand about five feet back, off-camera, ready to accompany her off-stage as soon as she finished. Thora was very amusing, very entertaining. The first three minutes passed. Then the four-minute limit. Then five minutes, then six, then seven and then eight. I noticed the floor manager gesturing to me to bring her off. I thought, 'Well, how can I? She's in full flow!'

I did this thing that children and ostriches do: if they can't see you, they think you can't see them. I turned my back on the audience so I couldn't see them, put my head down and sidled towards Thora. Just as I was going to mutter to her, 'Thora, I think they need you to finish,' I saw in my peripheral vision that the floor manager was signalling that it was OK to let her go on, because she really was being very funny and the audience were loving her. We reached something like twelve minutes, and Thora was in her element. Now I saw the floor manager frantically making cut-throat gestures, so I went forward again and as she was coming to the end of a story I murmured, 'Thora, I think they want you to end now.' As soon as she reached the tag-line and the laughter began, the floor manager signalled for final applause, which was long and loud, and I escorted Thora triumphantly off the stage to an ovation. I'm not sure if she knows to this day that all that had been going on. It was quite clear that she had settled in for the evening. What would you have done?

In the mid-eighties, I returned to radio work for the first time since 1960. I was in a play directed by Enyd Williams and it led to a great deal more work in a medium which I have come to love. On 20 July 1989 I read the letters that Barbara Pym had written to Philip Larkin. Delightful John Moffatt read Larkin's letters. The programme was called *Intimate Exchanges*; it was compiled by Anthony Thwaite and won the Sony Award. I loved doing it. I've always been fascinated by Barbara Pym. I was introduced to her books by David Cecil long before many people had heard of her, that is to say, before she wrote her come-back novel. Since then I have hugely enjoyed doing more and more radio work. My next broadcast was with Alan Bennett, in which we both read *Prophetic Book*, a seven-part autobiographical poem by Craig Raine, an extraordinary work which means a lot to me. The poem's coda is:

> Just before you die you are given the sun
> And all your mistakes – then they are taken away.

22. Waiting for God

I was in *Waiting for God* for five years. I was first contacted by Gareth Gwenlan in 1989, who sent me some scripts by Michael Aitken, and wanted to know if I was interested in making a pilot. I read a couple of the scripts, loved the character of Diana, and said I would do it. Tom was to be played by Graham Crowden, a blessed eccentric himself, like the character, and a delight and a joy.

I think we all felt that it was highly unlikely that a series about two elderly people, one completely loopy and the other chronically crotchety, living in an old people's home, could capture the imagination of the great British public. The BBC didn't think so either. It was the last of several pilots they had made, but none of the others had really worked, and they were left with ours. They looked at it, and within a fortnight, the first series was in production. This meant that the wig that I had worn for the pilot, which had come out of stock and resembled nothing so much as a lank tea cosy, had to be used for the whole of the first series, because there wasn't time to have a proper one made. To everybody's surprise, it took off. (The series, not my wig.)

I've played so many elderly parts through my career. Even Beatrice in *Tenko* was older than me – she was supposed to be in her fifties when I was only just forty; in *Open All Hours* I was an old crone; I did the old lady in the first tour of *Driving Miss Daisy*, and I've had a lifetime's experience of repertory, playing much older characters, so it's like second nature to me. But it was only after *Waiting for God* that people started to think I must really *be* old, and so to say, 'But you look so young in real life!'

Working with Graham was heaven. I mean he is a screwball, but extremely intelligent, and I adored him. I'd never met him before, but we got on well immediately. All the cast got on tremendously well.

The home, Bayview itself, was in Oxfordshire, but we used to film all the street scenes in Brighton or Bournemouth. On one occasion, during the third series, we were filming in Brighton on a beautiful, sunny day. They were setting up a shot and I was in full fig: costume, wig and make-up, with the stick, just standing there quietly, not talking to anybody, uncharacteristically minding my own business. An elderly lady came up to me.

When you are filming in the streets, you come across three sorts of members of the public. There are the ones who are absolutely fascinated, and want to find out what's going on, and talk to you. They are lovely and always welcome. There are the ones who walk by, studiously ignoring you, as if this is an everyday occurrence, and there is nothing of the least interest to be looked at. They are also fine. And then there are the ones who are absolutely furious that you are there, and what is more, that you appear to be enjoying your work. There are people in this world who think that if something is 'work' the workers should be seen to be having a frightful time.

This lady was one who felt we should not be there, and that if we had to be there, we certainly should not be enjoying ourselves. After watching us all crossly for a few moments, she came up to me and she said accusingly, 'What's all this then?'

I said, 'Well, we are with the BBC, and we are filming something.'

'Oh, yes? What's that then?'

'Well, it's a series, called *Waiting for God*.'

'Oh, yes? Who's in that then?'

I said, 'Well, Graham Crowden and Stephanie Cole.'
'Oh, I know Stephanie Cole. She's George Cole's mother.'
As I say, it all helps to keep one's feet on the ground.

In an early episode, Tom and Diana decide to earn some money using her expertise as a photographer, by taking aerial shots of houses and selling the results to the owners. This entailed going up in a helicopter. The day came and we found ourselves sitting in a helicopter on the tarmac shooting the scene. The door on my side had been taken off to help the cameraman.

'Now,' said the director, 'we will take the 'copter up about twenty feet and shoot Diana with her camera taking the aerial photos. OK?'

'Yes,' I replied, and Graham and I fastened our safety belts. The assistant floor manager appeared to ask if we were ready.

'When you've put my door back on we will be,' I replied, but she said nothing and disappeared. Seconds later the pilot appeared and clipped me, but not Graham, into an extra harness, and warning lights started to flash in my mind.

'What about the door?' I asked the director.

'Ah,' he murmured. 'Yes. We can't have the door, you see, because you have to lean out so we can see you take the photos. You'll be okay, won't you?'

Knowing the cost of hiring the helicopter for the day and the necessity for the shot, what could I say?

We rose slowly into the air and over the cans came the order for me to start taking the photos. I leaned out very slightly, camera to my eye and pretended to be snapping away.

'Lean out further, Steph . . . further . . . further!' came the instructions in my ear. So I did. Finally came the order, 'OK. We've cut. You can come down now.'

I took the camera from my eye, and nearly fainted. Through the lens I had had no idea of the distance, and I found myself leaning right out of the plane, with just one foot hooked round poor Graham's leg, and we were about two hundred feet up in the air!

'You all right?' chirruped the pilot. 'We're going down now, just a little banking on the way.' Round we went, banking, leaving me completely horizontal with the ground. When we eventually touched down I felt like doing a Richard II and kneeling to kiss the earth.

There was an episode in which Tom and Diana finally went to bed together. It happened to coincide with the publication of a book by Age Concern called *Living, Loving and Ageing*, in which they talk about sex in old age. Young people think that the moment you pass forty or fifty, certainly sixty, you must cease to want sex or to have anything to do with it. It's absolutely untrue, and it can continue to be immensely enjoyable until your dying day. It's like good food and good wine, one of the joys of life.

During *Waiting for God*, I became patron of Age Concern. It's run by a wonderful woman called Sally Greengross, who has boundless energy, and it means a great deal to me. I also became patron of the Bristol Research into Alzheimer's disease. I began to receive, and I still do, hundreds and hundreds of invitations to visit old people's homes, and when I go I always tell them that I regard myself as an honorary old-age pensioner. And I get invited to the lunches that Richard Ingrams' *Oldie* magazine holds, so I am officially an Oldie now.

I'd say I am more an 'equalist' than a feminist, but I do sometimes get angry about the glass ceiling. As you get older, in our business as in life, it is far less easy for a woman than it is for a man. It is changing, too slowly, but it seems to me that the way to make change happen is not to hit out at the men. It has to be all of us moving forward together, not entrenched on opposite sides.

In *Waiting for God*, we had a male writer, a male director, and a male co-star. I'm fond of Michael who wrote it, Gareth who directed it, and I love Graham dearly, but just as I have my militant feminist side, they have their male chauvinist side. When we were all sitting round talking, I became aware that, in order to make my voice heard, I was becoming an honorary feller. They would all probably disagree violently with this, because I know I come across as a very strong woman. They would probably say that I could be heard no matter how I said it, but I know that that was what I was doing. I didn't like that, so I decided to stop; but then I realised that what I was doing next was using feminine wiles, and I equally despise that. I had to find a way of being me, not being an honorary feller and not being 'little me', just straight down the middle, and it's jolly difficult.

I've always been political, gone on marches, and was the Equity deputy all through *Tenko*, and on several other productions I've been in. I've read the *Guardian* from the age of seventeen, when it was the *Manchester Guardian*. I must have mellowed in my middle age – I now read the *Independent*.

People talk disapprovingly about 'champagne socialism', but I think that's a load of old piddle. It is nonsense to say that just because you have been successful, and made a bit of money, you have lost all your ideals and stopped caring for anybody else. When people get any degree of celebrity or wealth, and the two often go together, what they often do is good by stealth. People don't know about it, because they don't shout about it. I know this to be true of at least 90 per cent of the people who have earned a degree of celebrity in my profession; they do an enormous amount of good and never talk about it. They give money, or do voluntary work, or both, but it would be like some sort of ghastly boast if they kept talking about it. Anyway, socialism isn't about charity, it's about equality of opportunity.

There are people in our society, and through working for organisations like Age Concern and the NSF I've met many of them, who mentally, emotionally or physically are not capable of looking after themselves, because they have not been blessed by good health, or they've had a lousy education and start in life, or there are all sorts of reasons, and it is up to those of us who are luckier to take care of them. I sincerely believe that, and to say otherwise is a load of cobblers and it makes me angry.

Towards the end of *Waiting for God*, after we'd done five series over five years and a couple of Christmas specials, we'd all had a wonderful time, but Michael, the writer, wanted to go on to other things, and I, personally, very much wanted to go on to other things. I loved Diana to death – acerbic, difficult, a feisty fighter, never letting anything get the better of her, fighting authority, a complete maverick, but actually with a very kind heart – but I'm not very good, as an actor, at doing just one thing for a long time. Little did I know, as Diana's stick and wig (vastly improved after the first series) were put away for the last time, that an even greater maverick role was awaiting me on television in 1997 – but I'll keep mum about her for now. Diana was terrific, she became a role model for many of the elderly, but it was time to move on. She has, however, remained a useful alter ego for me from time to time, as will be revealed in the next chapter.

23. Waiting for Sai Baba

Make voyages, attempt them. There is nothing else.

I wish I knew who originally said that – I think it might have been Byron. I found it in a book by John Berger. I've always been fascinated by travel, but as I've said, I never had the opportunity to really travel until I was in my early forties. It was then that I became aware of how the outward journey and the inward journey are equally important. However terrifying the waters look, however wild and churned and frightening, for me, it is necessary to explore. I don't know another way of being. I can't live any other way.

In 1991 I decided, as a fiftieth birthday present to myself, to take myself to India. I didn't want to do the touristy things, and it so happened that three people I knew from Findhorn, a spiritual community I had come to know in Scotland, by the Moray Firth, had lived and worked in Southern India, and they had decided that they would like to take a small party to visit and help in the places they knew there. So I joined them. During 1985 and 1986 I had visited Findhorn quite regularly for the odd week, and had learned a lot and made many good friends. I don't go there any more, but at that time it was an important landmark on my spiritual journey. So in November 1991 I met up with the Findhorn group of two Americans, two Germans, two

Swedes, and four Britons, from a wide variety of backgrounds and professions, and flew out from Heathrow for a
two-month sojourn in India.

We were a disparate group, often living in quite difficult
circumstances, in a country that makes you question yourself all the time. I love India with a passion, but for many
people it is not a comfortable place, and for me, even though
I adore it, it is not entirely comfortable. Our plan was to fly
to Bombay, go straight on to Madras and work our way
from there all round southern India.

We landed in Bombay at night, over the orange, gold, red,
white and blue lights of the city, and stepped off the aeroplane into a bath of warm air, and a throng of people
offering taxis, porters, hotels, and loudly proclaiming,
'Paisa' (Indian pennies), 'Rupees', 'Where you from?' and,
rather startlingly, 'Hello, Auntie!' which I was assured was a
term of great respect. We careered through the streets of
Bombay in an Indian bus. The driving in India gives a whole
new meaning to the phrase 'road sense'. The few rules are:
always drive in the middle of the road; always overtake on a
bend or straight into the oncoming traffic; sound your horn
very loudly at all times; and if the other bloke is bigger than
you and won't give way, drive into the ditch very fast.

We awoke the following morning to a view of sand and
sea, which looked glorious but was actually filthy, of children
doing handstands, of camels loping by, and of racehorses
being exercised on the beach. We then drove back to the
airport for our flight to Madras. In the morning light, India
finally hit us in full Technicolor, along with the pungent
smells of animals, frangipani, incense and drains. Cows,
camels, dogs, goats and loaded bullock carts crowded the
roadside, and there were beggars everywhere.

There was a five-hour delay to our flight. We got on to the
plane, were fed, and taken off the plane. Finally we reached
Madras very late at night, and then drove at top speed south
down the main road along the Coromandel coast to
Auroville, near Pondicherry. Barely avoiding wandering

cows, goats, water buffalo, and the endless line of peripatetic foot travellers, we overtook lorries painted with bright flowers and brighter gods – it was really not at all like the M1. We stopped for refreshments at a wayside stall. It looked rather grubby, but we risked the tea, which is made with sweet, hot milk. We also tried the small, hard, but sweet locally grown bananas, while Tamil lorry drivers grinned and stared at us incredulously. Eventually we turned off the main road and bumped for some miles along dirt tracks, seeing rats and bandicoots scurrying across our path in the headlights.

We arrived at the Auroville Guest Centre, which was to be our home for the next two weeks, and I fell asleep listening to a cacophony of night sounds – birds, howling dogs, wild cats, jackals, bullfrogs, a cricket that sounded as if it was sawing down a large tree, owls, geckos, the wind in the trees and the patter of light rain, the last few showers of the recent monsoon.

Auroville is a scattering of houses and villages, covering a huge area to the south of Pondicherry. It is a spiritual community, but it is also very much involved in the hands-on business of working with the people and the land, to make life on earth better. They have reforested and re-energised the land, using solar power and wind power, for they make use of all the knowledge there is of the regeneration of desert places and the education of farming people in agricultural techniques. There are schools for all the children in the area. The movement started with Sri Aurobindo, a Victorian Indian, a highly intellectual man brought up and educated in England. He returned to India and became a great spiritual leader, founding his big ashram, or spiritual centre, in the middle of Pondicherry, which is a very beautiful, French-colonial style city. The original ashram is very lovely, and people from all over the world go to visit it. Many stay on to live and work there. Auroville, the complex of settlements with names like Hope and Revelation, was started as an adjunct to Aurobindo's ashram and then, like Topsy, just grow'd. The original dwellings were traditional mud huts on stilts in containers of water to keep out termites, and thatched with palm leaves. They have long since been superseded by concrete, though most are no less picturesque.

The centrepiece of Auroville is rather sad in a way. In the latter part of his life Sri Aurobindo was joined by a French woman, who was always called 'the Mother', a deeply spiritual lady. The Mother had a vision of a great *Matramandir*, a temple of the Mother, which would be a temple to God, and would take the form of a huge multifaceted globe mounted on legs, and in the centre of the globe would be the biggest crystal in the world. The globe is still being built, and is absolutely huge. It takes five minutes to walk up to the entrance. Then there is a long spiral climb into the meditation chamber, and there *is* the biggest crystal in the world – as big as a room, and round, and extraordinary, a single piece of crystal grown in Switzerland. The first one they grew shattered, so they had to grow another one.

But like so many dreams, the original dream has gone rather wrong somewhere along the way. There is always a great danger when you become a guru that your followers will distort your teaching. Followers have to live by the letter of the law, by what the Mother wrote down, or by what is in the Gospel. We always hope for Utopia, but there is no such thing and never will be, and we have to grapple and cope with the fact that we are all human, and things aren't always, can't always, be what we hope for.

When the Mother was asked where the *Matramandir* should be, she had a vision that it should be sited beside an old banyan tree. She found the tree in Auroville, with an old woman sitting under it, and she said that this was the place. The old tree is still there, and the *Matramandir* is next to it. Why it is rather sad is that the *Matramandir* seems futuristic and bleak, in spite of all the people working in it and on it and round it and visiting it. The warm, holy place with the still centre is to be found by sitting under the old banyan tree next to it.

One of the main buildings in the Pondicherry ashram houses the tomb of the two founders. There, people were prostrating themselves before a huge marble sarcophagus covered in flowers. Inside the house, the founders' living-rooms are full of large turn-of-the-century vulgarities, heavy mahogany furniture, tiger rugs and odd ivory artefacts, all dark and rather dusty. The scene was enlivened on the day we visited by a very old man with a long white beard and hair, dressed in a white lungi lying on the floor, praying . . . and farting.

Soon we were finding our own way around Auroville on bicycles, along the tracks of golden earth through palm and neem trees, jasmine, frangipani and hibiscus, passing bullock carts, women with huge bundles of twigs or vast water pots on their heads, huge multicoloured butterflies, yellow bulbul birds, bright turquoise kingfishers, chipmunks, mongooses, the biggest bees and caterpillars I have ever seen, and uncountable children, who all wanted to find out who we were and where we came from. I acquired a few words in Tamil: 'Hello', 'Thank you', 'Very, very good' and 'See you tomorrow'. All I can remember now is that '*Rumba rumba nulla*' is 'Very, very good' – although perhaps it isn't spelled like that. These few words, along with a reasonable gift for mime and making a fool of myself, allowed for many long and hilarious conversations.

The accommodation was communal and primitive, but we ate delicious home-grown, home-made food, sitting underneath another giant banyan tree. At night the wildlife sounds were punctuated by the music of *bhajans* – songs to God – sung late at night and at dawn by pilgrims setting off on their once-in-a-lifetime pilgrimages to various temples around southern India. They all wore black with the symbol of Shiva in ash on their brows.

Once we were settled in at Auroville we could help in any of the places we had been shown round in the centre, or in the various surrounding villages – wherever we wanted or thought we would be of most use. The place that appealed to me was a little hut where I had found five Hindu women sitting working leather. It was owned and run by a wonderful young man called Vemkadesu, a Tamil. We became great friends, and I met his wife and two little babies and his Mum and Dad. He had been taught by an American woman, and believed that if women did the work of men, they should be paid the rate for the work of men, and that's how he managed things.

I spent a week bicycling to work on a terrible old bone-shaker that had no brakes, over the rough red lanes to the little village where Vemkadesu's workshop was. I would sit on the hard floor and work with them, making handbags, belts and key-rings. Because I am reasonably artistic we swapped patterns, and I learned from them some of their skills of working leather, polishing, punching, patterning, staining and embossing. We managed to chat away despite having no common language and I was struck, not by the differences between us, but by the multitude of things we had in common. I remember Sundri, at least twenty years younger than me, talking about her daughters, and I talked about my daughter, and it was all the same. This was one of the fascinating discoveries of the trip – the glory of the sameness, discovering that people everywhere, of every culture, share the same joys, worries, sorrows.

There was only one man, apart from Vemkadesu, an elderly man who worked on the old treadle machine outside, and he did all the sewing up. Chickens, cows and goats would wander in and out of the little hut. At midday we would stop and go out the back and drink 'tea'. They called it tea, but in fact it was runny semolina with cardamom seeds floating in it, heated up over an open fire. It is an acquired taste, and I don't think I would like it at all over here, but sitting under a palm tree, with chickens and goats scratching around, in the intense heat and dust of India, it was delicious.

Vemkadesu had great difficulty getting enough leather-working tools. It took me six months, but when I got back to England I eventually found somewhere that still makes the traditional tools and I sent several sets out to him, as well as continuing to support the business in a small way. Three years later, in 1995, I went back to India for a programme in a series that Arthur Smith was doing for BBC Radio 4, about people revisiting places that have meant a great deal to them. When I arrived back at Auroville with 'Arfur' we found that Vemkadesu had built a new temporary workshop, which now housed twenty workers, and was selling the leather goods in Pondicherry and Madras, and establishing a wide network of outlets.

There are 'four o'clock' schoolchildren in India, whose parents can't afford to send them to proper school all day, but they can work to earn money until three o'clock, and then go to school for a couple of hours. As well as more women workers, Vemkadesu was training several of these children in leather-working, and he would always let them go well before three to get their schooling. It's a great success story and has helped the economy of the whole village.

Christmas Eve 1991 was spent in Chidambaram, a town some 120 kilometres south, the most exhilarating celebration of Christmas Eve I have ever shared in. There was a great ceremony in the giant main temple, a short ritual dedicated to Vishnu, the protector, followed by the main attraction, the ceremony for Shiva, the destroyer. It took hours, with the sounds of bells, gongs, shawms and the scent of incense wafting everywhere. The front of the golden statue of Shiva was anointed with fire, water, rice and coconut milk, accompanied by chanting and bell-ringing. The heat, the noise and the crush of people were quite overpowering. We were blessed and anointed and given temple food, and then taken back to the home of the staggeringly beautiful young priest, for a feast prepared by his wife and mother. The temple musicians arrived to play for us, the priest's five-year-old son sang some pujas – devotional chants – and his nine-year-old daughter danced traditional temple dances.

After Christmas, we moved on to the city of Mysore. Our bus drove through a countryside dotted with sudden mountains and silkworm farms, with their fields of mulberry trees. The city itself is beautiful, full of silk and sandalwood, with a magnificent maharajah's palace. All the houses have tiled roofs, and the hotel was clean and functional, each room with its own bathroom, which was luxury indeed after living at Auroville, sharing a loo and a shower that wasn't always working. Mornings started early in Mysore, with devotional music on very loud speakers rousing the whole city at 5 a.m. Noise is life there, and privacy an alien concept.

While we were there we got caught up in a riot. They are much given to demonstrations and riots in India – well, it is jolly hot – and there is a continual on-going battle between the state of Tamil Nadu and the state of Karnataka over the rights to a river that runs along the border. It happens every year and gets very emotional; occasionally people get killed. I was in a little tailor's shop where I'd bought some silk, which is very cheap and very beautiful, and was having it made up. Suddenly we heard shouting and chanting, and there was a huge demonstration marching down the street towards us. There were about four or five tailors in the shop, and they all dashed out and brought down the steel shutters, so we were safe inside, while this demonstration slowly passed. Then they went to open up again, but they had somehow managed to lose the key, and we were locked in. There was I, with another woman from the Findhorn group and the tailors, all trapped in a tiny silk shop in Mysore. After we had done a lot of banging and shouting, somebody from the outside helped us and we burst out into the sunshine.

There was an old man in the city who read palms, a figure of legend. We eventually found him sitting on a pavement, this old, old man. I sat with him and he read my palm. All I can remember him saying was, 'Oh yes, yes. You are living very long life . . . until you are ninety!' Then he looked at me shrewdly and added, 'If you are exercising.' Right. So no chance of ninety, kiddo.

For New Year's Eve at the end of 1991 we moved on to Bangalore, where we shared the celebrations with several Indian families, among them a very fat and jolly Sikh who insisted on dancing with all the Western women – all fourteen of us. The main event of our visit to Bangalore was that we were given the opportunity to work as helpers at Mother Teresa's establishments. She had two houses there: a home for unwanted adults and an orphanage. The adults were 'unwanted' because they were either physically or mentally disabled. We spent a day with them, talking, playing and singing, and I found once again that I was able to enter their reality without any difficulty. Then we went to the orphanage.

I hardly know how to describe it. It was not particularly clean. There was one small room with all the tiniest babies in, some very ill. Along a corridor was a big room full of cots with the older children in, all of them skinny, and many were very badly disabled, mentally or physically or both. Outside at the back was a small dirt area with a swing and a roundabout, but it was only used when someone was free to take the children out there. There were no toys for them to play with. The only pictures were fairly gruesome images of the crucifixion high up on the walls. The babies wore little bits of rag for nappies, and the towels were just tea towels.

There was no sign of any nuns when we arrived. Mother Teresa was gravely ill, so all the sisters were in their convent praying for her. I thought, 'You can pray as you work. You don't have to be on your knees in a chapel fingering your rosary and thinking of Mother. You can be feeding and comforting and holding and hugging and giving love to a child at the same time.'

There were a couple of lay helpers, and two of the older Down's Syndrome girls were full of willingness and smiles.

Eventually a rather po-faced nun did appear, who turned out to be the mother superior.

It made no sense to me at all. Where were all the funds that were constantly being channelled towards Mother Teresa's charities? I was very, very upset and disturbed by it, and that was where I chose to work. We asked them if there was anything we could bring with us, and they asked for towels.

The next day we bought and took along lots of thick towelling, which we cut up for nappies and towels. We also took some plastic pants and Babygros, plus stacks of paper and packs of crayons for the toddlers. A couple of us sat outside with the three- and four-year-olds, who had obviously never had crayons before, and the delight with which they drew pictures with these coloured pencils was a joy to watch. There was a little boy called Radhu – they called him Joseph, but his real name was Radhu – who was a hunchback, bright as a button. I sat him on my knee to play, 'This is the way the farmers ride', and after singing it to him three times, he could sing the words with me. He spoke no English, but he picked up the words.

We worked from 7 a.m. until about 12.30 p.m. each day. The next morning when we arrived, there no nappies or towels to be seen. We were told they were 'in the wash'. None of the children's pictures were on the walls. They had been taken down and locked away. The following day there was still no sign of any of the towels we had brought, but as we were feeding the babies the young sister-in-charge rushed in and swept away the dirty nappies and bits of cloth, whispering urgently to us, 'Quick! Quick! We are getting all the children up very quickly now please, very beautiful, all in their lovely new things.'

'Why?'

'The Father is coming. Bring out the towels. Bring out the nappies. Everything lovely for Father.'

The priest was coming. It was a place, it seemed to me, that was the absolute antithesis of the word 'love'.

There was a little baby with hydrocephalus – water on the brain – very thin with big staring eyes. I would pick her up as soon as I got there in the morning, and I would carry her round with me all the time. I just hoped that might make a difference to what would be a very short life, because there was no chance at all of her getting an operation. You can actually do a great deal for hydrocephalus, but she was not going to get anything done, and she was going to die. I remember I had her in one arm, and one of the other babies in the other, and I was feeding it and holding it and singing to it, and one of the sisters came in and said, 'No, no. You are not to do that. That baby is old enough to hold his own bottle.'

'This is fine. I'm happy to do it.'

'No, no. Because then they are wanting it all the time. This is not a good thing to do. Put down in the cot. Not hold the bottle. If they are old enough – not hold.'

Somewhere along the line, everywhere in the world, people instinctively know that it is important to hold and touch, so that the baby has eyes to look into when it feeds. It is vital. And somewhere in its soul it always remembers that. In every village in India, every mother knows this. We were foolish enough to forget it in the West, and mothers used to put themselves and their babies through unnecessary misery because of a foolish fashion but, thank God, we've learned to follow our deep instincts again. But here I was, in India, being told by Christian nuns that this was not a good thing to do. I took no notice. We were only there for a week, but even if it was only for once in their life, they were held and cuddled and gazed at by somebody, and perhaps somewhere they would remember that.

I had got to know some children on the streets of Bangalore that I passed every day on the way to the orphanage, in particular the two children of a rag-picker. They lived on the street, and their parents earned a meagre living by picking up rags and rubbish. These street children, hungry and poor as they were, had far more than the babies in the orphanage, because they played catch with balls made out of paper, they chased around and made up little games. They had life in them.

They say that the late Mother Teresa will soon be made a saint, but what I saw on that visit was something that was very far removed from sanctity. We offered to pay, if they would arrange it, for little Radhu to have an operation for his hunchback in Bombay, with the best surgeons, or for him to come over to England to have it done. It's not an easy operation, but it can be done. When I went back with Arthur Smith three years later, nobody had done anything about Radhu's hunchback, and he was living with the monks, because he was now too old for the orphanage.

The orphanage itself had been rebuilt and refurbished. We walked into a lovely sunny place with toys everywhere. The children were clean and wore nice clothes. It was almost as if I had dreamed it, or as if the other place had been completely wiped off the face of the earth, and this had taken its place. My first feeling was one of enormous relief. Yet it was the same po-faced mother superior who greeted us, all smiles this time, 'Oh yes, I remember you when you were visiting us. Yes, very nice to see you again.' I was astounded. A little girl, who had been in her very early teens when I'd been there before, very disabled and with great difficulty in speaking, came running across the room to me crying, 'Oh Auntie, Auntie! How are you? Good to see you back!' which was very touching. I never saw Radhu again. All I can do is pray for him and wish him well.

On our wanderings, we visited various ashrams. We visited the Singing Guru at his Sachidananda Ashram, where everything was all very jolly. He was very fat and smiley in a lovely garden with little deer in it, and his followers sang *bhajans* all day long. It was delightful.

We went from Bangalore to a place in the mountains called Puttaparthi, where we were going to visit the gigantic ashram of one Sai Baba. We loaded mattresses on to the top of our bus, because we were going to be sleeping on the floor in sheds when we got there. The eight-hour journey took us across beautiful, increasingly mountainous countryside with fewer and fewer people or laden bullock carts on the roadside. We passed an old man, miles from anywhere, walking slowly along carrying his begging bowl, with a sitar slung across his back – an itinerant musician.

On the way we dropped in on an orphanage at Somnathpur, started by a man who had been a follower of the Shirdi Sai Baba, the predecessor to the present Satya Sai Baba. This man had been a thief and a drunkard and had had an overnight transformation through meeting or, some said, seeing a picture of Shirdi Sai Baba, and had built an orphanage on the banks of the River Cauvery, the border river over which there is so much dispute.

This was a very different place from Mother Teresa's, full of gloriously happy, chubby, lively, loved children. There was a beautiful temple. In the garden there was a plinth, covered in glass and sealed, and inside the glass dome was a black alabaster foot, a cast of the foot of Shirdi Sai Baba. As I approached it, I could smell the scent of jasmine, quite overpowering and not unusual in India, except there were no jasmine trees around, and I realised that the foot seeped jasmine oil. I could see it running down, and the scent, even from under the glass, was overwhelming. At first I thought, 'Good heavens!' Then my good old pragmatic, Western mind thought, 'There must be a good explanation for this.'

We went inside and there was a shrine to Shirdi Sai Baba and the Hindu priest in charge asked us if we would like to see the Miracle Medallion. Of course we would, so we all stood in a line and he came along holding out this little medallion on which was a picture of Shirdi Sai Baba, and from it was pouring amrit, a substance like nectar. He caught it underneath in a dish, and you could dip a spoon in the dish, and it tasted like honey. I was thinking, 'Ho, humph,' and when he got to me he looked me in the eye and said, 'You hold it.' He put this medallion in my hand –

and I swear it was the size and thickness of a sixpence, no more – and it sat there and went on pouring out more and more amrit. After some minutes he took it back.

I had an overpowering sense of exactly what it must have felt like, if indeed it happened, at the famous feeding of the five thousand – what it must have been like to sit there, maybe as one of the disciples, seeing Christ multiplying the loaves and fishes to feed all those people. It was like a bodily experience. It was not, 'Yes, my imagination can follow that, and good heavens, how clever!' It was, 'Christ! I don't understand!'

I don't have an explanation. It isn't that I believe that it is a miracle. It isn't that I don't believe. It is simply that that is what happened. I don't know why, I certainly don't know how, and yet I find I am happy not knowing.

We got back on the mattress-laden bus, which toiled on up into the mountains, a journey which became bleaker and bleaker as the landscape grew emptier and emptier, until we turned a corner, and there on a hillside was a larger-than-life-size statue of Christ, in what I can only describe as ice-cream colours – pistachio and strawberry, blue and cream – and another statue, in the same shades, of Krishna. On the other hillside stood an enormous statue of Hanuman, one of my favourite gods, the naughty monkey god from the *Ramayana*, who tore his heart out to help Ram and Sita, and made a bridge with all his monkey friends between Tamil Nadu and Sri Lanka, in order that Ram and Sita should escape from the dreaded ogres.

Next we came to the beginnings of what will be an enormous airport, and then a nearly completed, huge hospital. When I say enormous and huge, I mean mammoth. More buildings, a university, various schools, all in ice-cream pink, pale blue and cream, rather like Disney World in the grip of religious mania, and then, passing under a vast arch, we entered the little Indian village where Sai Baba was born, and where various miracles apparently happened to him as he sat beside the river. The village is quite ordinary, except that every little stall and shop is called the Sai Baba something.

We drove through the main gate into his huge ashram, which can sleep over five thousand people. It contains a temple with an enormous square in the middle where he gives daily darshan, the sight of a holy person. There are little stalls around the square, and then big huts the size of aircraft hangars and blocks of high-rise flats where you sleep. The Indians, even English Indians, stay in one lot of apartment blocks, and the white Westerners stay in another. Now there's interesting.

We lived for ten days in one of the huge aircraft hangar huts, each sleeping roughly one hundred people, and each visitor had a six-foot-by-three-foot space marked out in whitewash on the concrete floor, where we laid out the bedding rolls we had brought with us on the bus and there we slept. Just beside each hut there were 'showers': a cold-water tap in the wall, a jug, and a drainage channel for a loo. There were a lot of things that scuttled about in the night: hungry cats, wild dogs and curiously plump frogs.

Here is a typical day in the life of a Sai Baba devotee:

Up at roughly 3 a.m., stumbling through the unlit shed to the washhouse for a cold shower. Across the compound, being careful to avoid the dog shit, down the main street to the back of the mandir – temple – to sit cross-legged in lines on a cold, stone floor, huddled in a blanket, waiting to be let in for the *omkars* – invocations before prayers. Then we are packed into the temple by the *seva dahls* (a 'friendly' police force, women for the women, men for the men, with not a smile between the lot of them).

Next, singing the twenty-one *aums* – the most sacred words in the Hindu religion – plus a few other chants, we shuffle out to the great statue of Ganesha, the elephant god (my personal absolute favourite in the pantheon of Hindu gods, always plump and smiling, the god of scholars and prosperity). Here, in two queues, women and men segregated, although standing shoulder to shoulder (until I came here I thought it was the English who were the masters of the art of queuing) we process round the ashram with musicians on the gong, drum and shawm, chanting *bhajans* (hymns of praise, some remarkably bouncy). Then fall into yet another queue for the darshan – the sight of the holy person.

The queue is led into the outer courtyard and formed into lines. The head of each line picks a number from a bag, and if it's number one, your line goes into the inner courtyard first, and you get to sit in the front. (Even with all this queuing, there's still a mad dash at the end and I saw one poor old dear nearly trampled to death in the devotional rush.)

It is now about 7.15 a.m. and finally the moment arrives and the avatar appears, Sai Baba himself, whom I can best describe as a suntanned David Jason in a fright wig and a long, ill-ironed, orange frock. He would appear, and wave to us very graciously, not unlike our own dear Queen Mother, although apparently in his case the gesture means, 'Come on! More devotion!' He accepts the letters which are handed to him, and sweets, which he then throws back into the crowd (a bit like Les Dawson in the Palladium panto) and the devotees ooh and aah and try to kiss his feet. Having paraded around smiling for a bit, he works his miracles for us. Any five-year-old, given a few lessons by Paul Daniels, could do what he does – materialising sweeties and *vibhuti*, which is holy ash and supposed to be a cure-all (which I can tell you from personal experience doesn't cure all, because I had some mosquito bites that went sceptic when I applied *vibhuti*). Then he goes back inside. He doesn't speak a word. I found the whole business very disturbing.

After the darshan it is time for breakfast, at about eight o'clock, and another queue for meal tickets, then another queue to get the food on a metal dish in the canteen, a large, dark building with stone trestles and benches, not a place to linger, but then neither is the food to be lingered over. It is 'made by devotees for devotees' and it is lousy. There are more *bhajans* and then lunch – same as breakfast – and then at twelve noon back to the sheds for two hours of silence. Up again at two and more queues, this time sitting cross-legged for hours on red-hot concrete in the broiling sun. I decided at this point that I would become qualified to sit in the disabled seats at the back, so whenever I got in line I would ostentatiously run my hands through my grey-and-getting-greyer hair, and affected a Diana-from-*Waiting-for-God*-style limp. That did the trick. I would be escorted to a chair.

The afternoon darshan was exactly the same as the morning one, except hotter and stickier. It is followed by more *bhajans*, and you can't get away even if you want to opt out, because it is all broadcast at full volume over tannoys. After that there is time for a little wander round the stalls selling holy trinkets, more queuing for supper and lights out at nine.

There was the head of the hut, a shed sister- or brother-in-charge, usually somebody who had been on the ashram for some time. We had the ineffable pleasure of a Swiss woman called Elizabeth, who spoke eight languages, and whose whole life was ruled by 'Swami'. Every night before lights out she treated us to a lecture on Swami's ideas. Once, in gloriously idiosyncratic English which swooped and swerved like a yodel, she went on talking for at least twenty minutes about the importance of silence in order to save energy for devotion – which brought all sorts of comments to mind. Then, lying in the dark, listening to the rustling of nameless small animals (which I always hoped were scavenging cats) we would all sing the *lobkar*, the evening prayer – The nearest I could ever get to it was: '*Om, Om, Om, Shanti, Shanti, Shanti, Lobkar, Samaskar, Loopy Loo, Baba Too.*'

The thing that I found very difficult to stomach was almost five thousand people giving over all their power and self-responsibility to Sai Baba. He says he is an avatar.

Hmm. I think if you are an avatar, you don't have to say so. You just teach. I hadn't gone unprepared. I had read what Sai Baba teaches, and what he says cannot be faulted, concerning tolerance and love and respect for other religions. But people there would say, 'I will do this if Sai Baba allows . . . I will achieve that if Sai Baba allows . . . I don't know what to do, I will ask Sai Baba.' I went for a walk alone one day, to meditate under the meditation tree, where, after a peaceful half-hour away from the din of the ashram, the noisiest place in India, I was moved on by a *seva dhal*, who said, 'Swami says no meditating under the meditation tree.'

At one point there was an open day at an enormous stadium, with all the well-drilled schoolchildren and university students in bright costumes, singing and dancing and marching – a tad chilling, I found it – and then Sai Baba came in, wheeled on what in India is called a juggernaut – not a huge lorry, but a glittering vehicle, highly decorated, and pulled along by hand. It kept getting stuck and he got very cross and ungodlike and in the end had to walk to the podium.

I couldn't wait to leave. Ten days seemed an impossibly long time to have to endure it. I planned to leave early and had actually hired a taxi to take four of us of like mind straight to our next port of call, Hospet, the nearest town to Hampi, a great ruined city in the desert, and wait for the others there. But the night before we were due to leave, I was lying amid the scurrying creatures, thinking about the whole thing, and I suddenly realised that the only way I was going to make any sense of what it evoked in me was to stay and see it through, and perhaps I would begin to understand why these people needed it so much, and why it created such strong feelings of rage and antipathy in me. So I stayed. In my persona of Diana, I hobbled angrily into the presence of Sai Baba, morning and afternoon, for ten days, and sat glaring crossly at him from my seat at the back.

Staying on didn't provide me with any answers. I loathed

the way the devotees gave over all their power to this man, and were incapable of making a move without 'Swami'. A good day and it was, 'Oh, bless Swami, thank him!' and on a bad day it was, 'Oh, Swami is teaching me a lesson.' He lives in splendour and drives around in a Mercedes and expects all to prostrate themselves before him, and yet his writings about love and tolerance and embracing all faiths seem so wise. There appears to be an enormous chasm between the ideal and the reality. Krishnamurti said, 'Look within yourself for enlightenment. No man outside can set you free.'

There was a little girl who gave you garlands at the gateway of the ashram, and at the end of your stay you were obviously expected to give her some money. She had given me one or two garlands, and on our last day she came up to me saying, 'Auntie, Auntie, paisa, paisa.' And foolishly – it was the only time I'd ever done it in India, and I can't think what made me do it this time – I took out my purse, and in order to get at a few coins to give her, I took out a one- or possibly it was a two-rupee note. Worth about tuppence. I held this note in my hand, and suddenly there was a rush of children. It was like Hitchcock's *The Birds*, or *Suddenly Last Summer*; they were running and grabbing at the note, at me, at my purse, and I couldn't stop them. Little hands were grabbing everywhere. I held on to my purse and shouted at them. I completely lost my temper. A friend from the group came up and also shouted at them and they all ran away. But the few notes they had managed to grab at were all in pieces on the ground at my feet. They had all snatched, and so had received nothing. It was a very odd, disturbing experience.

We left and drove west across the desert to Hampi, which is Hanuman the monkey god's birthplace, an awesome ruined city spread over acres of boulder-strewn land, with temples and bathhouses, elephant stables, and the temple with seventy-six singing columns, each sounding a different note.

The nights were cold. At the hotel in Hospet I asked for an extra blanket, and one arrived, so recently and swiftly removed from another bed, it was still entangled in a dirty, warm sheet.

The next lap of the journey was a twelve-hour bus ride to Goa, stopping occasionally at crossings to allow Indian steam trains to pass in front of us, overburdened with passengers. We crossed various borders into mountains and jungle that are home to tigers and elephants. We were ferried over the smelliest river in the world ('Will we be eating fish?' I asked nervously) and at last entered Paradise Village, Calangute Beach. Unfortunately 'Paradise' wasn't quite finished, with no furniture, and showers that didn't work, but 'this is India', and with miles of silver sand and warm blue sea and the best, freshest seafood anywhere, not to mention the cheapest, who needs paradise?

My last few days in India were spent in Bombay, exploring the city, after getting there by train, in the ladies' carriage, which was marginally less crowded than the men's, or at least no one was hanging outside the windows. Arriving in Bombay, we had lunch at the Taj Mahal Hotel, overlooking the Gateway to India Arch and the harbour, with its peacock-feather sellers and sugar-cane vendors. And then, home.

Home. By Singapore Airlines to Heathrow, to be met by Em with the news that she had got her place at the Bristol Old Vic Theatre School to do the stage management course the following September. Home. Cool, fresh air, three hundred letters to be opened, and four cats furring my legs in greeting. Home. Lying for an hour staring at the ceiling in a steamy, hot, bubble bath, and then my own bed. Home. The end of an extraordinary, self-awarded fiftieth birthday experience. Home.

24. A time to mourn

I decided to look for my father again some years ago. My marriage was over, I was in the middle of analysis and it seemed important. After we'd been in touch when I was twenty-one, he had fairly soon afterwards broken off the connection, for there is no question but that it was he who had ended our correspondence, who had stopped replying to my letters. This second rejection seemed to me to be piling Pelion upon Ossa, although I hadn't been aware of that at the time. I tend to do a slow burn on things that hurt me enormously, and not to let them in properly.

In my early twenties, when it had happened, I had been very busy, working hard, enjoying my life, and I hadn't let myself experience the pain, so it passed almost without my noticing. But years later, when I went into analysis, I realised how angry I was that he had abandoned me a second time. I thought, 'Well, I'm going to find him again, and try to discover the whys and wherefores.'

I had an address in Stratford-upon-Avon, but he wasn't there. I told my mother that I was trying to find him and hadn't been able to, so she did her best, but she couldn't find out where he'd gone either. I then got in touch with Ariel Bruce, a professional seeker-out of people's families. She was one of the first people in the field, and is probably one of the best. She takes endless pains, and is very good at counselling. It's a sensitive thing, and sometimes it takes years and years from the beginning of the search to the finding and the meeting.

I remember her telephoning me quite soon after I'd first gone to her with all the details I had. It had apparently been very easy for her to trace him. He came from a Stratford-on-Avon family, and had never left the town. She telephoned me and said, 'Steph, I'd like you to come over because I've got some news.'

I knew right away that he was dead, but I went over anyway. She told me to sit down, and she said that he'd died seven years before. The same year that my stepfather had died.

I took the news in. I thanked her and I left. I got back in my car and sitting there parked in a London street, I suddenly found myself sobbing uncontrollably. At one point I thought, 'Why am I weeping for this unknown father who behaved so badly towards me and my mother? What is this grief? Is it because we never did get to know each other properly?'

I thought of the picture of him I had from my mother. She had always said that they could never have got on. I believe her. There would have been an awful clash of temperaments. I have quite a different picture of him from various relatives of his whom I've met since, of a pleasant, affable, charming man. And I have yet another image of him from the builder who came to work on my flat, a Warwickshire man called Philip Jones, commonly known as Fluff. Entirely coincidentally, he had known and remembered my father from years ago as a friend who he used to drink with in a pub in Stratford. Everybody liked my father, apparently. He was very gregarious and tremendous fun, a popular man. Yet in his private life he was so very, very reserved. I didn't even know exactly how old he was. All I knew from Ariel was that he had senile dementia towards the end, and then died of pneumonia, probably in his mid-seventies.

My relationship with my stepfather Colin had always been one in which I didn't feel that he cared for me very much, although I thought he was reasonably proud of me, and even though he was always kind and sweet, and would help me with things like putting my car right if it had gone wrong . . . So we rubbed along, but there was a part of me, of which I am ashamed, that despised his weakness. I suddenly realised, sitting weeping in my car, that I was crying not for my father, but for Colin. I was crying because for the first time, with my actual father finally dead, it left the stage clear for me to love my stepfather. For the first time I could allow myself to realise how much I had always loved him, which I had never been able to admit to myself when he was alive, or to show him, because it would have been denying my real father. Had my father ever come into my life, and been there for me, it would have been much easier to put into balance the love I felt for both of them – the innate love for my father simply because he was my own flesh and blood, and the real love for my stepfather, because he had been, as I now allowed myself to admit for the first time, a smashing Dad.

Over the ensuing weeks I was able to acknowledge how much I had loved him, and then began the process of what I could do to repair the damage, as he was now dead, for the way I had behaved towards him, not only throughout his life, but at his death and even after his death, when I had just thought, 'Good.'

I wrote my mother a letter, thanking her for being the mother that she had been. I thanked her for choosing to give birth to me, when her life would have been so much easier if she'd had an 'accident'. I was able to understand – for the first time – why I had been sent away to boarding-school so young, and from understanding it, to reach a point of forgiveness. I thanked her for marrying Colin. I put it all in this letter, which we've never talked about, but from that moment our relationship became better than it had ever been. It was a very cathartic time.

There is no point in saying, 'Oh, if only . . .' It's a waste of emotional energy, spiritual energy, even physical energy. You have to find a place of acceptance for what you've done, and for what other people have done to you, understand it, and then, if you are very lucky, from understanding you can find a way to forgive. Sometimes, when things have been really hideous, forgiveness can never be on the agenda. But for me it was, because although the damage and the hurt had been deep, and had been very hard, it was ultimately understandable, and so forgivable. I couldn't bear the thought of my mother dying without our coming to a place of understanding, of forgiving each other; it was too ghastly to contemplate. But I also knew that if it were left alone we wouldn't say or do anything about it. So it had to come from me.

When Ariel told me that she had discovered that my father had died, she had also said, 'But don't forget – you have a half-sister.'

I said, 'Yes, I know, but I really don't want to do anything about that. She probably doesn't know about me. I don't want to upset the apple-cart. I think it's best left.'

Ariel said, 'Well, let me just find out. Just in case. Let me make the odd enquiry.'

We segue forward a few weeks, and I was getting ready to fly to America, the trip to Taos that I have already described. It was just after midnight and I was asleep, because I was leaving the next day, and the telephone rang. It was Ariel.

She said, 'Steph, I've just been talking to your half-sister. Would you like to speak to her? I've found her. She's married and lives not far from Stratford-upon-Avon. She's home at this moment and would like to talk to you.'

I took down the number, put the receiver down, took a deep breath, dialled the number and got through to her husband. I said, 'I'm Stephanie.'

Steve, her husband, said, 'Oh great! Just a minute. She's outside, going through the dustbins.'

I thought, 'Hallo? A bit iffy in the mental area? It must run in the family.'

It transpired that all Ariel had told her was that she had a half-sister, named Stephanie, and that I was an actor. I had been absolutely right, she hadn't known until that moment that a half-sister existed.

When you're in panic or shock, your mind does all sorts of strange leaps, and because they had been to see *Aspects of Love* some few weeks previously, she had thought, 'Actor – play – she might have been in it – I'd better look at the programme.' So at that moment, in the middle of the night, she was going through the dustbins with a torch, trying to find it.

She came to the telephone and we started to talk. Her name is Cordelia Sarah and she is ten years my junior. And I, who was once an only child, now have two brothers, and a sister whom we all call Wiggy.

25. *Wiggy*

When my father stopped writing to me, I assumed, rightly I think, that I was an embarrassment in his new family, for he married again. He had told my sister's stepmother of my existence. In fact, she has told me that she actually encouraged him to ask me to come and meet my half-sister and get to know her, but he never would. When my sister was growing up she didn't know of my existence, and when we eventually met she told me how she used to sit with our father and watch *Tenko*, and her favourite character was my character, but he still never told her.

He was a bit of a Victorian father to Wiggy. Was he ashamed for her to know about his past? When I hear my half-sister talking about the kind of old-fashioned, very autocratic father that he was, I'm very thankful that I was not brought up by him, because I would not have stood for it. I have too much of my mother in me, and too much of him in me, for that matter, so there would have been God-awful rows. Perhaps it was just as well that he and my mother parted when they did.

That first night, on the telephone, Wiggy and I talked and talked, we laughed and we cried. We tried to cover so much ground, but there were two lifetimes to tell. She said, 'You know, my greatest fear is that you are about to fly out of the country.'

I said, 'I am. I'm flying to America tomorrow at lunch-time.'

'Oh, no! But we must meet before you go. Where are you flying from?'

'Gatwick.'

'We'll come down to Gatwick tomorrow. Steve will run me down. What time are you flying?'

'One o'clock.'

'Would it be all right if we met you at eleven o'clock? We could meet at the Gatwick Hilton?'

'Right. OK. You're on.'

I didn't get a lot of sleep that night. My mind was whirling. The next day I drove down to Gatwick on the dreaded M25. I'm always, always on time or early, but this time, for once, because of the motorway traffic, I was about twenty minutes late. I parked the car, went into the Gatwick Hilton, where you go in at ground level, then up an escalator to the foyer. This area, which is enormous, is always crowded with people flying in, people flying out, people meeting people, air stewardesses and pilots. I looked at all these crowds and across the foyer I saw . . . myself – ten years younger and two stone lighter, but definitely me, sitting there. I knew at once it was her, but I said to myself, 'Don't be so silly, Steph. How can you know? You cannot possibly know.' But the family resemblance is extraordinary. I saw her get up, and it had to be her.

The lovely thing was, while she and Steve had been sitting there, up the escalator just at the moment I should have arrived had come Claire Rayner, who as it happens I know slightly, a lovely, warm person. Wiggy didn't think, 'That's Claire Rayner.' She saw a well-known face and thought, 'Is that her? Is that my sister the actor?' My sister got up and waved to her and smiled, and Claire, because she is always sweet and friendly, waved back. For a brief ten seconds, my sister thought that was me. Claire passed on elsewhere, and my sister realised her mistake. Then I came racing up the escalator, and as soon as she saw me, we both knew.

We tried to cram in the story of our lives. Steve bought champagne and we sat there talking and crying and laughing and bringing out photographs. I suddenly remembered the time and realised that I was going to be late for my flight, so we whisked over to the airport proper. I was flying PanAm and their security was very rigorous. I had to go through a security cordon just to check in my bags. Wigs asked if she could come through with me, just while I checked in the bags, and the security guard said, 'No.'

Wigs said, 'But this is my sister – and we've only just met . . .' And she told him the whole story, and he started to cry, and he called all the other people to gather round to hear the story, and they were all weeping. So we all went to put my bags in. Then he telephoned through to the departure lounge to say that I was a bit late but I was on my way, and he told them the whole story again, down the telephone, and by the time I arrived everybody on the aeroplane knew the story as well, and as I went to my seat they all looked at me as I passed them with tears in their eyes.

I went to Taos, the red-earth land of my dreams, and when I came back Wigs and I met up again, and started to build up a friendship.

A great friend of mine called Vilma Hollingbery was in an episode of *Waiting for God*. We were filming in Oxfordshire, where Wiggy then lived, and we all had dinner together and told Vilma the story of our meeting. Vilma is also a writer and said it would make a riveting television play. We started discussing the possibilities of dramatising it, and came up with ideas for a sitcom, to be called *Dot and Carrie*, which we eventually sold to the BBC. They axed it at the last minute, along with a number of other projects, when there was a change of head of comedy. Fair enough. It happens. There's a lot wrong with the series, but I hope it sees the light of day eventually, particularly for Vil, who put in an enormous amount of work. For the moment it is under consideration by one of the big independent producers for ITV. It's 'in process', as we say.

Wigs helped me find a cottage in Warwickshire, where I used to stay while I got to know my new extended family. I have a niece, Alice, who was four when we first met. Steve also had three children by a previous marriage, my sister's stepchildren. They've been through some quite hard times. Steve's property business crashed in the late eighties when a lot of people were hit, but things are going well for them now.

I have never met Wigs' mother, who lives in Wales and breeds ponies, because she left when Wigs was two, and Wigs stayed with her – our – father. We're like a mirror-image of one another – she was without a mother and I was without a father. Wigs in a way has been less lucky than I have, because she is immensely creative and very good with people, but she has either never had or never taken the opportunity to make much use of her gifts. If we had met much sooner, I sometimes wonder whether she might not have been liberated, and become less afraid of losing our father's approval. We had many happy times together whenever I was able get down to the country to see them.

My cottage in Warwickshire was just an ordinary little two-up, two-down, but the previous owners had opened up the attic as well. It overlooked the glebe fields around church and the churchyard, and at the bottom of the garden was a little river. Beside it was what had been an old orchard, and was now the maternity ward for the sheep. The farmer, Michael, would put the very pregnant, about-to-lamb ewes in there and, overnight, from being a few very fat sheep, there would be dozens of little white lolloping, jumping things.

That cottage felt like a person. I used always to say, 'I'm here,' to it when I arrived. It had a tiny barn attached to it, where pipistrelle bats and house martins roosted. I would sit on the dry stone wall with my back against the barn for hour after hour, watching the sun go down, with the bats flying round my head. I created a tiny orchard at the bottom, and let the grass and the wild flowers grow, and I would go and lie in the long grass and watch the sky. A great place to dream.

About four years ago, Steve's work – buying and selling property – took him to Florida, and he and Wigs and the children have lived there ever since, and will probably stay there. We've been out there, Em and I, and stayed with them, but we rarely meet now. I've sold the Warwickshire cottage. Leaving it was very hard. It was the first time in my life that a place had exerted an emotional pull on me.

Wigs' and my relationship has reached an equilibrium, mainly because we live so far apart. Also, the initial enthusiasm cools off. I think that's natural. She is still my sister, and I care about her, but it is not quite as important a relationship for either of us as we perhaps thought it was going to be at the beginning. There are links: we look so alike, and we have both inherited certain character traits from our father. But we don't have a common background, and we haven't gone about things in the same way. It's the old nature–nurture conundrum: in spite of the ties of blood, we can't compensate for all those years when we didn't know each other because we don't have a shared history. Nevertheless, I won't ever quite get over the thrill of now being able to bring the words 'my sister' into a conversation, and I am glad we found each other.

26. 'On tour with Stephanie Cole'

At five-thirty in the morning, two men looking like space-men, in leather jackets, leather gauntlets and huge helmets, arrived out of the pitch darkness on Harley Davidson motorbikes, to pick up Kerin Parfitt, my PA, and me. Most people go sightseeing by coach or by car, but here in Australia in 1992 I had found a leaflet in my hotel saying that you could ride to our chosen destination on a Harley Davidson bike. I had booked the bikes.

We donned all the leather gear, and I gingerly got on the back of one of them, clasping my driver tightly round the waist and as we roared off, I clung on to him for dear life . . . We were about halfway to our destination, Uluru (Ayers Rock), a sacred site of the Aborigines, when I noticed that Kerin was rather nonchalantly leaning back in her seat, holding on to a sturdy handlebar on the backrest behind her. Feeling rather foolish, I let go of my clutches of my poor rider, and copied her.

It is very cold at that time of the morning. The world is completely quiet and it was still pitch dark when we set off, no sign of dawn at all, not even a thin glimmer of light on the horizon. Then, above the roar of the bikes, we suddenly heard the thrilling sound of the bell-bird that starts to sing when he knows that dawn is about to break, rather like our blackbird. During the twenty-minute drive the horizon slowly began to lighten.

You are taken round to the east of the rock at dawn, where

you stand and watch it change colour as the sun rises. The rock goes from absolute black, when all you can make out is a dark shape in the star- and moonlight, to deep purple, to mid-purple to red, to glowing terracotta, brighter and brighter, until it is a deep, shining gold, breathtaking in its beauty and one of the wonders of the world. It's very high, nearly 900 feet. Many people climb to the top. I didn't want to, because the summit is a holy place for the Aborigines, and I thought it would be like abseiling from the dome of St Paul's for a laugh.

I did walk round it, a very long walk, and on the west side it folds in on itself and there is a miraculous spring with a pool of the clearest, coldest water, which I tasted. There were blue and red dragonflies darting around, and tadpoles and tiny fish in the pool. And round about are rock paintings. I don't have words for it, it is so ancient it sings, it shifts something very deep down in you.

It was here that I discovered that I had taken dozens of photographs over the past two days with no film in my camera.

We were on our way to a tour of New Zealand. The week's stopover in Australia *en route* was part business, largely pleasure. The business bit was seeing Geoffrey Atherden, the author of *Mother and Son*, a hugely popular sitcom on Australian television that I wanted to do in Britain, but of that more anon. The pleasures were seeing Sydney, a city which is so stunning everyone should visit it once before they die; being at Ayers Rock at dawn; and, for my last twenty-four hours, staying with Sister Angela, my friend and sister in spirit, at her convent in the outback.

All the time I was doing *Waiting for God*, I was in great demand by charities for the elderly. I had been approached both by Age Concern, New Zealand, and by the New Zealand Rotarians, asking me to go over and do some after-dinner speaking to help them to raise money. I wanted to go, but after-dinner speaking did not appeal to me, so with my agent, Michael Ladkin, I decided that it might be more fun, both for me and for them, if I were to perform my Alan Bennett 'Talking Heads' monologue, 'Soldiering on', and they agreed. The monologue alone would not make a full evening's entertainment, so Michael had the idea of me simply talking and answering questions about my career for the second half.

After a week in Australia, Kerin, Michael and I flew into Wellington, making what felt like an impossible landing on an absolutely tiny airstrip with the sea on all sides. We came through customs and immigration, to be greeted by a huge crowd of people all wearing jolly straw boaters and holding up a row of placards saying: THE NEW ZEALAND ROTARIANS WELCOME STEPHANIE COLE. Waiting for God was a very big hit over there, which was why I'd been asked in the first place, so I suppose some people may have known who on earth Stephanie Cole was.

We went out to the tour vehicle they had provided, which was to carry us, our props and equipment across New Zealand, and emblazoned on the sides, in huge red and white painted letters, were the words ON TOUR WITH STEPHANIE COLE. It was very touching, but quite alarming. As in America, they have quite a low speed limit compared with ours, and when there was nothing for miles but open road and a couple of sheep, it was hard to keep to fifty miles an hour, so I'm sorry to say that we broke the speed limit sometimes, and it wasn't long before we were caught. With my name in red on the side of the car, there was no chance of going for the low-profile approach. Sometimes when the police recognise you it can work in your favour, but sometimes it can work against you. Fortunately 'our' policeman was sweet and let us off with a caution.

I was very, very nervous as the time drew near for my first performance in Auckland. I'd had one or two quite overwhelming spiritual experiences in Australia, and here in New Zealand I'd been enjoying myself, being entertained royally, eating too much and talking my head off on radio and television interviews, as well as meeting more and more new people as we were taken round the day care centres and homes for Alzheimer sufferers that we were raising money for. The carers all seemed to have boundless energy, young and old, and expected me to be the same. I realised I was getting overtired and hadn't spent nearly enough time thinking about my show. I hadn't even finally sorted out what I was going to say in the second half.

I woke up on the morning of the first performance with a migraine. I went over to the Aotea Theatre in the late morning to check things out, and felt a bit better. It was all looking good. We had a technical run at three in the afternoon, which was fair old chaos and which got me worrying and neurotic again, but then we had a dress-rehearsal at about four-thirty, which went fine. Kerin had never done anything quite like this before – neither had I for that matter – but she coped brilliantly and there was a very supportive theatre manager and team for the sound and lights, and Michael, who was acting as tour organiser, was extremely effective at getting everything under control. He went home after the first week of performances and Kerin was in charge. She is a New Zealander and we had met when she was make-up supervisor on *Waiting for God*, and we had become great friends.

The audience couldn't have been better. I did 'Soldiering on' for the first half, which they clearly loved, and for the second half, I decided to fly without a parachute – no script or notes on bits of card. I remember standing in the wings thinking, 'Once I've done the little bit of opening – I don't know what I'm going to say next.'

I have never got such a buzz in my life. I went on the stage, sat on a bar stool and I just talked and told them stories. I had thought that I could perhaps manage twenty minutes, but I suddenly found that I had been going merrily on for forty-five minutes. At the end I asked if anyone wanted to ask any questions – which they did – which gave me inspiration for the next night, for other stories to include, so the show gradually evolved. I kept a sort of free flow feeling about it. We went all over New Zealand with it, from Auckland to Hamilton to Wanganui, then down to the South Island, Christchurch, Nelson – everywhere. We walked among geysers in Rotorua, white-water rafted at Queenstown, whale-watched at Kaiora and climbed the Fox Glacier.

Throughout the tour everyone was tremendously hospitable and flatteringly welcoming. One lady came up to me after the show and said that she thought *Waiting for God* was absolutely wonderful, because there was one moment when Diana had said something that had brought her father back vividly for her, as he always used to say the same thing.

I said, 'Oh, what was it?'

'Bollocks!' she said.

New Zealand is the most exotically beautiful country, with a tremendous climate, splendid, dynamic people, delicious food and wine, but unfortunately the theatres, on the whole, apart from the ones in Auckland, Wellington and Hamilton, are pretty much all a nightmare. Or were then. They don't seem to have a strong theatre tradition over there, and everything was done by the seat of the pants, by not overwhelmingly enthusiastic amateurs. We had one near disaster after another.

My favourite example is our arrival at Nelson, on South Island. There was nobody about; a filthy, dusty stage; sweet wrappers strewn everywhere; it was ghastly. There was a blackboard in the wings, displaying the legend, 'Please no ice creams, no ice pops and no mothers on stage.'

Kerin and I set to, rolled up our sleeves and scrubbed down the stage. Our requirements were minimal and were always faxed through in advance, but often there was nothing ready at all. We only needed very basic lights and a simple sound system and Kerin was always in charge of this. How she didn't have a nervous breakdown I don't know; I nearly did. At Nelson there were only two lights and no sound system at all. The young man in charge, when he finally arrived, said, 'Hang on a minute,' went off and came back with his own sound system from home, with a couple of tiny speakers. It was ridiculous. Unfortunately this sort of experience was repeated almost wherever we went: programmes weren't printed or weren't delivered, and occasionally, because the publicity was so badly organised, nobody in town even knew we were coming, so hardly anyone came.

I had said to the Rotarians, at the beginning, 'If you make this work, you will be able to do it again and again with other people who are in popular television series.' They were given the opportunity to employ, for a relatively low fee, one of the best tour operators in New Zealand. It would have been a much greater success if they'd allowed a professional to run things, and paid him a small percentage out of the profits, but they wouldn't, and as a consequence they didn't make anything like the profit they had hoped for. It was a basic lesson: if you're going to do something you've never done before, take advice from the experts, because it's worth paying out a little in order to get back twice as much.

However, it was a great learning experience for me, and even though it was utterly exhausting and occasionally a nightmare, Kerin and I both had enormous fun. What really made it worthwhile was meeting the old people in the various day centres, for whose benefit it was meant to be, and who so obviously appreciated everything we were doing. With certain provisos, I would do it again.

What meant most to me on that entire hectic trip weren't the successes and calamities, the highs and the stresses of the actual tour, nor even the almost mystic, dawn, bike ride to Ayers Rock, but a short trip I made before I left Australia. It was a life-changing experience. I visited Sister Angela, the nun that I had come to know as a result of reading her letters to Helen Joseph on the radio. I went to see her at her monastery of Poor Clares, out in the bush. I took a train from Sydney up to the north of New South Wales and spent a night at the convent, which the sisters had built with their own hands.

The convent nestles into the side of a hill, with a little chapel built underneath, looking down across a wild valley, cleared at the bottom by early settlers, where cattle now graze. It's a wonderful, slightly higgledy-piggledy place, miles from civilisation, although a supportive lay community seems to be growing round it, and the sisters have an increasing number of visitors. They grow all their own vegetables and herbs, bake their own 'Clare' bread and keep geese and hens, and they've made a big pool for ducks, in which two ducklings were bobbing about when I arrived. A few yards away there is a monastery, with the same number of monks as there are nuns in the convent.

Angela showed me where she'd done her 'vision quest'. At a time of great doubt and uncertainty she had gone on solitary retreat for six months, in a little hut in the woods. The sisters would deliver food for her, but she wouldn't see them. She was quite alone.

She went through some very hard times while she was there, and one day she hit rock bottom. She had a little table and a chair at the window, with a pencil and paper and the Bible, and the cross and a bed, and that was all. Nothing else. She was sitting there, in utter despair, when a little bird came and sat outside her window and looked at her. She looked at it, and it did a little dance outside her window. Every day for three days the little bird visited her, until at last she understood that it was a messenger. That was her turning-point. She spoke to it, 'Thank you, you've come and given me peace and you've done your job well. Thank you.' The bird flew away, and Sister Angela returned to her community with a lighter heart.

We went for a walk through the woods to the top of the hill, called Holy Hill, where Angela has fashioned a simple cross in wood; she was a sculptor before she became a nun and still works in wood. The evening I arrived, all the sisters and I sat and ate convent-baked 'Clare' bread and drank cocoa and watched a video about Bede Griffiths. It was my idea of heaven. When I was going to bed, Angela said, 'Don't be worried by the sounds you hear in the night.' Their nun-made duck-pond has become a meeting-place for creatures of the forest and you can hear the sounds of Australian animals – kangaroos, koalas and wallabies – coming and talking and arguing and lapping the water at night. I didn't see them, but I heard them and sensed their presence.

The next day I received Holy Communion for the first time in many years. There were seven of us in the chapel; we sang songs and I read a lesson, and we all gave the bread and wine to each other. Angela is an ordained priest, so it started with her, she passed it to the person on her left, and it went all the way round, first the wafer and then the wine. I was deeply moved, and for the first time in my life I began to understand, in my body, what Holy Communion means.

27. A Passionate Woman

After *Waiting for God*, Michael Ladkin and I were looking for other series and plays I might do. I wanted to do something in the theatre. I had become great friends with David Pugh, the producer of *Steel Magnolias* in London, and he too was trying to find something for me to do in the West End. We began the search even before *Waiting for God* had finished, and we were all reading dozens of scripts, possible revivals as well as new plays. About halfway through the process, Ned Sherrin came on board. His knowledge of theatre is encyclopaedic, which was a great help.

At last, early in 1994, we found something that we all wanted to do, a revival of a play by a dead author. David Pugh, as our producer, was negotiating to buy the rights. The literary agent dealing with the play had gone away on holiday, leaving the negotiations in charge of an assistant, who proceeded to sell the rights to someone else and, to cut a long story short, we lost the play. I was very cast down, because reading script after script is wearying work. I remember getting on the telephone to moan to Ned, who said, 'Never mind, dear, because when something like that happens, it means you are not meant to do it, and something better will come along.'

I said, 'I know. It's just that I'm having difficulty touching that belief at this moment.'

Two months later, when I had read more plays than I'd had hot dinners, when my beautiful seventeenth-century sideboard was groaning under the weight of new scripts, old scripts, every sort of script, the telephone rang, and it was David Pugh. His office is down in Shaftesbury Avenue, and he said, 'Steph, come down and have a drink at the Café Royal, because I think I've got a script for you.'

'Oh, David! Not another one. I don't think I can read another one . . .'

'No, come on, come on, come on, come on down!'

I stumped off to meet him and he handed me a script saying, 'Don't look at it now. Wait until you get home.'

So after a pleasant drink, I went home and undid the script, thinking, 'Oh, dear! Here we go again.'

I started to read it, and after two pages I was thinking, 'Yes! This is the one. This is the character.'

It was a new play, called *A Passionate Woman*, beautifully written by a Yorkshire woman called Kay Mellor, who had written for television, and has a brilliant ear and a unique voice. The 'passionate woman', Betty, is an ordinary housewife, about my age, slightly daffy, quite naive, very vulnerable, who, on the wedding day of her son on whom she dotes, has come to realise how empty her marriage is. Betty doesn't hide her vulnerability. I've played a lot of women who covered up their vulnerability in a rather aggressive or fierce way, and I have done it myself, too, in real life, but I knew I also had another side to me, and that this would give me a chance to explore this warmer, more overtly emotional side. The theatre is a wonderful place to discover all the facets of your own character by acting them out. It's like a big therapy workshop, really.

So that was it. We'd found the play. Ned was to direct and David to produce. We cast it quickly with Neil Morrissey, James Gaddas and Alfred Lynch, who respectively played my son, my dead lover who returns as a ghost, and my husband, and they were all just perfect. We had tremendous fun during rehearsals, although Ned Sherrin's diaries that were published at the time record that our high spirits were as much to do with what we ate and drank as anything to do with the work. Ned's account rings absolutely true, so, with his permission, here's a taste of it:

London:
Tuesday 6th September 1994
. . . Gaddas has the biggest appetite, especially for puddings. Nick-names and catch phrases emerge early on in the rehearsal. I can't remember Morrissey's name and at one point call him Mulrooney, which sticks. Later he boasts that he can move on the roof that takes over the set on Act 2 'like a gazelle'. From then on he became Bambi Mulrooney. Stephanie never speaks of one long-gone actor who could not remember his lines without a qualifying 'bless his heart'. This phrase became essential whenever anybody screwed up.
. . . The big news is that there is a new menu at the Bar Central next Monday.

Monday 19th September 1994
New menu *not* quite ready.

Thursday 22nd September 1994
New menu finally arrives. Chef congratulated (bless his heart) . . .

Bath:
Tuesday 4th October 1994
Discover excellent brasserie, The New Moon, opposite stage door. Fortified for smooth dress rehearsal and imminent first night. London friends, lovers and followers descend. Cast on terrific form, much laughter and applause. Keith Waterhouse declares that one of Stephanie's Act 2 speeches has authentic 'Broadway-bound' ring . . .

Richmond:
Monday 10th October 1994

... Excellent Italian restaurant opposite stage door. Access through kitchens – warm welcome. Ideal for post mortems.

Guildford:
Monday 24th October 1994
A woman bursts into Stephanie's dressing-room to announce that her performance has confirmed her decision to leave her husband. Cast's spirits, already high, bolstered by praise from Albert Finney and Cameron Macintosh.

London:
Tuesday 1st November 1994
First preview in West End . . . Five restaurants adjoin the theatre. Hurrah!

All the while we were rehearsing *A Passionate Woman*, the only two people in the cast and crew who didn't smoke were Ned and me. I had given up smoking when I was twenty-eight, because Henry's much older brother had died of cancer, and I had been so horrified by the manner of his dying that I definitely didn't want it to happen to me. Giving it up had been a very hard battle over about a year during which I had been extremely difficult to live with. The main reason I didn't ever go back to smoking was because I knew I'd have to give it up again, and it was the hardest thing I'd ever done in my life. I was never evangelical about it. It was fine with me if other people wanted to smoke around me, but eventually I became what I considered to be a non-smoker. I never gave it a thought, except that about once a year I would have a dream in which I was smoking a cigarette, and I would wake up thinking, 'Oh, God! Oh, no, I don't. I haven't for years.'

For the last week of rehearsals we had moved to the Queen's Theatre in Shaftesbury Avenue, which was 'dark', meaning it didn't have a play on, so we leased it and put up our revolving set on the stage, so that we could rehearse with it before opening down in Bath. The set was first a loft, and then revolved and became a rooftop. The loft, which was on quite a steep rake, turned out to be so narrow that it was quite impossible to move about on it. When we got out on to the roof, for the second act, I discovered I would have to spend most of the time standing on a six-inch-square surface by a chimney, and then would have to climb up on to a roof ridge which was about eight inches wide, and about fifteen feet above ground. There were no safety measures the first time we went up there, and I completely freaked out. We finished rehearsal at about six o'clock, and I was in tears.

They took me over the road to China Joe's, a cocktail bar in Shaftesbury Avenue and plied me with innocuous-tasting cocktails, which hit me in the knees within seconds. While we were talking about what could be done to make it all possible, I remember leaning over to David Pugh and saying, 'Oh, David, give us a cigarette, darling.' For twenty-five years, during which I had been through birth, marriage, divorce and deaths, I had never wanted to smoke. But now I took a cigarette, and I smoked it as though I had never stopped.

After that I would just have the occasional one a day, two a day, and then it slowly worked up to about twenty. I've given up again now, and that's it, but I've learned something – and that is that once a smoker, always a smoker. I will always be a smoker, like an alcoholic is always an alcoholic, though they never drink again.

After our opening in Bath, we went on to Guildford and Richmond before moving to the West End and the Comedy Theatre. At the climax of the play my character, Betty, has to decide whether to settle for her passionless marriage, commit suicide and join the ghost of her dead lover, move in with her son and his new wife, or to go off on her own. In the end she chooses to get into a passing hot-air balloon and goes up, up and away. Parts of the play were obviously

232

fantasy, but it was a metaphor for real and serious things, and it resonated not only with middle-aged women but also with young women who were seeing their mothers going through it, and older women who had been through it themselves in the past, or something similar, and even with the men, because it was a very even-handed play. Alfred Lynch, as my faltering husband, showed how much Betty herself was responsible for the emptiness of their marriage, and the lack of love.

We ran for nine months in the West End and it was a joyous experience. Through Michael Medwin who is David's business partner, Albert Finney and Sean Connery were our very starry backers, and they both came to see it. At Christmas I switched on the lights in Regent Street with Jonathan Price, Lynda Bellingham and Lionel Bart. I got very tired during those nine months because the whole thing was so exciting, in a way that even an enormous success on television can never be. Television never has that immediacy, that buzz, that close encounter with an audience, that spinning excitement every time the house lights go down and the curtain goes up.

On the final curtain call we were waiting for the curtain to fall, but it didn't, and in my peripheral vision I saw a man coming from the wings. I thought that it was John Berger, our company manager, and that something had happened. Then I realised that it was Michael Aspel with the Big Red Book. I thought it must be for Neil, but I looked at him and no, it wasn't. Well then, it must be Jimmy. No. It must be Alfie. No. Michael approached me, the audience laughed and cheered, and I was so genuinely caught out that I am sorry to have to confess that I am one of the few people who, on being presented with the Big Red Book, responded with an unprintable – and untransmittable – expletive deleted. I apologised to the BBC producer afterwards, and she said that I was not to worry as they would cut it out, but they didn't. You couldn't hear it, but anyone with any lip-reading skills could have seen very clearly what I was saying.

I was completely taken by surprise. My mother and Emma had been secretly working with the researcher for weeks. Afterwards I managed to piece together clues that I probably should have picked up, but because I was working so hard, I hadn't. For instance, Emma had had a friend to stay for a couple of nights, and one morning they were both looking terribly bleary-eyed. I said to them, 'What have you two been up to?' and they said, 'Oh, we sat up talking until four in the morning.' What they had actually been doing – Emma having crept into my bedroom and taken my Filofax out of my handbag when I was asleep – was sitting up until four in the morning, copying out all the names and addresses of my friends. Then my mother came to stay and casually asked to borrow back some of the albums of photographs and reviews – she and Great-Aunt Peg have been the family archivists over the years, collecting all the cuttings, but they have always handed over the completed albums for me to keep. She said she needed them to show to two very old friends who were coming to stay. I didn't think anything was peculiar about that either. I just said that of course she could take them home. They, too, were riffled through by the researcher, and photographs removed.

My mother and Emma had been brilliant about insisting that they not only include famous names, but other people who they knew I'd really want to see. So as well as the *Tenko* gels and my friends from *Waiting for God*, and Rudi Shelley, we had Sister Angela, my Great-Aunt Peg, my brothers came over from Keynsham, and they flew Wigs over from America.

I was sure that Sister Angela would be on a film clip, but on she came at the end, in her brown Poor Clare robes and sandals, saying 'Hallo, darling!' as if it was the most normal thing in the world.

Angela has been very involved in work on the new feminist theology being done by an American university, and had gone over there to lecture for a couple of terms a few years earlier. They had asked her to go back for a reunion, and she was in the chapel at her convent, talking to God about it and saying, 'I know I can't afford it, but I want to go, and if I'm meant to go, show me if there's a way.'

At that moment the telephone rang. It was a Friday, and a voice said, 'This is the BBC in London. Are you busy just now?'

And she said, 'Well, I'm preparing my sermon for Sunday.'

They said, 'Ah . . . Do you have to do it?'

'Why?'

'Because we want you to fly to England on Sunday to be on Stephanie Cole's *This is Your Life*.'

She immediately said, 'Oh, yes, I'll come for Steph.'

They told her she would be able to pick up her return ticket to England at the airport, and she thought very quickly and said, 'The ticket from Australia to England and back – could I cash it in and get a "round the world"?' They said that she could, and that's what she did. She flew to England, appeared on *This is Your Life*, flew on to America for her reunion, and then back home to Australia, all for the same price, courtesy of the BBC.

After the recording, we all partied on until four in the morning. When we came downstairs, the poor cabbies who had been booked for us were all sound asleep at their wheels. This was in 1995, when Great-Aunt Peg was ninety-five, and too frail to travel all the way to London. They had sent a film crew down to the Harriet Nanscowen Home in Braunton, North Devon, where she lived. She was then a little more compos mentis than she was by the end of her life, but even so they had to do thirty-seven takes. At the end, when they thought they had probably just about got enough to put something together for a thirty-second clip, they told her, 'Thank you very much, Miss Hirst. We've finished now.' To which, Great-Aunt Peg replied, 'Well! Thank heavens for that! If that's television – I won't be doing any more.'

28. 'Blow dat sax'

Albert Finney came to see *A Passionate Woman* when we were in Guildford. He came backstage to talk to me afterwards, and was utterly enchanting. We talked for about half an hour about acting and the theatre. He is completely passionate about the business and unaffected by his own celebrity. Then he said something, and it seems silly when you think that I'd been in the business about thirty-six years when he said this, but it was one of the best bits of advice anybody's ever given me. It wasn't really offered as advice, we were just talking about acting, and he said, 'I sometimes think of acting as like being a jazz musician.'

'How so?'

'Well, you know how to play your instrument superbly, you know what the music is, and when you get to actually perform, you get out there and – you just blow dat sax.'

He sent me a first-night card for the West End run saying, 'Dear Steph, Get out there and blow dat sax. Love, Albie.'

If I hadn't been an actor, I might have wanted to be a philologist, a linguistics expert. Words are very subtle. You can have a line of script, and you know what the character is trying to say, but there is one word in that line – and it could be an 'and' instead of an 'if' or a 'but' – which, because English is probably one of the most subtle languages in the world, will alter the whole nuance of the sentence. I love that; it gives me such pleasure. That is one of the reasons I love poetry so much – because of the importance of the exact choice of words.

In real life we talk in clichés much of the time, but when you hear a cliché in theatre or television drama or in the cinema, it is quite ludicrous. This is why I get so irritated when people admire Agatha Christie's plays so much, because frankly she was a sublimely bad writer of dialogue.

Although, having said that, in the days when I was teaching at weekend workshops with young would-be actors, when they arrived for the first class I would always say to them, 'Would you *like* to be an actor? Or do you *have* to be an actor? Because if you would just like to be an actor, please go and be an accountant. But if you have to be an actor, then at least you'll have the fire that you'll need to overcome some of the problems.' One girl, when I asked her why she wanted to be an actor, said, 'Because I want to get famous, so that I can save seals.' That was the single most bizarre motive that I have ever come across.

I recall a young man who came for a weekend workshop. We talked a little, and it transpired that he had grown up in the country and that he had never ever been to the theatre, or read a play, in his life. I said, 'I don't quite see how you can want to be an actor if at the age of seventeen you've never even been to see a play. I think what you need to do, now you are in London, is to take yourself off to see a play in the West End. You can get yourself a seat in the gods very cheaply.' He wanted to know what I thought he should see, but I told him to look through the listings in *Time Out* or something, read the descriptions, and decide for himself.

We met again for the next lesson. He was beside himself, with all the shining-eyed ecstasy of the born-again. He said, 'I've been! It is wonderful! I had the best evening! The best time!'

I said, 'Oh, this is great. I'm so delighted. What did you go and see?'

'*The Mousetrap*!'

But I thought, 'If that's what it takes to turn one person

on to the theatre, to go and see more plays then, good old Agatha. That's fine by me.' He was never going to be an actor, this lad, but I hope that he is now a regular theatregoer and gets great pleasure from it.

While I was playing *A Passionate Woman*, a very great friend of mine, the writer Barrie Shore, who lives in Salisbury, wrote to me to say that there was a very successful writers' festival there, now in its third year, and to ask if I would be willing to take part in it. I said I would be happy to, as long as it was on a Sunday, the only day in the week I had free.

After some time she sent me the script of a one-woman play by Peter Shaffer called *Whom Do I Have the Honour of Addressing?*, and asked if I could read it for an audience. I was incredibly busy, but I said, 'Yes, of course' and we made a date for me to go down. Peter Shaffer himself would be there, and Michael Billington, the *Guardian* theatre critic. The first part of the evening would be my reading and the second half would be the three of us in discussion with the audience.

To my shame, because I was very busy, I simply did not have time to read the play through beforehand more than twice. It wasn't laziness, I genuinely did not have the time. However, one thing I am quite good at is reading off the cuff, so there was a part of me that was not too nervous, because I knew I could make it work.

I went down and met Peter Shaffer, and was quite over-awed by him because he is one of our great writers, and Billington, whom I'd met before. When *A Passionate Woman* opened, one or two of the critics on the broadsheets, including Michael Billington, had reviewed it somewhat dismissively as being a populist play, and I had thought, 'Why is it that so many critics live only from their necks upwards?'

During the discussion at Salisbury someone asked Peter Shaffer, 'You always used to write primarily for men. You've now started to write for women. Why?'

He replied, 'Well, I think I write for both. But one of the

reasons I've started to explore the woman's point of view is that I've become interested in it. I wrote *Lettice and Lovage* simply because Maggie Smith asked me to write something for her, and then I wrote *Whom Do I Have the Honour of Addressing?* especially because it explores the woman's angle.'

Billington said, 'I think one of the great things about Peter is that he is so good at writing for both sexes.'

Someone in the audience asked, 'Do you think men are as good at writing for women as women are at writing for men?'

And Billington said, 'I'm not sure how good women *are* at writing for men.'

I immediately perked up and said, 'Some women are very good. For example, I'm in a play at the moment, *A Passionate Woman*, about a woman in her early fifties finding out who she is, in which the second half is beautifully written from the men's point of view, her son's and her husband's. It's very even-handed. The husband's part in particular is movingly and sensitively written, so you are absolutely clear how he feels, and that is a perfect example of a woman writing brilliantly for a man.'

I felt that for once an actor had had the chance to answer a critic.

Without telling you the whole plot, one can say that Peter Shaffer's play, a wonderfully moving piece, is more or less based on a true story about an intelligent, middle-aged woman, a very conventional, ordinary woman, whose life has been changed by meeting a young American film star, a relationship which has ended in a shocking and traumatic way. At the start of the play she sits on the stage – alone, of course – and has turned on a tape recorder to tell her story. She is drinking whisky, which she has never drunk before in her life, and she has a bottle of pills ready, so when she has drunk enough she'll take the pills with the whisky. At the end we don't know whether she is going to leave the incriminating tape and commit suicide, or wipe the tape and stay alive. Because it is also very funny, it is extra-ordinarily affecting.

A year after the reading in Salisbury, Duncan Weldon decided to take it down to Chichester and stage it properly, and asked me to play it. I knew from July 1995 that we were going to do it. We were to start rehearsing in October, so I had six weeks to learn it. It was not easy to learn because Peter, who writes wonderfully and is a brilliant stylist, always uses the unexpected word, or the unexpected inversion of a sentence. Come October I had not once got through the script without drying and I was scared.

Just like many actors, one of my major fears throughout my career has not been, 'Will I be good or bad or absolutely lousy?' but, 'Will I dry?' I had once or twice had minor dries, but when you're acting with other people they'll cover it up, and of course you cover up for them. In a single-character piece, you are on your own.

At Chichester I had an excellent deputy stage manager, Jane Seamark, and I was directed by Bill Bryden, who was both allowing, and yet feeding me ideas all the time; he was both supportive and bolstering. Came the opening night and, although I was very frightened, I got through it.

We did three weeks down at Chichester, a week in Guildford, and then a week in Malvern, which has a lovely little refurbished theatre. I did the Monday night at Malvern – and it was a great success. By this time I am five weeks into the run and beginning to be able to get out there and 'blow dat sax'.

On Tuesday the first act goes fine and I'm into the second act, and suddenly I hear Jane in the prompt corner riffling through pages of script. I think, 'Blast, I've jumped . . . OK, what have I cut?'

It's extraordinary how your mind can operate on different levels. I'm still performing for the audience, while my mind is racing backwards through the play to work out what I've cut, whether I've missed something important, whether I can get the information in somehow. Is this bit important?

Yes . . . Is that bit important? No . . . Five minutes later, I stop. I don't know where I am.

I lean forward and take a drink from the prop whisky. When you dry, the best thing to do is to relax . . . which is easier said than done. I'm sitting there thinking, 'It'll come' and I take another drink, but it doesn't come. Nothing comes. I've got an agreement with Jane that she'll only give me a prompt if I ask for it, because I tended to pause in different places and for a different duration on different performances.

Eventually I said, 'Yes?' to Jane. She gave me the cue, and I started, but even as I started I realised that, in the panic, she had given me the cue from where I had just stopped, rather than from the beginning of the bit that I'd missed out. I dried again, stopped again and said, 'Ladies and gentlemen. I'm really sorry. But I have inadvertently cut a chunk of this play, and if you don't know what's gone on in that chunk, it will spoil your enjoyment of the rest. So what I'm going to do is ask Jane, my prompter, to take me back, and I'll start again.'

It was all very well, but I was aware that there was a slight frisson in the audience, and I would have to break it somehow, for me and for them. I picked up the glass of pretend whisky and said, 'You see what too much of this does for you!'

There was a big laugh, Jane found the right cue, we started again, and got through to the end. Everyone applauded warmly. It was fine. I was fine. I talked and laughed about it afterwards in the bar with the crew. I went back to the hotel, still absolutely fine. I woke up the next morning – and it was as though I had been in an accident. I was in a mild state of nervous shock.

I talked to myself and said, 'Steph, this is the best thing that could have happened to you. You now know that after the biggest, worst, most public dry – you are still alive. And you finished the play. And it was a good performance. What's your problem?' Slowly, I recovered.

A Passionate Life

For the audience, the world of the play is like watching a parallel universe. They can switch from one level of reality to another. I discovered this when I was doing *A Passionate Woman*. If something went wrong, like our revolving stage jamming, which happened twice, I found that I could talk to them until it was fixed, and that that was within the bounds of possibility. The same was true of the Shaffer, and it is nearly always so. You don't have to be afraid. You've just got to go out there and *blow dat sax*.

29. Keeping Mum

My mother and I have talked about death and dying quite often. For me, for quite some time now, thinking about it has become an essential part of everyday life. I don't fear death but, very selfishly, I fear losing other people. When my mother dies I shall miss her horrendously. I hope she has a good death. I'd hate it for her if she had a long-drawn-out, painful time, with years and years of mental confusion, like my poor great-aunt. I've become a member of the Voluntary Euthanasia Society and I've made a living will, because I can't bear the thought of being kept alive for years and years to no purpose.

I would like to be alert to the journey. I would like to have the courage to live the journey, to go through all its stages, the anger, the grief; looking back over the stuff of my life; being able to let go of the people and the places and the things that I love, and to get to a point where I can say, 'Now I can go.'

My mother is utterly, tranquilly, unafraid of death, often talks about whom she will leave what to, and how it is to be done, and constantly has clear-outs so that we don't have to face piles of papers and so on. She wants to be cremated. She hasn't made up her mind where she wants her ashes to go, just as she hasn't made up her mind which residential care home she eventually will go into in Keynsham, because it rather depends on which one has the best cook when the time comes. She is resolutely determined never to be a burden.

I can't make up my mind, either, about where to be buried. While I love the idea of slowly sinking back into the earth, and re-energising the ground that I'm buried in, what also appeals is the cleanliness and the fresh beginningness, or endingness, of burning and then being scattered. I think I would like to be scattered off Baggy Point, over the North Atlantic Ocean, where I was brought up.

I was on a radio programme not so long ago called *Looking Forward to the Past*, talking about epitaphs or memorials. We were each asked, 'If you could have a monument, what would it be?' I said that I would like a poem written for me by Kathleen Raine, to my mind one of the greatest poets of our century, with her intense mystic vision of the vitality of the natural world. And that is what I would like my epitaph to be: a poem. And if someone wanted to chisel it on to a tombstone, well and good, but I don't think I would care.

Memento Mori, which means 'a reminder of death', is the rather bleak title of a very funny and perceptive novel about old age by Muriel Spark. In the 1990s I played Dame Laetitia Colston in an excellent television adaptation of the book, alongside a very starry cast, many of them golden oldies themselves – Michael Hordern, Renée Asherson, Thora Hird, Cyril Cusack and Maurice Denham – and a few youngsters like John Wood, Maggie Smith and Zoe Wanamaker. Jack Clayton was the director. As one critic put it, 'You laugh till you spill your cocoa.'

All the actors playing the 'oldies' were getting on a bit in years – except me. Even knowing the brilliance of the make-up team, I must admit that when I watched a preview of the film, I was a bit dismayed. I was far too convincing as the aged Dame Letty, and I kept saying sadly, 'Oh dear! Do I really look like that?'

There was one quite violent scene where Dame Letty, in her bedclothes, is attacked by a late-night intruder, and I had a stand-in stuntwoman. She and I were dressed identically in dreadful flannelette nighties and hairnets over our rollers. At one point, during a break in the filming, we were standing together having a chat. We turned to see the cameraman and crew watching us, literally weeping with laughter.

I took part, one Sunday morning some years ago, in a programme on Radio 2 with Don Maclean. After the programme was over, we carried on chatting and he asked me if I'd look at some videos he had of an Australian sitcom called *Mother and Son* by a writer called Geoffrey Atherden. (This was before my trip to Australia and New Zealand.) Don told me, 'I would like to do it over here, with me as the son, and you as the mum.'

I took the videos home and looked at them. The production values were not good, but as I closed my eyes in disappointment, I found myself listening to the dialogue and realising that it was really good. I went into rehearsal the following day for *Waiting for God* and asked if anybody had seen it, because a few episodes had been shown over here, although it hadn't been a success and had soon been taken off. Mike Aitken, our writer, said, 'Yes. Geoff Atherden is a great friend of mine.'

I told him that I wanted to get hold of some scripts. Mike said, 'I can do even better than that. He's coming over to England next week, and he has asked if he can come and watch our rehearsal, to see how Brits make sitcoms. You'll meet him.' I met Geoff, and liked him. He brought some scripts with him, and that was the start of it. Then we met again when I was over in Australia.

It had been Don's idea originally. It was going to be him and me, and I kept him in touch with what was going on every step of the way. Then, after a lot of negotiating by my agent, Michael Ladkin, with the BBC, they said they didn't want to do it after all. ITV shilly-shallied about, and the whole project rather died on us. The only person who kept it alive over the next year or so was Michael, who every now and then would pick up the telephone and asked different people to think about it.

Then Geoff Perkins took over as Head of Comedy at the BBC. Michael persuaded him to read the scripts and he decided that it was worth doing. The title was changed to *Keeping Mum*. The producer was to be Stephen McCrum and the brilliant Sylvie Boden the director. Their ideas for casting were for the sons to be much younger than in the Australian version, so in the event Don was not asked to do it.

I have always felt terribly guilty about that, and I knew I should write to him straight away and explain, but I never did, because I am a coward. Not very long after it started I got the most gracious letter from him saying, 'It's a wonderful piece of work and thank you so much. I'm sorry I can't be part of it, but it's terrific.' I thought that showed a largeness of spirit and generosity of mind that was quite extraordinary in our often, but not always, egotistic business.

Sylvie Boden wanted to make some technical innovations. It was the first time a sitcom has been done with a widescreen, filmic finish. We had eight cameras, including a Steadicam, which we used a lot. We sometimes did as much as a twelve-minute sequence on one single long-shot on the Steadicam, which is pretty rare in television and unknown in sitcoms. We also had a set which was built as an exact replica of the bungalow where we filmed on location. On top of the set was built a gantry, so there was no problem of the sound getting in – they were actually fifteen feet above us all the time. In a minor, strictly technical way, the show made television history, using techniques never tried before.

Early on I said that I didn't think I should play it in Received Pronunciation English, because something said to me that Peggy has innate intelligence, but has not had the education that her sons have had. Looking at who she is, in her many moments of lucidity, the things she likes reading, the things she likes doing, they are those things that people like who have not had the advantage of a really good education. Given the English class system, she is probably lower-middle class.

I put in my bid for a Bristol accent, the accent I would have had myself if I'd had any. I wanted it to be Bristol rather than Somerset or Devon, because I didn't want her to sound like a stage Mummerset village idiot. I wanted her to have a city accent, with a little bit of a cutting edge to it.

Because *Keeping Mum* is about an elderly lady who is a bit befuddled, there was a danger, that in fact was borne out, that some people might think she had the beginnings of Alzheimer's disease or senile dementia and that we were making fun of that. As patron of Age Concern that would look terrific, wouldn't it – if I were to make fun of the ill and elderly?

I'd like to hit that on the head once and for all. My character, Peggy, has an extreme form of 'benign senescent forgetfulness', which we all suffer from as time goes by, when, for example, we go into the kitchen and say, 'What on earth have I come in here for?' It started to happen to me when I was about fifty. I often put my glasses on my head and almost immediately wonder, 'Where on earth have I put my glasses?' Peggy's problem, of course, is more extreme, because she's older. In my own family, my mother is worse than me. I have coined a phrase which I use in my speeches for Age Concern: '*If you're not one, you've got one, or you're going to be one.*' It was taken up and used for the publicity for *Keeping Mum*. We were not laughing at Peggy. We were putting forward a story about a mother-and-son relationship which is exacerbated by the mother's benign senescent forgetfulness.

I have visited many residential homes since it started and the patients and carers have all said they enjoyed it because it made them laugh. Whenever I visited my great-aunt, the nurses and helpers in the home always had hilarious stories of what the elderly people had been up to. Laughter is a way of coping, much better than rage or suicide. I do appreciate that some people still find it too much. If so my answer is, please don't watch it.

In Australia, when the series first came out, they had much the same sort of reaction as we have had, with several people up in arms, 'How can you laugh at something like this?' They have a *Right to Reply*-style programme on which a middle-aged lady, looking after a mother in the early stages of Alzheimer's, said, 'I don't know how you can do it. It's just appalling.'

Nothing they said could placate her, so in the end they said, 'Well, this is a hard thing to say, but please, just don't watch it.'

She replied, 'But I have to watch it – my mother loves it!'

Peggy isn't a victim, she's a survivor. She's devious. There are times when she does things unconsciously, but just as often she's quite aware of what she's at. I adore her.

I found some of the scripts painful to do, particularly the scenes between her and her son, when he's trying to break it to her that he's going to have to put her in a home, and she's absolutely terrified. When we recorded them, the studio audience fell silent. The show mixes tragedy with comedy; it mirrors what goes on in everybody's life.

One of those scenes in particular exemplifies the 'does she or doesn't she know?' question. When her son Andrew is persuading her to try the home, he says, 'It'll be like staying in a lovely luxury hotel.' The next thing you see is Peggy coming down the corridor dragging a huge bag of golf clubs.

'Where are you going with that?'

'I'm taking my golf clubs.'

'But you can't play golf.'

'How do you know I can't play golf? I don't know whether I can play golf or not, so how do you know?'

'But they're not going to allow you to take golf clubs there . . .'

'I thought you said it's a luxury hotel. I've never heard of a luxury hotel where you can't take your own golf clubs.'

I loved playing that scene. Is she doing it deliberately to discomfit him? Or does she really think it's a luxury hotel that she's taking her golf clubs to? I don't know. Sometimes she knows and sometimes she doesn't know what she's doing. I also love her friendliness. She is a frequent visitor at the local fire station because she loses her way so often, and they always give her a lift home. 'Hallo, boys! Hallo, er . . .'

'It's Colin.'

'Oh, yes. Hallo, Colin and hallo, um . . . boys.'

I know so many women and men like that; they are to be celebrated.

My own mother is very active, very fit, and a great gardener. There's nothing she loves more than a good house move. She'll come and organise and pack and unpack and provide endless tea and sandwiches. She's always been a great goer at things, and she hasn't quite taken on board that in her late seventies it might be a good idea to take things a little more easily. Her heart is strong, but she overdoes things and then wonders why she feels a little peculiar, so our constant refrain is, 'Please will you take it easy.' She's very good at seeing the bright side, and being positive. Her life is full of friends and recently she has begun a new career – going round various clubs and organisations giving talks on *This is Your Life*.

I've always been quite temperamental and volatile. When I was an angry teenager, in fact until the age of about forty, she always put down my behaviour to being 'difficult – just like your grandmother'. Since forty it has been put down to 'the menopause'. Actually we are terribly alike, and Emma is cast in the same mould!

I'm not always as tolerant of Em as I might be, even now that she's twenty-four and living her own life. I can still enrage her, too. We have worked together, indeed she was the deputy stage manager for a tour I did of *A Passionate*

Woman. She's extremely good at her job, wise, grown-up and able, yet I would still find myself leaving the theatre at night, saying goodnight to everybody and then saying to her, 'Now, darling, do make sure you eat properly tomorrow.' She would give me such a black look and I'd think, 'Now, why did I say that?'

Working with her has been good for me, because I am able to see her objectively, this very young woman being incredibly efficient, conscientious and hardworking; it has given me a great respect for her. I think we all ought to see our children at work, either in their careers, or being parents perhaps, to see how well they do it. It teaches respect, and that is such an important part of love – respect for the other.

I used to think how sad it was that our performances, especially in the theatre, are here today and gone tomorrow for, unlike other art forms, live performances cannot be kept. But now I don't regret it. I was very struck about two years ago at the Royal Academy, at an exhibition of Tibetan art which I visited because I find mandalas fascinating and beautiful. I once spent months making and painting my own mandala, with everything that meant something in my life in a geographical circular pattern.

Throughout the exhibition, some Tibetan monks were making a huge sand mandala. They funnelled different coloured sands very delicately to make fine and intricate patterns. The exhibition was on for six months, and at the end of it, they took this exquisite piece of work – which had taken eight hours a day for six months to create – to the Thames and blew it away into the river.

They had made their beautiful mandala out of the sand, and then it was gone, because that is what a human life is like. I understood it. You try and make it a good life, in some way or another, and then it's gone. All the people who saw the mandala shared it and experienced it, have it in their bodies and minds. But you don't cling to it, you let it go.

I'm surrounded by an accumulation of things – paintings, musical instruments, books, videos, all those things that adhere to us through our lives. I love being surrounded by them, but now I hold to that thought, that you can love something while it is here, and find it beautiful, but you must always be prepared to let it go. And so with people. Caring hugely, loving greatly, while they are with us, but still being able to let go if they go before us – that is what we have to learn.

30. Love again

When a marriage ends, it leaves you with a huge sense of failure, whoever was to blame – and it's never just one person's fault. Or if it ever is, in Henry's and my case it was definitely six of one and half a dozen of the other, a mutual drawing apart of two lives. But that is hindsight; at the time I thought that maybe I didn't have it in me to make a relationship work. I wasn't good enough, not giving enough, not loving enough, simply not enough.

So after my marriage was over, I was happy to be on my own. It was a relief. However, after a couple of years I began to wonder if I wasn't being unduly hard on myself. I had a few friends with very good, loving marriages that had lasted thirty or forty years, and I could see how they made their marriages work, by pulling together through the bad times as well as the good. They worked at it together, liked yoked oxen. I wanted some of that. I remember ranting and raving at God, saying, 'It's no good. I've read all the books. I know the theory. Now please put me in the laboratory and let me see if I can make a long-term relationship work.'

I suppose everybody goes through it. There's a part of me that knows, when I look back over my life, that every now and again God has given me a tap on the shoulder about these things, and I didn't learn, and so it was as though, finally, God had said, 'I am determined you are going to get it this time, so this time you're going to get it in spades. Now you've *got* to learn.'

I did get it in spades. I had the most disastrous love affair. I did learn. And now I know. After that I thought, 'OK. Now I can look at my life and think, Steph, what are you? You're fifty-four, you've got a great daughter, a lovely home, a terrific career and wonderful friends. What more do you want?' And the answer was, 'Nothing. That'll do; that'll do for me.' Then, just at the time when I finally realised I was perfectly happy and self-sufficient, along came Peter.

I met him, or rather, re-met him, at the fiftieth anniversary celebrations of the Bristol Old Vic Theatre School, to which over four hundred past students were invited. I was renaming one of their studios, so I was going officially, as well as for pleasure. It was an all-day event, on a glorious day in early June. We were all milling round. I was standing talking to someone, and I saw a man come in and I thought, 'Now I know him. Oh, I know. It's Peter Birrel.'

I had first known him over thirty years ago, when I was just beginning life as a humble ASM, and he was a rather flash young actor – a bit arrogant I thought – in the Bristol Old Vic Company. We hadn't seen a lot of each other in those days, because he was never a party-goer like me. We had both been in a production of *Richard II*, when all the scenery had collapsed; and I remembered him as a brilliantly sinister, silent figure in *The Killer* by Ionesco. We'd seen each other very occasionally over the years since then, at the Acton 'Hilton', as they call the BBC rehearsal rooms, but just to say, 'Hi! How are you doing?' We hadn't ever really communicated.

We started chatting at the reunion, and I found him rather attractive and charming. He said, 'What are you doing this summer?'

I said, 'Well, I'm supposed to be writing my auto-biography.'

He was interested, because he's a writer as well as an actor, and he said, 'How are you writing it?'

'Well, I've tried long-hand, and I've tried recording stuff into a tape recorder and getting it transcribed, but nothing really works, but I've now got a programme on my computer which acts as a sort of secretary. I dictate, and it is supposed to print it up on the screen. Unfortunately it doesn't actually work. I keep getting a completely lunatic stream of consciousness filling the screen, page after page, like something from James Joyce, that has nothing whatever to do with what I've said.'

He said, 'How extraordinary! Twenty-five years ago I wrote a short story, based on that premise, that a computer took over and started printing out stuff that the man had not dictated.'

I said, 'I'd love to read it.'

'I'll send it to you.'

Actually, the reason my computer does it, or rather doesn't do it, is not because it's trying to take over the world, but because it is trying to convert every sound it hears into words. When the telephone rings, when the clock ticks or chimes, it tries to make words out of those noises and then adds them into whatever I am dictating.

We hadn't swapped addresses, so Peter went to some trouble to send me his story via my agent's office. I read it, thought it was very good, and found, to my amazement, that the computer in his story was called by the acronym for Computerised Over Lord Electorate. I sent it back saying that I had enjoyed it, and do let's meet again. It was really more or less just out of politeness, so we could natter about the Vic School and various old friends we'd discovered we had in common.

Some time later I telephoned him because I had some people coming to dinner who I thought he'd be interested in meeting. I left a message on his answering machine asking if he'd like to come on such-and-such a day. I didn't hear back. The dinner party came and went. My friends came to dinner and Peter didn't, but I didn't think a lot about it.

Some time later I got a telephone call from him saying, 'I'm terribly sorry. I've been away in France and have just got home and got your message.'

I said, 'Oh, well. The dinner's been and gone.'

'Yes, I realise that. I am sorry.'

There was a bit of a pause, so I said, 'Well, look, I'll tell you what. Why don't you come to dinner anyway?'

And he said, 'I'd love to.'

At first I decided to ask some other people and make it another dinner party, but I was rather tired so I thought, 'Oh, bother it. He can just come on his own.'

He arrived at about quarter past seven; we had a drink and sat and talked. He has a different way of looking at the world from me. He tries to be scientific and analytical, a clear-headed, atheist Jew, whereas I go more by my feelings and instincts, and I do have a faith, albeit a rather searching, unorthodox one. We had dinner, and talked. We discovered we had a shared passion for poetry. We had our coffee and talked. We found, in his Jewish and my Celtic backgrounds, a shared sense of rootlessness.

Eventually he said, 'Well, I suppose I'd better be going. What's the time?' We looked at our watches, and it was half past four in the morning. We'd had no idea.

I think that night we both knew. I remember him saying, 'I didn't think this was going to happen to me.'

I said, 'Neither did I.'

And we both said, 'Maybe it isn't. Maybe it isn't.' But we both knew that it was, right from the beginning. Everything had changed.

He rang me when he got home. Then he rang me again the next day. Then we went out to the National Film Theatre and saw *The Seven Samurai* which I hadn't seen for years, and which he had seen several times and loved. And that was the start of it.

Peter had been married, and that had ended, and he'd had various relationships, but he was like me in that he didn't think that there would be anybody else and he didn't particularly want there to be, his life was quite settled. We were both at exactly the same stage, and it was as if we were both being given this one last opportunity. I feel so blessed.

Even when we hit a rocky place, we can talk, and because, as one gets older one gets more experienced, we've both made mistakes that we can recognise, so we can avoid a lot of pitfalls. I have never before been with anybody who is so easy to be with. Within a year he has become my best friend, my best everything, both of us able to talk and tolerate and be tolerant. It is a wonderful gift.

Peter told me later that he very nearly hadn't gone to Bristol that day, because the rail fare from London to Bristol was something outrageous like fifty-six pounds return, because it was a Friday and there are no cheap day returns on Fridays. Being rather low on funds, he had thought he wouldn't bother, but then he had thought, 'Wait a minute. What about the coach? Because I would quite like to go . . .' So he rang up the coach company and they said it was eight pounds return. If he hadn't done that, we might never have met again.

I once had a belief – completely irrational, a superstition you might say, but which still lingers a bit – based on the fact that when my career started to go downhill was when I got married and had my daughter, and that when my career started to take off again, I lost my marriage. I began to think that you couldn't have both. There is still a bit of me that still can't really believe that I am going to be allowed to have both at the same time. I still sometimes feel that I'm treading on very thin ice.

I love the fact that we have a shared past. One of our great delights has been going back to Bristol to see Paula Spielman, who had been secretary at the Vic School when we were there. We had been students at different times, but she had known us both and we had both been very fond of her. We see her quite often now, and that's something very special, because she knew us both when we were young. All our pasts are intertwined.

In my favourite episode of *Keeping Mum*, Great-Uncle William had died, and two very diminutive elderly people were seen as part of the funeral group, both at the graveyard and back at the house. They never spoke or were spoken to and they were never mentioned. They were just seen walking along in the graveyard, or sitting in the house with plates of food. They were probably friends of Great-Uncle William, so they just wandered in and out of the scenes, sometimes right in the foreground of the shot, but never explained. I thought they were the most gloriously comic creation.

They were played by two extras called Robert and Edna who came from Devon. They were both in their eighties, had been married for over fifty years, with children, grand-children, etc. Totally devoted. I asked them what their secret was, and they said, 'Well, we never stop talking. We wake up in the morning, and one of us goes and gets the tea, and then we sit in bed drinking our tea and talking, talking, talking, until one of us says, "Good heavens! It's nine o'clock – the day's almost gone. We'd better get up." ' I just loved that. If Peter and I never stop talking – and I hope we never will – perhaps we can be like that one day.

The first time that Peter and my mother met, we went to Keynsham for tea, stayed for a couple of hours and then left. Emma telephoned my mother that night and said, 'What did you think?' Because they're terrible gossips, my mother and Emma. They can both talk the hindleg off a donkey, and keep the telephone company in profit. My mother said, 'Well, very nice, dear. But they both talked so much I couldn't get a word in edgeways!'

I can think of nothing worse in the whole of one's life than dying alone, with no one there to hold your hand, as you take the step over. This is why I am so happy that Peter and I are together. I've been given a chance to see if I can get it right. Peter feels like that too: this is the best relationship that's ever happened, let's make it work. One day we shall leave London and live in the country by a river and have a rescued donkey – well, two, because they like to have a

companion – and a rescued pig; that's my dream. I want to
live by water with Peter, and build dams and things like a
child in my own bit of river. Some days we will walk
upstream, until we can see where the river bends.

Curtain Speech

I've always thought that the important thing in life is to follow your bliss, to stick at doing the thing you really want to do, even if people try and put you off, and even if you aren't the world's best at it. I feel extremely lucky, that I've been allowed to do that, and not struggled to get to the top of a ladder only to discover it was leaning against the wrong wall. People too often get turned away from their passions to follow a safer path, and nearly always live to regret it.

I was recently asked by Janine Duvitski if I would go and hand out prizes and give a little end-of-term talk to the eleven-year-olds who were leaving the primary school where her children go. I thought I'd just be chatting informally to a little group of eleven-year-olds, but when I got there I discovered that I had to stand on a platform and give my talk in front of the entire school, from the five-year-olds upwards, plus all the parents and all the teachers. I had to think a bit quickly of something to say that would appeal both to five-year-olds and to forty-five-year-olds.

I started burbling on. I told them the story of how I'd been expelled – which perhaps was not the best thing to tell bright, mischievous primary school children. However, I did, and then I said, 'The most important thing, when you leave school, is that you follow your bliss. Do you know what I mean by that? Well, what do you love doing? Hands up anyone who would like to tell me what they really love doing – anything from splashing about in the bath to making mud pies to reading Roald Dahl . . .' They were all a bit shy, but eventually a young lad at the back put up his hand and said, 'Yeah, Miss. I like football.'

I said, 'Great. Now, look – you might or might not be lucky enough to be a professional footballer one day, but even if you aren't, you might be able to teach football, or be a referee, or write about it, or become a sports commentator, or simply play it as your hobby. Don't let anybody put you off. Don't let anybody tell you that you aren't good enough or you can't do it. If that's what you love, you stick at it. That's what I mean when I say you must "follow your bliss".'

They all filed out afterwards and I was standing talking to Jan and some others when a little lad came up and said, 'Miss, can I talk to you please, Miss? You know that thing about following your bliss? I'll tell you what I love doing – and my Mum won't let me do it.'

I said, 'What's that?'

He said, 'I love climbing up on the high wall and jumping off it. I really love it. And my Mum won't let me do it.'

I thought, 'Oh, Steph! Wrong! You've really got yourself into this.'

I said to him, 'Yes. Well, the problem is, what I *should* have said to you was: follow what you love doing *as long as it does not hurt others or yourself*.'

Children are so literal. I could imagine them all going home and saying to their mums, 'I love eating ice lollies and watching TV, and climbing up high walls and jumping off 'em, and the lady says you've gotta let me do it.'

Thank you for sticking with me to the end. I don't know what is going to happen next. One of the things about being an actor – about life, really – is that you never know what's round the next corner, what the next telephone call, letter, fax is going to contain, if there will be any work. We all get bogged down and depressed sometimes, but it's also quite exciting, because all you know is that whatever comes next will be whatever comes next.

Do I have any ambitions? Not as such, no. I don't have

any of that 'I want to play Hamlet at the National' kind of ambition. Being with Peter; seeing my daughter grow happier; spending time with my friends; enough interesting new work to keep me out of mischief; and beyond that, whatever comes along is fine by me. I suppose as far as work is concerned, I am more interested in performing new writing, about people I recognise, than doing revivals.

I used to do so much reading and journeying and real hands-on stuff, trying to learn and experience everything I could about spiritual things. That doesn't seem to be where I am for the moment, although that's not to preclude it for the future. I am still a searcher, and hope that I always will be. The day I think, 'I've got there, I've done it,' is the day that I'll have to start all over again. But I don't plan things as much as I used to. Just to be seems very important.

I have said to Peter that all I want is for there to be more days when we can just sit and watch the sun come up, travel across the heavens and go down again. It's right when you are in your twenties and thirties to be out there, strutting your stuff, but now I'm in my fifties it seems more and more important to go inside myself. Not to opt out of life, but to have more time, like Sister Angela's eagles, to play in the thermals and simply be.

Acts One and Two happened yesterday. Now I feel remembered out. Now I feel the need to go back out there and start following my bliss, blowing dat sax. They're calling Beginners for Act Three.

Programme Note:

Stephanie and Peter got married on 5th October 1998 in Bath.